POPE FRANCIS

The Gospel of Matthew

POPE FRANCIS

The Gospel of Matthew

A Spiritual and Pastoral Reading

Foreword by Daniel P. Horan, OFM

ORBIS BOOKS
Maryknoll, New York 10545

Founded in 1970, Orbis Books endeavors to publish works that enlighten the mind, nourish the spirit, and challenge the conscience. The publishing arm of the Maryknoll Fathers and Brothers, Orbis seeks to explore the global dimensions of the Christian faith and mission, to invite dialogue with diverse cultures and religious traditions, and to serve the cause of reconciliation and peace. The books published reflect the views of their authors and do not represent the official position of the Maryknoll Society. To learn more about Maryknoll and Orbis Books, please visit our website at www.maryknollsociety.org.

Published by Orbis Books, Box 302, Maryknoll, NY 10545-0302.

Edited and adapted from the original Italian publication: *Matteo: Il Vangelo del compimento, Lettura spirituale e pastorale* © 2016 by Libreria Editrice Vaticana, Città del Vaticano.

The texts (homilies, meditations, speeches, Angelus, etc.) after the beginning of the pontificate are taken and adapted from: http://w2.vatican.va/content/vatican/en.html. The Italian sources are listed in the bibliography and were translated by Orbis Books.

Manufactured in the United States of America

Library of Congress Cataloging-in-Publication Data

Names: Francis, Pope, 1936- author.
Title: The Gospel of Matthew : a spiritual and pastoral reading / Pope Francis.
Other titles: Matteo. English
Description: English edition. | Maryknoll : Orbis Books, 2020. | Includes bibliographical references. | Summary: "Based on the Gospel of Matthew, this collection of written and oral sources of Pope Francis, a master of prayerful silence, guides us through the Gospel so that we may embrace a simple and living intimacy with Jesus, the Word made flesh"—Provided by publisher.
Identifiers: LCCN 2019030846 (print) | LCCN 2019030847 (ebook) | ISBN 9781626983540 (paperback) | ISBN 9781608338191 (ebook)
Subjects: LCSH: Bible. Matthew—Criticism, interpretation, etc.
Classification: LCC BS2575.52 .F7313 2020 (print) | LCC BS2575.52 (ebook) | DDC 226.2/0—dc23
LC record available at https://lccn.loc.gov/2019030846
LC ebook record available at https://lccn.loc.gov/2019030847

Contents

CONTENTS

Foreword

by Daniel P. Horan, OFM

One of Pope Francis's many attributes is that he is consistently a man of scripture, a follower and preacher of the Gospel. From his informal daily homilies and extemporaneous remarks to his formal apostolic exhortations and encyclical letters, the Holy Father goes out of his way to tie his message back to the proclamation of the good news of Jesus Christ and ground his worldview and pastoral guidance in the word of God.

Early in his pontificate, Pope Francis published his first apostolic exhortation, *Evangelii Gaudium*—"The Joy of the Gospel." Deep within this beautiful and challenging document the pope calls our attention to the centrality of scripture in the life of the church and the living of Christian faith. Disturbed that so many Christians, including the church's ministers, qualify and distort the clear and direct message of Christ in the Gospel to suit their own ends and comfort, Pope Francis offers a stern corrective to the accommodating gloss many people apply to interpreting scripture.

> The message is so clear and direct, so simple and eloquent, that no ecclesial interpretation has the right to relativize it. The Church's reflection on these texts ought not to obscure or weaken their force, but urge us

> to accept their exhortations with courage and zeal. Why complicate something so simple? Conceptual tools exist to heighten contact with the realities they seek to explain, not to distance us from them. This is especially the case with those biblical exhortations which summon us so forcefully to brotherly love, to humble and generous service, to justice and mercy towards the poor. Jesus taught us this way of looking at others by his words and actions. So why cloud something so clear? (*EG* 194).

This consistent refrain to interpret scripture seriously and honestly echoes in everything Pope Francis says and does. And readers of this inspirational and exhortative volume of the Holy Father's reflections on passages from the Gospel of Matthew will find this to be true in the following pages.

In addition to taking seriously the unsettling simplicity of the Gospel, these pages highlight several key themes. One of the more subtle yet significant threads is Pope Francis's firm conviction that the Holy Spirit continues to speak to the church through the Gospel. The Bible is not a static document, a museum piece or rare book to be admired for its inertness. Rather, the Bible is the historical medium of divine revelation, alive with the dynamism of Spirit continually speaking to the people of God in each generation and in every context. In his 2018 apostolic exhortation on the universal call to holiness, *Gaudete et Exsultate,* at the outset of his lengthy reflection on Matthew's account of the beatitudes, Pope Francis challenges us to "listen once more to Jesus, with all the love and respect that the Master deserves. Let us allow his words to unsettle us, to challenge us and to demand a real change in the way we live" (166). In order to take the inspired word of God seriously, we must open ourselves not only to the consoling and encouraging aspects of the Gospel, but also the disturbing and discomfiting summons of the Spirit in our lives.

Another persistent theme in the pope's reflections on scripture in general and the Gospel of Matthew in particular is the historicity of divine revelation. As the Second Vatican Council's dogmatic constitution on divine revelation, *Dei Verbum,* reminds us, revelation is first and foremost about God's self-disclosure and invitation to divine relationship extended to each of us in every age. The Bible is the historical medium of divine revelation. It is the concretized narration of God's gift of self to humanity as seen through the eyes first of the people of Israel and then of the early followers of Jesus Christ. These texts, which began as oral tradition passed on for generations, proclaim a powerful—and at times, scandalous—truth of a God who enters into the messiness of our reality, and who does so out of love. As Christians, we believe that the fullness of this revelation—this divine disclosure—is accomplished in Jesus of Nazareth. God literally enters into creation and human history. Far from being simply a curious fact, this is something that instead bears ramifications for how we view ourselves and our world each day. God continues to draw near to us even amid great suffering and pain. Yet God also desires the salvation of all creation, which is the culmination of history. Pope Francis sees these concurrent truths of our faith reiterated throughout the pages of Matthew's Gospel and invites us to consider how being a Christian disciple requires our cooperation in the inbreaking of God's reign here and now.

Finally, Pope Francis's reflections on the Gospel of Matthew are relatable and accessible because he always sees the evangelical call as practical and not just theoretical. This is clearly evident in his reflections on the famous "Last Judgment" scene in Matthew 25. Recognizing that many fear the end of their lives, Pope Francis says: "Dear brothers and sisters, may looking at the Last Judgment never frighten us: rather, may it impel us to live the present better." He reminds us that Jesus's proclamation is an invitation to "begin again, for up until now we have done little," as Saint Francis of Assisi is remembered to have said to his brother friars. We always have the opportunity to begin again, to start anew, to live the Gospel better by putting into practice what it is we say we believe.

This collection of Pope Francis's engaging and challenging reflections on the Gospel of Matthew is a guidebook for all who long to follow Christ more fully, understand scripture more clearly, and love God and neighbor more completely.

Introduction

The Word Is Fulfilled Today

This book does not represent a systematic exegetical reading of the Gospel of Matthew or a progressive *lectio divina* of passages from the Gospel; rather, it represents a broad, reflective meditation by Francis—Jesuit, superior, pastor, bishop and, today, pope—based on the scriptures; not developed organically, but woven together from fragments, words spoken or written by Francis at various times. His thoughts are arranged here according to the succession of the chapters of the Gospel of Matthew. Together these reflections form a commentary in which the Word resounds sometimes as a light that illuminates circumstances of personal, ecclesial, and social life and at other times as an invitation to go out and "walk through courtyards and see grasslands, looking at fragments but contemplating forms"—yet always as an echo of the voice of the Divine Master, who today speaks to his people and to each person. No one is excluded, believer or non-believer, good or bad; all are called to announce the fulfillment of the Word in his person.

The purpose of this book is to help those who, both for personal enrichment and deeper understanding, read and meditate on the Gospel of Matthew. It is meant to draw them closer to Jesus and to discover the hidden treasure in the words of the Gospel, words that can make the heart burn again today.

These pages are not intended for study, or necessarily for preaching, but simply for letting ourselves be guided by Francis, a master of prayerful silence, to enter into a simple and living intimacy with him who is the Word "full of grace and truth" (John 1:14), the Word made flesh.

Noticeable throughout the selection of reflections is the familiarity of Pope Francis with the Word and hence his untiring concern to announce it as "the master of a household who brings out of his treasure what is new and what is old" (Matt 13:52). Perhaps all this can be summed up in what the apostle John, advanced in years, wrote: "We declare to you what we have seen and heard so that you also may have fellowship with us; and truly our fellowship is with the Father and with his Son Jesus Christ. We are writing these things so that our joy may be complete" (1 John 1:3–4).

The "Word" thus takes on a double meaning or dimension: the eternal Word incarnate, Jesus of Nazareth, and the Word contained in scripture. Perhaps each may seem separate in meaning; in reality, they are like two sides of the same coin that refer to each other in a continuous dynamic that can be understood as "Word in abeyance" waiting to become "Word accomplished"—"Word that becomes flesh."

The Word Is Mercy Made Flesh

From the mouth of Jesus, almost like a refrain, we often hear the expression of mercy: "I desire mercy, not sacrifice" (Matt 9:13; 17:7). He is the One who not only reveals the mercy of God, not only announces the coming of the time of mercy, but also implements it in many ways, in many gestures, and in many encounters. The love of the Father "has now been made visible and tangible in Jesus's entire life. His person is nothing but love, a love given gratuitously. The relationships he forms with the people who approach him manifest something entirely unique and unrepeatable. The signs he works, especially with regard to sinners, the poor, the marginalized, the sick, and the suffering, are all meant to teach mercy. Everything in him speaks of mercy. Nothing in him is devoid of compassion."[1] "In Christ, the Father pours forth his boundless mercy even to making him 'mercy incarnate.'"[2]

The Word Resounds and Is Fulfilled

The Word of scripture is presented as a great story of the relations between God and humanity, a history of encounters, clashes, and escapes. When we read this story today, when we hear it, when we celebrate it, it is no longer something of the past, an archaeological residue. Rather, it lives on in our present: it is the word of God, the word of the Lord, it is a new event. We are no longer strangers, but we are involved participants and actors in this story. In fact, we read in the prophet Isaiah: "For as the rain and the snow come down from heaven, and do not return there until they have watered the earth, making it bring forth and sprout, giving seed to the sower and bread to the eater, so shall my word be that goes out from my mouth; it shall not return to me empty, but it shall accomplish that which I purpose, and succeed in the thing for which I sent it" (Isa 55:10–11). In summary: the Word resounds and is fulfilled today. It is from this perspective that we reflect on the Gospel of Matthew and the various reflections of Francis.

—Translated from the original introduction by Gianfranco Venturi

1
Origins of Jesus

How Jesus Was Born (1:18–24)[1]

God makes history and we make history

In those "bad times" that inevitably arise in life, you must take on problems with courage, placing them in the hands of a God who makes history even through us, and corrects it even though we are unable to understand and we make mistakes.

In yesterday's liturgy, we reflected on the genealogy of Jesus. And with this morning's passage from the Gospel of Matthew (1:18–24) the reflection concludes by telling us that salvation is always in history: there is no salvation outside of history. Indeed, before arriving at the point we read about today, there was a long history, a remarkably long history. The point of this history was—as the church chose to tell us symbolically in yesterday's reading of the genealogy of Jesus—simply this: God wants to save us in history.

Our salvation, the one God wants for us, is not aseptic, manufactured; it is "historical." God made a journey in history with his people. The first reading, taken from the prophet Jeremiah (23:5–8), says something beautiful about the phases of this history: "The days are coming, says the Lord, when men shall no longer say, 'As the Lord lives who brought up the people of Israel out of the land of Egypt,' but 'As the Lord lives who brought up and led the descendants of the house of Israel out of the north country and out of all the countries where he had driven them.'"

This was another step, another phase. History is made step by step: God makes history, and *we too make history*. And when we make mistakes, God corrects history and leads us onward, onward, always walking with us. After all, if this isn't clear to us, we will never understand Christmas; we will never understand the mystery of the Incarnation of the Word, never. For it is all a history of walking, and obviously, it doesn't end with Christmas, because now the Lord is still saving us in history and walking with his people.

This is why we need the sacraments, prayer, preaching, the first proclamation: in order to continue with this history. We also need sins, for they are not lacking in the history of Israel; in Jesus's own genealogy there were many considerable sinners. Yet Jesus went forward. God goes forward, despite our sins.

The Lord inconveniences us to make history

In this history there were a few bad moments: bad times, dark times, troublesome times that caused problems for the chosen ones, for those people whom God had chosen to guide history, to help his people move forward. Abraham, a calm ninety-year-old, with his wife: they had no son, but had a beautiful family. However, one day the Lord intervened in Abraham's life and commanded him to leave his land and set out on a journey. Abraham was ninety years old and that was definitely inconvenient for him. But this is how it was for Moses too. After fleeing from Egypt he had gotten married. His father-in-law had a huge flock, and Moses shepherded that flock. He was eighty years old and he was thinking about his sons, about the inheritance he would leave them, and about his wife. And then the Lord commanded him to return to Egypt to free his people. This was definitely inconvenient for him, comfortable as he was there in the land of Midian. But the Lord bothers us, and it was useless for Moses to ask: "But who am I to do this?"

So, the Lord bothers us in order to make history. Often he makes us take paths we would not have chosen. Recall the story of Elijah: the Lord impelled him to kill all the false prophets of Baal. Then, when the queen threatened him, he was frightened. The man who had killed four hundred prophets was terrified of one woman! He ran away, scared to death. He didn't want to continue moving. It was truly a bad moment for him.

Joseph is also put to the test

In today's passage from the Gospel of Matthew we read of another bad time in the history of salvation: there are so many of them. In this reading the main character is Joseph, betrothed to Mary. He really loves his bride-to-be, and she goes to help her cousin. And when she comes back the first signs of pregnancy can be seen. Joseph suffers. He sees the women of the village gossiping at the market. In his suffering, he says to himself about Mary: "This woman is good, I know her! She is a woman of God. What has she done to me? This isn't possible! But I have to accuse her and she will be stoned. They will say all sorts of things about her. But I can't lay this weight on her, about something I don't understand, because she isn't capable of infidelity."

Therefore, Joseph decides to take the problem on his shoulders. And this is what the "gossipmongers" at the market will say: "Look, he left her with child, and then ran away so he wouldn't have to take responsibility." Joseph instead prefers to look like a sinner, like a bad man, in order to avoid casting a shadow on his betrothed, whom he really loves, even though he doesn't understand.

All who are chosen are put to the test

Abraham, Moses, Elijah, Joseph, God's chosen ones, make history in their difficult times by shouldering the problem without understanding. Moses, standing on the shore, saw

Pharaoh's army approaching: the army over there, the sea over here. He might have said: "What do I do? You misled me, Lord!" But then he takes the problem upon himself and says: "I can go back and negotiate, I can fight and be defeated, or I can trust in the Lord." Facing these alternatives, Moses chooses to trust, and the Lord makes history through him.

Or consider Joseph, the son of Jacob. Out of jealousy, his brothers wanted to kill him. Then they sold him, and he became a slave. Later he had a problem with the administrator's wife, but he didn't accuse the woman. He was a noble man, and he knew that it would have destroyed the poor administrator to have known his wife was unfaithful. And so Joseph kept his mouth shut, bore the problem, and went to jail. But the Lord freed him.

Returning to the gospel reading, Joseph, betrothed to Mary, finds himself at the worst time of his life, the darkest moment. He takes the problem upon himself, willing to see himself accused by others in order to protect his bride. (A psychoanalyst might say this was the extremity of his anguish seeking release.) He might have thought, "Let them say what they want!" In reality, however, Joseph took his bride with him, saying: "I don't understand a thing, but the Lord told me this, and this child is going to appear as my son!"

We are also put to the test, and we continue the story

That is why, for God, making history with his people means walking and putting his chosen ones to the test. Indeed, throughout history, his chosen ones have generally gone through dark, painful, bad times, like these that we have seen; but in the end the Lord comes. The Gospel tells us that he sends an angel. And this is—let's not say it's the end of the story, because history continues—precisely the moment before the next: one history before Jesus's birth, and then another history.

In consideration of these reflections, let us always remember to say, with trust, even in the worst of times, even in moments of illness, when we realize that we have to ask for extreme unction because there is no way out: "Lord, history did not begin with me nor will it end with me. You go on. I'm ready." And thus we place ourselves in the hands of the Lord.

This is the attitude of Abraham, Moses, Elijah, Joseph, and also of so many other chosen people of God: God walks with us, God makes history, God puts us to the test, God saves us in the most difficult moments, because he is our Father. Indeed, according to Paul, he is our dad.

May the Lord enable us to understand this mystery of his journey with his people in history, of his testing of his chosen ones, of those with the greatness of heart to take upon themselves the suffering, the problems, even the appearance of sinners—think of Jesus—in order to carry on with history.

In the Little Things (1:1–25)[2]

> Give us, Lord, the treasures of your mercy
> and because the Virgin's motherhood
> marked the beginning of our salvation,
> the feast of his Nativity makes us grow
> in unity and peace.

God's style: reconciliation and peace...

God reconciles: he reconciles the world to himself through Christ. Jesus, brought to us by Mary, makes peace, gives peace to two peoples, and of two peoples he makes one: Hebrews and Gentiles. One people. He makes peace. Peace in their hearts. How does God reconcile? In what "manner" does he do this? Does he perhaps make a great assembly? Does everyone come to an agreement? Do they sign a document? No, God uses a specific method to make peace: he reconciles and makes peace in the little things and on the journey.

From littleness comes peace

God chooses little things, humble things, to do great works: "But you, O Bethlehem Ephrathah, who are one of the little..." (Micah 5:2). In other words, you are so little, but you will be great, because your ruler will be born from you and he will be peace. He himself will be peace, because from that *littleness* comes peace. This is the manner of God, who chooses little things, humble things, to do great works. The Lord is "the Great One" and we are "the little ones," but the Lord advises us to make ourselves little, like children, to be able to enter the kingdom of heaven, whereas the great ones, the powerful, the arrogant, the proud cannot enter. God, however, "reconciles and makes peace in littleness."

God walks in history

The Lord does not want to make peace and reconcile with a magic wand: today—boom!—all done! No. He journeys with his people. An example of this action of God is found in today's gospel. The passage regarding Jesus's lineage may seem somewhat repetitious: "This one begot that one, that one begot this one, this one begot that one..." It's a list, yet it is God's journey: God's journey among men, good and bad, because on this list there are saints and there are sinful criminals.

Thus, it is a list that contains even much sin. However, God is not afraid: he journeys. He walks with his people. And on this journey he makes hope grow in his people, hope in the Messiah. This is the "closeness" of God. Moses said it to his people: "Think about it: what nation has a God as close as ours?"

Thus, this journeying in littleness, with his people, this walking with the good and bad gives us our way of life. We know the way in which we must walk as Christians in order to "make peace" and "reconcile" as Jesus did: with the beatitudes and with the measure by which we will all be judged. Matthew 25: We must do likewise. This means "in littleness and in journeying."

...guarding dreams

The people of Israel dream of being set free; they have this dream because it was promised to them. Even Joseph dreams, and his dream is somewhat like a summary of the entire history of God's journey with his people. However, it is not only Joseph who has dreams; God also dreams. God our Father has dreams, and he dreams beautiful things for his people, for each of us, because he is Father and as Father he thinks and dreams of the best for his children.

In conclusion

This great and almighty God teaches us to do great works of peacemaking and of reconciliation in littleness, by walking, and by not losing hope, with the capacity to dream "great dreams," to have "vast horizons."

In this commemoration of the beginning of a crucial phase of salvation history, the birth of Our Lady—we seek the grace of unity, of reconciliation, and of peace. To be "always on the path, close to others" and "with great dreams." With *littleness*, the littleness that is found in the eucharistic celebration: "a little piece of bread, a little bit of wine..." In this *littleness*, there is everything. God's dream is there, his love is there, his peace is there, his reconciliation is there, Jesus is there.

Small and Holy (1:1–16, 18–23)[3]

God is "the Lord of history" and also of "patience." He "walks with us": for this reason, the Christian is called to not fear great things and to also pay attention to small things.

History entrusted to human freedom

When we read the story of creation in Genesis, we risk thinking that God was a magician, complete with a magic wand, able to do all things. But that is not how it was. In fact, God made things—each one—and he let them go with the intrinsic, internal laws he gave to them so that they would develop, so they would reach fullness. Thus, the Lord gave autonomy to the things of the universe, but not independence. In this way, creation unfolded over eons and eons, until it got to how it is today. And so God is not a magician; he is Creator.

With respect to humanity, however, the case is different. When on the sixth day of the story God creates human beings, he gives them another kind of autonomy that is a bit different: not independence but an autonomy that is freedom. And he tells them to go on in history. God puts them in charge of creation so that they can exercise stewardship over it and bring it to the fullness of time. The *fullness of time* is what God had at heart: the coming of his Son.

The path of humanity

God predestined us, every one of us, to be conformed to the image of his Son (Rom 8:28–30). This is the path of humanity: God wanted us to be like his Son and his Son to be like us.

And this is how history continued, as is also seen in the passage of the Gospel of Matthew (1:1–16, 18–23), which presents the genealogy of Jesus: This one was the father of this one; this one fathered this one; that one fathered that one . . . In this list there are saints and also sinners; but history goes on because God wanted human beings to be free. The day that they misused their freedom, God drove them out of Paradise. The Bible tells us that he made them a promise and they left Paradise with hope: sinners, but with hope.

God walks with us through history

As humanity moved through history it experienced problems, war, hostility, sin—but also hope. The journey was not made alone: God walked with his people. He created an option, an option for time, not for the moment. He is the God of time. He is the God of history. He is the God who walks with his children until the "fullness of time," that is, when his Son is made man.

Although the genealogy is repetitive, it contains this treasure: God walks with the just and with sinners. And if we recognize ourselves as sinners, we know that God also walks with us, with all of us, until we reach our final encounter with him.

God is in the great things and the small

The Gospel, which contains within it this centuries-long history, ends in a tiny thing, in a small village, with the story of Joseph and Mary: *she was found to be with child of the Holy Spirit*. Therefore, the God of the great history is also in the little story, there, because he wants to walk with every single person.

In the *Summa Theologica,* Saint Thomas has a beautiful phrase about this. He says: "Not to fear great things, but also to acknowledge the small ones, this is divine." God is in the great things, but also in the small ones, in our small things. Moreover, our God is also the Lord of Patience: the patience that he had with all these generations, with all these people who lived their history of grace and sin. God is patient. God walks with us, because he wants all of us to come to be conformed to the image of his Son. And from the moment of creation in which he gave us freedom—not independence—until today, he continues to journey.

The birth of Mary

Today we are in the antechamber of this story: the birth of Our Lady. And let us thus ask the Lord in prayer to grant us unity to walk together, with peace in our hearts. It is today's grace: it is how we have arrived here, because our God is patient. He loves us; he accompanies us.

Thus today, we can look to Our Lady, small, holy, without sin, pure, chosen to become the mother of God, and also to look at this history behind her, stretching back so far, over centuries.

We can ask ourselves several fundamental questions: "How do I journey in my story? Do I let God walk with me? Do I let him walk with me or do I want to walk alone? Do I let him caress me, help me, forgive me, lead me forward to reach the encounter with Jesus Christ?" Because this is exactly the point of our journey: to encounter the Lord.

There is one final question that we need to answer: "Do I let God have patience with me?" Only by looking at this great history and also at this small village of Bethlehem can we praise the Lord and humbly ask that he grant us peace, that peace of heart that he alone can give us, and that he gives us only when we let him walk with us.

All in Secret (1:18–25)[4]

God comes to save us. He finds no better way to do so than to walk with us, living our life. And at the moment of choosing the way to live his life, he didn't choose a great city of a great empire; he did not choose a princess or a countess or an important person for his mother; he didn't choose a luxurious palace. It seems as if everything was intentionally done in near obscurity.

Mary was a girl of sixteen or seventeen years of age, no older, in a faraway village on the outskirts of the Roman Empire, and certainly few people had even heard of that village. Joseph was a young man who loved her and wanted to marry her. He was a carpenter who earned his daily bread. All in simplicity, all in obscurity. And even the rejection—because they were betrothed, and in such a small village, you know how gossip is, it spreads. Joseph realized that she was pregnant, but he was a just man . . . The angel explained the mystery to Joseph: "The child that Mary bears is the work of God, the work of the Holy Spirit." When Joseph awoke from his sleep he did what the angel of the Lord had commanded him, and he went to her and married her (cf. Matt 1:18–25). All was hidden, all was humble. The great cities of the world knew nothing about it.

This is how God is among us. If you want to find God, seek him in humility, seek him in poverty, seek him where he is hidden: in the neediest, in the sick, in the hungry, in the imprisoned.

Joseph, "the right person" for a Grand Project (1:19, 20)[5]

On this Fourth Sunday of Advent, the Gospel tells us about the events preceding the birth of Jesus, and the evangelist Matthew presents them from the point of view of Saint Joseph, the betrothed of the Virgin Mary.

Joseph, a just man

Joseph and Mary were dwelling in Nazareth; they were not yet living together, because they were not yet married. In the meantime, Mary, after having welcomed the angel's announcement, came to be with child by the power of the Holy Spirit. When Joseph realized she was pregnant, he was bewildered. The Gospel does not explain what his thoughts were, but it does give us the essential facts: he seeks to do the will of God and is ready for the most radical renunciation. Rather than defending himself and asserting his rights, Joseph chooses what for him is an enormous sacrifice. And the Gospel tells us: "Joseph, being a just man and unwilling to put her to shame, resolved to send her away quietly" (1:19).

This brief sentence reveals a true inner drama if we consider the love that Joseph had for Mary! But even in these circumstances, Joseph intends to do the will of God and decides, surely with great sorrow, to send Mary away quietly. We need to meditate on these words in order to understand the great trial that Joseph had to endure in the days preceding Jesus's birth. It was a trial similar to the sacrifice of Abraham, when

God asked him for his son Isaac (cf. Gen 22): to give up what was most precious, the person most beloved.

A bigger project

But as in the case of Abraham, the Lord intervenes: he finds the faith he was looking for and he opens up a different path, a path of love and of happiness. "Joseph," he says, "do not fear to take Mary as your wife, for that which is conceived in her is of the Holy Spirit" (Matt 1:20).

This gospel passage reveals to us the greatness of Saint Joseph's heart and soul. He was following a good plan for his life, but God was reserving another plan for him, a greater mission. Joseph was a man who always listened to the voice of God. He was deeply sensitive to God's will, a man attentive to the messages that came to him from the depths of his heart and from on high. He did not persist in following his own plan for his life. He did not allow bitterness to poison his soul. Rather, he was ready to make himself available to the news that was being presented to him in a such a bewildering way. And thus, he was a good man. He did not hate, and he did not allow bitterness to poison his soul. Yet how many times does hatred, or even dislike and bitterness, poison our souls! This is harmful. Never allow it. Joseph provides an example: by refusing to allow his heart to be poisoned he becomes even freer and greater. By accepting himself according to God's design, Joseph fully finds himself, beyond himself. His freedom to renounce even what is his, the possession of his very life, and his full interior availability to the will of God challenge us and show us the way.

Let us make ourselves ready to celebrate Christmas by contemplating Mary and Joseph: Mary, the woman full of grace who had the courage to entrust herself totally to the Word of God; Joseph, the faithful and just man who chose to believe the Lord rather than listen to the voices of doubt and human pride. With them, let us walk together toward Bethlehem.

2
The Magi

The Star, Light of the Seekers of God (2:1–12)[1]

Faith and the search for God

The light of faith in Jesus also illumines the path of all those who seek God and makes a specifically Christian contribution to dialogue with the followers of the different religions. The Letter to the Hebrews speaks of the witness of those just ones who, before the covenant with Abraham, already sought God in faith. Of Enoch "it was attested that he had pleased God" (Heb 11:5), something impossible apart from faith, for "whoever would approach God must believe that he exists and that he rewards those who seek him" (Heb 11:6). We can see from this that the path of religious man passes through the acknowledgment of a God who cares for us and is not impossible to find. What other reward can God give to those who seek him, if not to let himself be found? Even earlier, we encounter Abel, whose faith was praised and whose gifts, his offering of the firstlings of his flock (cf. Heb 11:4), were therefore pleasing to God. Religious man strives to see signs of God in the daily experiences of life, in the cycle of the seasons, in the fruitfulness of the earth and in the movement of the cosmos. God is light and he can be found by those who seek him with a sincere heart.

The Magi, image of the seekers of God

An image of this seeking can be seen in the Magi, who were led to Bethlehem by the star (cf. Matt 2:1–12). For them God's light appeared as a journey to be undertaken, a star that led them on a path of discovery. The star is a sign of God's patience with our eyes, which need to grow accustomed to his brightness. Religious man is a wayfarer; he must be ready to let himself be led, to come out of himself and to find the God of perpetual surprises. This respect on God's part for our human eyes shows us that when we draw near to God, our human lights are not dissolved in the immensity of his light, as a star is engulfed by the dawn, but shine all the more brightly the closer they approach the primordial fire, like a mirror that reflects light. Christian faith in Jesus, the one Savior of the world, proclaims that all God's light is concentrated in him, in his "luminous life" which discloses the origin and the end of history. There is no human experience, no journey of man to God, which cannot be taken up, illumined, and purified by this light. The more Christians immerse themselves in the circle of Christ's light, the more capable they become of understanding and accompanying the path of every man and woman toward God.

The journey of faith

Because faith is a way, it also has to do with the lives of those men and women who, though not believers, nonetheless desire to believe and continue to seek. To the extent that they are sincerely open to love and set out with whatever light they can find, they are already, even without knowing it, on the path leading to faith. They strive to act as if God existed, at times because they realize how important he is for finding a sure compass for our life in common or because they experience a desire for light amid darkness, but also because in perceiving life's grandeur and beauty they intuit that the presence of God would make it all the more beautiful. Saint Irenaeus of Lyons tells how Abraham, before hearing God's voice, had already sought him "in the ardent desire of his heart" and "went throughout the whole world, asking himself where God was to be found," until "God had pity on him who, all alone, had sought him in silence." Anyone who sets off on the path of doing good to others is already drawing near to God, is already sustained by his help, for it is characteristic of the divine light to brighten our eyes whenever we walk toward the fullness of love.

A Breath of Universality (2:1–12)[2]

In today's Gospel, the narrative of the Magi coming from the East to Bethlehem to adore the Messiah conveys a breath of universality to the Feast of the Epiphany. This is the breath of the church, which wants *all peoples of the earth to be able to encounter Jesus,* to experience his merciful love. This is the desire of the church: that they may find Jesus's mercy, his love.

Christ is newly born. He does not yet know how to speak, and already people—represented by the Magi—can meet him, recognize him, worship him. The Wise Men stated: "We have seen his star in the East, and have come to worship him" (Matt 2:2). Herod heard this as soon as the Magi arrived in Jerusalem. These Wise Men were prestigious men of a distant religion and different culture, and they were on their way to the land of Israel to worship the newborn king. The church has always seen in them the image of humanity as a whole, and with today's celebration of the Feast of the Epiphany, the church almost tries to direct, respectfully, each man and each woman of this world to the Child who is born for the salvation of all.

Let us lift our gaze to heaven

On Christmas Eve, Jesus manifested himself to shepherds, humble and scorned men—some say brigands. They were the first to bring a little warmth to that extremely cold cave in Bethlehem. Then the Magi arrived from faraway lands. They too were mysteriously drawn by that Child. The shepherds and the Wise Men were very different from each other; however, *they had one thing in common: heaven*. The shepherds of Bethlehem immediately hastened to see Jesus, not because they were particularly good, but because they kept watch in the night and, raising their eyes to heaven, they saw a sign; they heard its message and followed it. It was the same for the Magi: they observed the heavens, saw a new star, interpreted the sign, and set out on their journey from afar. The shepherds and the Wise Men teach us that in order to encounter Jesus it is necessary *to be able to lift our gaze to heaven*, not to withdraw into ourselves, into our own selfishness, but to have *our heart and mind open to the horizons of God*, who always surprises us, to be able to welcome his messages and respond with readiness and generosity.

Let us be guided by the Gospel

When the Magi, the Gospel says, "saw the star, they rejoiced exceedingly" (Matt 2:10). For us too, there is great comfort in seeing the star, in other words in feeling guided and not abandoned to our fate. *The star is the Gospel*, the Word of the Lord, as the psalm states: "Thy word is a lamp to my feet and a light to my path" (119 [118]:105). This light guides us to Christ. Without listening to the Gospel, it is impossible to encounter him! The Wise Men, indeed, by following the star arrived at the place where they found Jesus. Here "they saw the child with Mary his mother, and they fell down and worshiped him" (Matt 2:11). The experience of the Magi exhorts us not to be satisfied with mediocrity, not to "cut corners," but to seek the meaning of things, to fervently explore the great mystery of life. It teaches us not to be scandalized by smallness and poverty but to recognize majesty in in humility, and to be able to kneel before it.

May the Virgin Mary, who welcomed the Wise Men in Bethlehem, help us *to lift our gaze from ourselves,* to allow ourselves *to be guided by the star of the Gospel* in order *to encounter Jesus,* and to be able to humble ourselves *to adore him.* In this way we will be able to bring to others a ray of his light and to share with them the joy of the journey.

Witnesses of Universal Salvation (2:1–12)[3]

On Christmas Eve, we meditated on the hastening of several shepherds of the people of Israel to the grotto of Bethlehem; today, the Solemnity of the Epiphany, we remember the arrival of the Magi, who came from the East to adore the newborn king of the Jews and universal Savior and to offer him symbolic gifts. With their act of adoration, the Magi bear witness that Jesus has come to earth to save not one people alone but all peoples. Therefore, on today's feast our gaze broadens to the horizons of the whole world in order to celebrate the "manifestation" of the Lord to all peoples, which is the manifestation of the love and universal salvation of God. He does not reserve his love for the privileged few, but offers it to all.

As the Creator and Father is *of all people,* so the Savior wants to be *for all people.* That is why we are called to always nourish great faith and hope for every person and his or her salvation: even those who seem far from the Lord are followed —or better yet "chased"—by his passionate love, by his faithful and even humble love. For God's love is humble, very humble!

Journey of the Magi, journey of the soul to meet Christ

The gospel account of the Magi describes their journey from the East as a journey of the spirit, as *a journey toward the encounter with Christ.* They are *attentive to signs* that indicate his presence; they are tireless in facing the trials of the search; they are *courageous* in interpreting the implications for life that derive from encounter with the Lord. This is life: Christian life is a journey, but one that involves being attentive, tireless, and courageous. A Christian journeys like this. A Christian journeys attentively, tirelessly, courageously. The experience of the Magi evokes the journey of every man and woman toward Christ. As for the Magi, so for us, to seek God means *to journey*—and as I said: attentively, tirelessly and courageously—focused on the sky and discerning in the visible sign of the star the invisible God who speaks to our hearts.

Guided by the star: the Word of God

The star that is able to lead every man and woman to Jesus is the *Word of God*, the Word that is in the Bible, in the Gospels. The Word of God is the light that guides our journey, nourishes our faith and regenerates it. It is the Word of God that continually renews our hearts and our communities. Therefore, let us not forget to read the Bible and meditate upon it every day, so that it may become for each of us like a flame that we bear inside us to illuminate our steps, as well as those of others who journey beside us, who are perhaps struggling to find the path to Christ. Always with the Word of God! The Word of God carried in your hand: a little Gospel in your pocket, purse, always to be read. Do not forget this: always carry the Word of God with you!

Mary, make us be ever more on the move

Now let us turn to the Virgin Mary and invoke her protection of the universal church, in order that the Gospel of Christ, the light of nations, the light of all peoples, might be spread through the entire world. May she help us to increasingly embrace the journey, and to continue on that journey attentively, untiringly, and courageously.

The Seeds of Truth (2:1–12)[4]

The Magi mentioned in the Gospel of Matthew are a living witness to the fact that the seeds of truth are present everywhere, for they are the gift of the Creator, who calls all people to acknowledge him as good and faithful Father. The Magi represent the men and women throughout the world who are welcomed into the house of God.

Before Jesus, all divisions of race, language and culture disappear. In that Child, all humanity discovers its unity. The church has the task of seeing and showing ever more clearly the desire for God that is present in the heart of every man and woman. This is what the church is called to do: with the light that she reflects, to draw out the desire for God present in every heart.

Like the Magi, countless people in our own day have a "restless heart" that continues to seek without finding sure answers. It is the restlessness of the Holy Spirit that stirs in hearts. They too are looking for a star to show them the path to Bethlehem.

"The star" that changes you

How many stars there are in the sky! And yet the Magi followed a new and different star, which for them shone all the more brightly. They had long peered into the great book of the heavens, seeking an answer to their questions—they had restless hearts—and at long last the light appeared. That star changed them. It made them leave their daily concerns behind and set out immediately on a journey. They listened to a voice deep within, a voice that led them to follow that light. It was the voice of the Holy Spirit who works in all people. The star guided them, until they found the King of the Jews in a humble dwelling in Bethlehem.

The question to be repeated

All this has something to say to us today. We do well to repeat the question asked by the Magi: "Where is the child who has been born the King of the Jews? For we observed his star at its rising, and have come to pay him homage" (Matt 2:2). We are impelled, especially in an age like our own, to seek the signs that God offers us, realizing that great effort is needed to interpret them and thus to understand his will. We are challenged to go to Bethlehem, to find the Child and his Mother. Let us follow the light God offers us—that tiny light. The hymn in the breviary poetically tells us that the Magi *lumen requirunt lumine* [seek the light of life by the light of the star]. That tiny light leads us to the light that streams from the face of Christ, full of mercy and fidelity. And once we have found him, let us worship him with all our heart, and present him with our gifts: our freedom, our understanding, and our love. True wisdom lies concealed in the face of this Child. It is here, in the simplicity of Bethlehem, that the life of the church is summed up, for here is the wellspring of that light which draws to itself every single person and guides the journey of the peoples of the world along the path of peace.

Go Out, Find the Star, and Proclaim the Gospel (2:1–12)[5]

The words of the prophet Isaiah—addressed to the holy city of Jerusalem—are also meant for us. They call us to rise and go forth, to leave behind all that keeps us self-enclosed, to go out from ourselves and to recognize the splendor of the light that illumines our lives: "Arise, shine; for your light has come, and the glory of the Lord has risen upon you" (60:1). That "light" is the glory of the Lord. The church cannot delude herself into thinking that she shines with her own light. Saint Ambrose expresses this beautifully by presenting the moon as a metaphor for the Church: "The moon is in fact the church . . . [she] shines not with her own light, but with the light of Christ. She draws her brightness from the Sun of Justice, and so she can say: 'It is no longer I who live, but Christ who lives in me'" (*Hexaemeron*, IV, 8, 32). Christ is the true light shining in the darkness. To the extent that the church remains anchored in him, to the extent that she lets herself be illumined by him, she is able to bring light into the lives of people. For this reason the Fathers of the Church saw in her the *mysterium lunae*.

We need this light from on high if we are to respond in a way worthy of the vocation we have received. To proclaim the Gospel of Christ is not simply one option among many, nor is it a profession. For the church, to be missionary does not mean to proselytize. For the church, to be missionary means to give expression to her very nature, which is to receive God's light and then to reflect it. This is how the church serves. There is no other way. Mission is her vocation; to shine Christ's light is what she is called to do. How many people look to us for this missionary commitment, because they need Christ? They need to know the face of the Father.

THREE QUESTIONS (2:16–18)[6]

"Adam, where are you?"

This morning, in the light of God's Word that has just been proclaimed, I wish to offer some thoughts meant to challenge people's consciences and lead them to reflection and a concrete change of heart.

"Adam, where are you?" This is the first question that God asks man after his sin. "Adam, where are you?" Adam lost his bearings, his place in creation, because he thought he could be powerful, be able to control everything, be God. Harmony was lost; Adam erred and this error occurs over and over again in our relationship with others. "The other" is no longer a brother or sister to be loved, but simply someone who disturbs my life and my comfort. God asks a second question: "Cain, where is your brother?" The illusion of being powerful, of being as great as God, of being God himself, leads to a whole series of errors, a chain of death, even to the spilling of a brother's blood!

God's two questions echo today as forcefully as ever. How many of us, myself included, have lost our bearings; we are no longer attentive to the world in which we live; we don't care; we don't protect what God created for everyone, and we end up unable even to care for one another. And when humanity as a whole loses its bearings, it results in tragedies like the one we have witnessed.

"Where is your brother?"

"Where is your brother?" His blood cries out to me, says the Lord. This is not a question directed to others; it is a question directed to me, to you, to each of us. These brothers and sisters of ours were trying to escape difficult situations to find some serenity and peace; they were looking for a better place for themselves and their families, but instead they found death. How often do such people fail to find understanding, fail to find acceptance, fail to find solidarity? And their cry rises up to God! Once again I thank you, the people of Lampedusa, for your solidarity. I recently listened to one of these brothers of ours. Before arriving here, he and the others were at the mercy of traffickers, people who exploit the poverty of others, people who live off the misery of others. How much these people have suffered! Some of them never even made it here.

"Where is your brother?" Who is responsible for this blood? In Spanish literature we have a comedy by Lope de Vega about the people of the town of Fuente Ovejuna who kill their governor because he is a tyrant. They do it in such a way that no one knows who the actual killer is. So, when the royal judge asks, "Who killed the governor?" they all reply: "Fuente Ovejuna, sir." Everybody and nobody!

Today too, the question has to be asked: Who is responsible for the blood of these brothers and sisters of ours? Nobody! That is our answer: It isn't me; I don't have anything to do with it; it must be someone else, but certainly not me. Yet God is asking each of us: "Where is your brother, whose blood cries out to me?" Today no one in our world feels responsible. We have lost a sense of responsibility for our brothers and sisters. We have fallen into the hypocrisy of the priest and the Levite whom Jesus described in the parable of the Good Samaritan. We see our brother half dead on the side of the road, and perhaps we say to ourselves: "Poor soul . . . !" Then we go on our way. It's not our responsibility, and with that thought we feel reassured, assuaged.

The culture of comfort, which makes us think only of ourselves, makes us insensitive to the cries of other people, makes us live in soap bubbles that, however lovely, are insubstantial. They offer a fleeting and empty illusion that results in indifference to others. Indeed, it even leads to the globalization of indifference. In this globalized world, we have fallen into globalized indifference. We have become used to the suffering of others: it doesn't affect me; it doesn't concern me; it's none of my business!

Here we can think of Manzoni's character, "the Unnamed." The globalization of indifference makes us all "unnamed"—responsible, yet nameless and faceless.

"Which of us has cried?"

"Adam, where are you?" "Where is your brother?" These are the two questions that God asks at the dawn of human history, and that he also asks each man and woman in our own day, that he also asks us. But I would like us to ask a third question: "Has any one of us wept because of this situation and others like it?" Has any one of us grieved for the death of these brothers and sisters? Has any one of us wept for the people who were on the boat? For the young mothers carrying their babies? For the men looking for a means of supporting their families? We are a society that has forgotten how to weep, how to experience compassion—"suffering with" others. The globalization of indifference has taken from us the ability to weep!

Rachel's cry

In the Gospel we heard the grieving, the wailing, the great lamentation: "Rachel weeps for her children... because they are no more." Herod sowed death to protect his own comfort, his own soap bubble. And so it continues... Let us ask the Lord to remove the part of Herod that lurks in our hearts; let us ask the Lord for the grace to weep over our indifference, to weep over the cruelty of our world, of our own hearts, and of all those who in anonymity make social and economic decisions that open the door to tragic situations like this. "Has any one wept?" Today has anyone in our world wept?

TEARS OPEN THE HEART (2:16–18)[7]

Knowing how to cry

Jonah helped people see, helped them to become aware. His call found men and women able to repent, and able to weep—to weep over injustice, to weep over corruption, to weep over oppression. Tears like this are tears that lead to transformation, that soften the heart; they are the tears that purify our gaze and enable us to see the cycle of sin into which very often we have sunk. They are tears that can sensitize our gaze, our attitude that has grown hardened and even dormant in the face of another's suffering. They are tears that can break us open, so that we become capable of conversion. This is what happened to Peter after having denied Jesus; he cried, and those tears opened his heart.

Ask for the gift of tears

Tears: a word that echoes forcefully today among us, a word crying out in the wilderness, inviting us to conversion. In this Year of Mercy, with you here, I beg for God's mercy. With you I wish to plead for the gift of tears, the gift of conversion.

We cannot deny the humanitarian crisis that in recent years has meant migration for thousands of people, whether by train or highway or on foot, crossing hundreds of miles through mountains, deserts, and inhospitable zones. The human tragedy that is forced migration is a global phenomenon today. This crisis, which can be described with numbers and statistics, we want instead to describe with names, stories, families. They are our brothers and sisters, expelled by poverty and violence, by drug trafficking and criminal organizations. Being faced with so many legal vacuums, they get caught up in a web that ensnares and always destroys the poorest. Not only do they suffer poverty but they must also endure all these forms of violence. Injustice is radicalized in the young; they are "cannon fodder," persecuted and threatened when they try to flee the spiral of violence and the hell of drugs. And what can we say about the many women whose lives have been unjustly robbed?

Let us together ask our God for the gift of conversion, the gift of tears. Let us ask God to give us hearts that are open like those of the Ninevites, open to his call heard in the suffering faces of countless men and women. No more death! No more exploitation! There is always time to change, always a way out, and always an opportunity. There is always the time to implore the mercy of the Father.

Conversion

Just as in Jonah's time, so too today may we commit ourselves to conversion; may we be signs lighting the way and announcing salvation. I know of the work of countless civil organizations working to support the rights of migrants. I know too of the committed work of so many men and women religious, priests, and lay people in accompanying migrants and in defending life. They are on the front lines, often risking their own lives. By their very lives they are prophets of mercy; they are the beating heart and the accompanying feet of the church that opens her arms and sustains.

This time for conversion, this time for salvation, is the time for mercy. And so, let us say together in response to the suffering of so many: In your compassion and mercy, Lord, have pity on us... cleanse us from our sins and create in us a pure heart, a new spirit (cf. Ps 51 [50]:3, 4, 12).

Knowing How to Rest and Dream (2:13–23)[8]

The scriptures seldom speak of Saint Joseph, but when they do, we often find him resting while an angel reveals God's will to him in his dreams. In the gospel passage we have just heard, we find Joseph resting not once, but twice. This evening I would like to rest in the Lord with all of you. I need to rest in the Lord with families, and to remember my own family: my father, my mother, my grandfather, my grandmother... Today I am resting with you, and together with you I would like to reflect on the gift of the family.

The dream of Joseph

First, however, let me say something about dreams. I am very fond of dreams in families. For nine months every mother and father dream about their baby... They dream about what kind of child he or she will be... You can't have a family without dreams. Once a family loses the ability to dream, children do not grow, love does not grow, life shrivels up and dies. So I ask you, each evening, when you make your examination of conscience, to also ask yourselves this question: Today did I dream about my children's future? Today did I dream about the love of my husband, my wife? Did I dream about my parents and grandparents who have gone before me? Dreaming is very important—especially dreaming in families. Do not lose the ability to dream!

How many difficulties in married life are resolved when we leave room for dreaming, when we stop a moment to think of our spouse, and we dream about the goodness present in the good things all around us? It is very important to reclaim love by what we do each day. Do not ever stop being newlyweds!

Rest and dream

Joseph's rest revealed God's will to him. In this moment of rest in the Lord, as we pause from our many daily obligations and activities, God is also speaking to us. He speaks to us in the reading we have just heard, in our prayer and witness, and in the quiet of our hearts. Let us reflect on what the Lord is saying to us, especially in this evening's gospel reading. There are three aspects of this passage that I would ask you to consider: First, *resting in the Lord*. Second, *rising with Jesus and Mary*. Third, *being a prophetic voice*.

Resting in the Lord

Rest is so necessary for the health of our minds and bodies, and often so difficult to achieve because of the many demands placed upon us. But rest is also essential for our spiritual health, so that we can hear God's voice and understand what he asks of us. Joseph was chosen by God to be the foster father of Jesus and the husband of Mary. As Christians, you too are called, like Joseph, to make a home for Jesus. To make a home for Jesus! You make a home for him in your hearts, your families, your parishes, and your communities.

To hear and accept God's call, to make a home for Jesus, you must be able to rest in the Lord. You must make time each day to rest in the Lord, to pray. To pray is to rest in the Lord.

But you may say to me: "Holy Father, I know that; I want to pray, but there is so much work to do! I must care for my children; I have chores; I am too tired even to sleep well." I know. This may be true, but if we do not pray, we will not know the most important thing of all: God's will for us. And for all our activity, our busy-ness, without prayer we will accomplish very little.

Resting in prayer is especially important for families. It is in the family that we first learn how to pray. Don't forget: the family that prays together stays together! This is important. There we come to know God, to grow into men and women of faith, to see ourselves as members of God's greater family, the church. In the family we learn how to love, to forgive, to be generous and open, not closed and selfish. We learn to move beyond our own needs, to encounter others and share our lives with them. That is why it is so important to pray as a family! So important! That is why families are so important in God's plan for the church! To rest in the Lord is to pray, to pray together as a family.

I would also like to tell you something very personal. I have great love for Saint Joseph, because he is a man of silence and strength. On my table, I have an image of Saint Joseph sleeping. Even when he is asleep, he is taking care of the church! Yes! We know that he can do that. So when I have a problem, a difficulty, I write a little note and I put it underneath Saint Joseph, so that he can dream about it! In other words, I tell him, "Pray for this problem!"

Rising with Jesus and Mary

Next, *rising with Jesus and Mary*. Those precious moments of repose, of resting with the Lord in prayer, are moments we might wish to prolong. But, like Saint Joseph, once we have heard God's voice, we must rise from our slumber; we must get up and act (cf. Rom 13:11). In our families, we have to get up and act! Faith does not remove us from the world but draws us more deeply into it. This is very important! We have to be deeply engaged with the world, but with the power of prayer. Each of us, in fact, has a special role in preparing for the coming of God's kingdom in our world.

Just as the gift of the Holy Family was entrusted to Saint Joseph, so the gift of the family and its place in God's plan is entrusted to us. Just like Saint Joseph. The gift of the Holy Family was entrusted to Saint Joseph so that he could care for it. Each of you, each of us—for I too am part of a family—is charged with caring for God's plan. The angel of the Lord revealed to Joseph the dangers that threatened Jesus and Mary, forcing them to flee to Egypt and then to settle in Nazareth. So too, in our time, God calls upon us to recognize the dangers threatening our own families and to protect them from harm.

Let us be on guard against colonization by new ideologies. There are forms of ideological colonization that are out to destroy the family. They are not born of dreams, of prayers, of closeness to God or the mission God gave us. They come from without, and for that reason I am saying that they are forms of colonization. Let us not lose the freedom of the mission that God has given us, the mission of the family. Just as our peoples, at a certain moment of their history, were mature enough to say "no" to all forms of political colonization, so too in our families we need to be very wise, very shrewd, very strong, in order to say "no" to all attempts at an ideological colonization of our families. We need to ask Saint Joseph, the friend of the angel, to send us the inspiration to know when we can say "yes" and when we have to say "no."

Being prophetic voices...

The gospel passage we have heard reminds us of our Christian duty to be *prophetic voices* in the midst of our communities. Joseph listened to the angel of the Lord and responded to God's call to care for Jesus and Mary. In this way he played his part in God's plan and became a blessing not only for the Holy

Family but for all of humanity. With Mary, Joseph served as a model for the boy Jesus as he grew in wisdom, age, and grace (cf. Luke 2:52). When families bring children into the world, train them in faith and sound values, and teach them to contribute to society, they become a blessing in our world. Families can become a blessing for all of humanity! God's love becomes present and active by the way we love and by the good works that we do. We extend Christ's kingdom in this world. And in doing this, we prove faithful to the prophetic mission that we have received in baptism.

. . . taking care of the poor

During this year, which your bishops have set aside as the *Year of the Poor,* I would ask you, as families, to be especially mindful of our call to be missionary disciples of Jesus. This means being ready to go beyond our homes and to care for our brothers and sisters who are most in need. I ask you especially to show concern for those who do not have a family of their own, in particular those who are elderly and children without parents. Never let them feel isolated, alone and abandoned, but help them to know that God has not forgotten them. Today I was very moved when, after Mass, I visited a home for children without families. How many people work in the church to make that home a family! This is what it means, in a prophetic sense, to build a family.

You may be poor yourselves in material ways, but you have an abundance of gifts to offer when you give to Christ and the community of his church. Do not hide your faith; do not hide Jesus, but carry him into the world and offer the witness of your family life.

3
John the Baptist

Repent (3:1–12)[1]

Why convert?

We ask ourselves, "Why do we have to convert? Conversion is about an atheist who becomes a believer or a sinner who becomes just. But we don't need it. We are already Christians. So we are okay." But this isn't true. In thinking like this, we don't realize that it is precisely because of this presumption—that we are Christians, that all is good, that we're okay—that we must convert: from the supposition that, all things considered, things are fine as they are and we don't need any kind of conversion. But let us ask ourselves: Is it true that in the various situations and circumstances of life, we have within us the same feelings that Jesus has? Is it true that we feel as Christ feels? For example, when we suffer some wrongdoing or some insult, do we manage to react without animosity and to forgive from the heart those who apologize to us? How difficult it is to forgive! How difficult! "You're going to pay for this"—that phrase comes from inside! When we are called to share joys or sorrows, do we know how to sincerely weep with those who weep and rejoice with those who rejoice? When we should express our faith, do we know how to do it with courage and simplicity, without being ashamed of the Gospel? There are so many questions we can ask ourselves. We're not all right. We must always convert and have the sentiments that Jesus had.

The Baptist still cries out in the deserts of humanity

The voice of the Baptist still cries out in the deserts of humanity today, which are—what are today's deserts?—closed minds and hardened hearts. And his voice calls us to ask ourselves if we are actually following the right path, living a life according to the Gospel. Today, as then, he admonishes us with the words of the prophet Isaiah: "Prepare the way of the Lord!" (v. 4). It is a pressing invitation to open one's heart and receive the salvation that God offers ceaselessly, almost obstinately, because he wants us all to be free from the slavery of sin.

The words of the prophet amplify this voice, portending that "all flesh shall see the salvation of God" (v. 6). And salvation is offered to every person, to all people, without exception, to each one of us. None of us can say, "I'm a saint; I'm perfect; I'm already saved." No. We must always accept this offer of salvation. This is the reason for the Year of Mercy: to go farther on this journey of salvation, along this path that Jesus taught. God wants all of humanity to be saved through Jesus, the one mediator (cf. 1 Tim 2:4–6).

Called to make Jesus known

Therefore, each one of us is called to make Jesus known to those who do not yet know him. But this is not to proselytize. No, it is to open a door. "Woe to me if I do not preach the gospel!" (1 Cor 9:16), Saint Paul declared. If Our Lord Jesus has changed our lives, and he changes it every time we go to him, how can we not feel the passion to make him known to those we encounter at work, at school, in our apartment building, in the hospital, in meeting places? If we look around us, we find people who, were they to encounter Christians in love with Jesus, would be willing to begin—or begin again—a journey of faith. Shouldn't we and couldn't we be these Christians? I leave you these questions: "Am I truly in love with Jesus? Am I convinced that Jesus offers me and gives me salvation?" If I am in love, I have to make him known! But we must be courageous: make low the mountains of pride and rivalry; fill in the ravines dug by indifference and apathy; make straight the paths of our laziness and our compromises.

Prepare, Discern, and Decrease (3:1–3)[2]

Prepare, discern, decrease. These three verbs describe the spiritual experience of Saint John the Baptist, who came before the Messiah "preaching the baptism of conversion" to the people of Israel.

Prepare

John worked above all to prepare, taking nothing for himself. He was an important man: the people sought him and followed him, because his words "were strong" like "a sharp sword," to use the words of Isaiah (cf. 49:2). The Baptist reached the hearts of the people. And if perhaps he felt tempted to believe he was important, he never gave in to that temptation, as can be seen in his response to the experts who asked him if he was the Messiah: "I am a voice, only a voice," he said, "of one crying in the wilderness. I am only a voice, but I come to prepare the way for the Lord." His first job, thus, was to prepare the hearts of the people for an encounter with the Lord.

Discern

But who is the Lord? The answer to this question lies in John's second vocation: to *discern* who the Lord was among so many good people. The Spirit revealed this to him. Therefore, he had the courage to say: "This is the one. This is the lamb of God, who takes away the sins of the world." While in preparing John said, "After me one will be coming . . . ," in discerning—in recognizing and pointing out the Lord—he said, "This is the one . . . who was before me."

Decrease

This is where John's third vocation—to *decrease*—comes in, because precisely from that moment of his life he began to humble himself, to decrease so that the Lord would increase, to the point of allowing himself to be humiliated. This was the most difficult challenge John faced, because the Lord had a manner that he had never imagined, even to the point at which, in the prison where Herod Antipas had incarcerated him, he suffered not only the darkness of the cell but also the darkness in his heart. He was assailed by doubts—"But is he the one? Have I made a mistake?"—so much so that he sent his disciples to Jesus to ask him: "Are you he who is to come, or shall we look for another?"

John's humiliation is twofold: the humiliation of his death as the price of a whim and also the humiliation of not being able to glimpse the history of salvation, the humiliation of darkness of the spirit. This man who had proclaimed the Lord's coming after him, had seen him before him, who knew how to await him, knew how to discern, now sees Jesus far away. That promise has become distant. And he ends up alone, in the dark, in humiliation—not because he loved to suffer but so that the Lord would increase. He ended up humiliated but with his heart at peace.

The vocation of the Christian

It's beautiful to think of the Christian vocation like this. In fact, a Christian doesn't proclaim himself, he proclaims another, prepares the path for another: for the Lord. In addition, a

Christian must know how to discern, how to differentiate the truth from what may resemble the truth but is not: he must be a person of discernment. Finally, he must be a person who knows how to humble himself so the Lord may increase in the hearts and souls of others.

The Baptism of Jesus (3:13–17)[3]

Today's Gospel emphasizes that, when Jesus had received baptism from John in the Jordan River, "the heavens were opened" to him (Matt 3:16). This fulfills the prophecies. In fact, there is an invocation that the liturgy has us repeat during the season of Advent: "O that thou wouldst rend the heavens and come down" (Isa 64:1). If the heavens remain closed, our horizon in this earthly life is dark and without hope. Instead, in celebrating Christmas, we once again receive the faith that gives us the certainty that the heavens have been rent with the coming of Christ. And on the day of the baptism of Christ we continue to contemplate the heavens opened.

The manifestation of the Son of God on earth marks the beginning of the great time of mercy, after sin had closed the heavens, raising itself as a barrier between human beings and their Creator. With the birth of Jesus the heavens open! God gives us in Christ the guarantee of an indestructible love. From the moment of the Word becoming flesh it becomes possible to see the open heavens. It was possible for the shepherds of Bethlehem, for the Magi from the East, for the Baptist, for Jesus's apostles, and for Saint Stephen, the first martyr, who exclaimed: "Behold, I see the heavens opened!" (Acts 7:56). And it is possible for each one of us, if we allow ourselves to be suffused with God's love, which is given to us by means of the Holy Spirit. Let us allow ourselves to be invaded by God's love! This is the great time of mercy! Do not forget it: this is the great time of mercy!

Jesus sent to share our condition

When Jesus received the baptism of repentance from John the Baptist, demonstrating solidarity with the repentant people—he without sin and with no need for conversion—God the Father made his voice heard from heaven: "This is my beloved Son, with whom I am well pleased" (Matt 3:17). Jesus receives approval from the heavenly Father, who sent him precisely that he might share our condition, our poverty. Sharing is the true way to love. Jesus does not dissociate himself from us; he considers us brothers and sisters and he shares with us. And so he makes us sons and daughters, together with him, of God the Father. This is the revelation and source of true love. And this is the great time of mercy!

Does it not seem to you that in our own time extra fraternal sharing and love is needed? Does it not seem to you that we all need extra charity? Not the sort that is content with extemporaneous help which does not involve or risk anything, but the charity that shares, that takes on the hardship and suffering of a brother or sister. What flavor life acquires when we allow ourselves to be inundated by God's love!

Let us ask the Holy Virgin to support us by her intercession in our commitment to follow Christ on the way of faith and charity, the path traced out by our baptism.

Participation in the Human Condition (3:13–17)[4]

The place where we are meeting commemorates Jesus's baptism. Coming here to the Jordan to be baptized by John, Jesus showed his humility and his participation in our human condition. He stooped down to us and by his love he restored our dignity and brought us salvation. Jesus's humility, the fact that he bends down to wounded humanity in order to heal us, to heal all our wounds— never fails to move us! On our part, we are profoundly affected by the tragedies and suffering of our times, particularly those caused by ongoing conflicts in the Middle East.

The Gospel of Mercy (3:13–17)[5]

A love open to all

After reflecting on the mercy of God in the Old Testament, today we begin to meditate on how Jesus fulfilled it. It was a mercy he expressed, realized, and communicated throughout his earthly life. Encountering the multitudes, proclaiming the Gospel, healing the sick, being close to the least, forgiving sinners, Jesus made visible the love that is open to us all: none are excluded! Open to all without borders. A love that is pure, freely given, and absolute. A love that culminates in the sacrifice of the cross. Yes, the Gospel is truly the "Gospel of Mercy," for Jesus is Mercy!

The merciful mission of Jesus

All four gospels testify that Jesus, before taking up his ministry, *wanted to be baptized by John the Baptist* (Matt 3:13–17; Mark 1:9–11; Luke 3:21–22; John 1:29–34). This event gives decisive direction to Christ's entire mission. Indeed, he did not present himself to the world in the splendor of the temple, although he could have done so. He did not announce himself with the sounding of trumpets, although he could have done so. And he did not come vested like a judge, although he could have done so. Instead, after thirty years of a hidden life in Nazareth, Jesus went to the Jordan River, together with many of his people, and there waited in line with sinners. He wasn't ashamed; he was there with everyone, with sinners, to be baptized. Therefore, from the very beginning of his ministry, he manifested himself as the Messiah who, moved by solidarity and compassion, takes upon himself the human condition. As he said in the synagogue of Nazareth by identifying with the prophecy of Isaiah: "The Spirit of the Lord is upon me, because he has anointed me to preach good news to the poor. He has sent me to proclaim release to the captives and recovery of sight to the blind, to set at liberty those who are oppressed, to proclaim the acceptable year of the Lord" (Luke 4:18–19). Everything that Jesus accomplished after his baptism was the realization of that initial design: to bring to all people the saving love of God. Jesus did not bring hatred. He did not bring hostility. He brought us love—a love that saves!

The fruit of God's mercy

Jesus made himself neighbor to the lowliest, communicating to them God's mercy that is forgiveness, joy, and new life. Jesus, the Son sent by the Father, is truly the start of the time of mercy for all humanity! Those present on the banks of the Jordan did not immediately understand the full extent of Jesus's gesture. John the Baptist himself was stunned by his decision (cf. Matt 3:14). But not the Heavenly Father! He let his voice be heard from on high: "You are my beloved son; with you I am well pleased" (Mark 1:11). In this way, the Father confirmed the path that the Son had taken up as Messiah, as the Holy Spirit descended upon him in the form of a dove. Thus, Jesus's heart beats, so to speak, in unison with the heart of the Father and of the Spirit, showing to all that salvation is the fruit of God's mercy.

From baptism to the cross

We can contemplate even more clearly the great mystery of this love by *directing our gaze to Jesus crucified*. As the Innocent One is about to die for us sinners, he offers his plea to the Father: "Father, forgive them, for they know not what they do" (Luke 23:34). It is on the cross that Jesus presents the sin of the world to the mercy of the Father: the sin of all people, my sins, your sins, everyone's sins. There, on the cross, he presents them to the Father. And along with the sin of the world, all our sins are wiped away. Nothing and no one is left out of this sacrificial prayer of Jesus. That means that we must not be afraid of acknowledging and confessing ourselves as sinners.

How many times have we said: "Well, this one is a sinner; he did this and that..." We judge others. And you? Every one of us ought to ask ourselves: "Yes, he is a sinner. And me?" We are all sinners, but we are all forgiven. We all have the opportunity to receive the forgiveness that is the mercy of God. Therefore, we mustn't be afraid to acknowledge that we are sinners, to confess that we are sinners, because every sin was borne by the Son on the cross. When we confess our sins, repenting, entrusting ourselves to him, we can be certain of forgiveness. The sacrament of reconciliation makes present to each one of us the power of forgiveness that flows from the cross and renews in our life the grace of mercy that Jesus purchased for us! We must not be afraid of our defects: we each have our own. The power of the love of the Crucified One knows no bounds and never runs dry. This mercy wipes away our defects.

Experiencing the mercy that transforms

Let us ask God for the grace to experience the power of the Gospel: the Gospel of mercy that transforms, that lets us enter the heart of God and makes us capable of forgiving and looking at the world with more goodness. If we accept the Gospel of the Crucified and Risen One, our whole life will be formed by his renewing love.

4

Jesus's Public Life Begins

Jesus is Tempted (4:1)[1]

The manifestation of Jesus Christ reveals the presence of the spirit of evil, of sin. Jesus says it openly: "The world cannot hate you, but it hates me, because I testify against it that its deeds are evil" (John 7:7). No one can approach the truth and the reality of sin except through the grace of God, that is, through the manifestation of Jesus Christ: "The Son of God was revealed for this purpose, to destroy the works of the devil" (1 John 3:8). Jesus is a sign of contradiction. His becoming flesh, his sacrifice is so that "the inner thoughts of many will be revealed" (Luke 2:35). The epiphany of Jesus Christ is ultimately a judgment. "And this is the judgment, that the light has come into the world, and people loved darkness rather than light because their deeds were evil" (John 3:19). In his presence, "Nothing is covered up that will not be uncovered, and nothing secret that will not become known" (Luke 12:2; Matt 10:26; Mark 4:22; Matt 5:5).

Jesus Begins with the "Galilee of the Gentiles" (4:12–17)[2]

Today's Gospel recounts the beginnings of the public life of Jesus in the cities and villages of Galilee. His mission does not begin in Jerusalem, the religious center as well as the social and political center, but in an area on the outskirts, an area looked down upon by the most observant Jews because of the presence in that region of various foreign peoples; that is why the prophet Isaiah calls it the "Galilee of the nations" (Isa 9:1).

It is a borderland, a place of transit where people of different races, cultures, and religions converge. Thus, Galilee becomes a symbolic place for the opening of the Gospel to all nations. In this sense, Galilee is like the world of today, characterized by the simultaneous presence of different cultures, the necessity of encounter, and the possibility of conflict. We too are immersed every day in a kind of "Galilee of the nations," and in this context, we may feel afraid and give in to the temptation to build fences to make us feel safer, more protected. But Jesus teaches us that the Good News, which he brings, is not reserved to one part of humanity; it is to be communicated to everyone. It is a proclamation of joy destined for those who are waiting for it, and also for all those who perhaps are no longer waiting for anything and haven't even the strength to seek and to ask.

. . . to show that no one is excluded

Starting from Galilee, Jesus teaches us that no one is excluded from the salvation of God, that it is from the margins that God prefers to begin, from the least, so as to reach everyone. Jesus teaches us a method, his method, which also expresses the content, which is the Father's mercy. "Each Christian and every community must discern the path that the Lord points out, but all of us are asked to obey his call to go forth from our own comfort zone in order to reach all the 'peripheries' in need of the light of the Gospel."[3]

. . . and also to meet low-profile people where they work

Jesus begins his mission not only from the outskirts, but also among people whom one would refer to as having a "low profile." When choosing his first disciples and future apostles, he does not turn to the schools of scribes and doctors of the Law, but to humble and simple people who diligently prepare for the coming of the kingdom of God. Jesus goes to call them where they work, on the lakeshore: they are fishermen. He calls them and they immediately follow him. They leave their nets and go with him; their life will become an extraordinary and fascinating adventure.

An Invitation to Mission (4:18–22)[4]

When the Lord comes into our life, when he passes into our heart, he always speaks a word to us and makes us a promise: "Go ahead . . . Courage, do not fear, for you can do this!" It is an invitation to mission, an invitation to follow him. And when we hear this, we see that there is something wrong in our lives that we must correct and leave behind. Or, even if there is something good in our life, the Lord inspires us to leave it behind, to follow him more closely, as happened [at the lake of Gennesaret]: the disciples left everything, says the Gospel. "When they had brought their boats to shore, they left everything and followed him" (Luke 5:11).

Jesus never says, "Follow me" without mentioning the mission. No! "Follow me and I'll do this to you." "Follow me for this." "If you want to be perfect, leave and follow me." There is always the mission. We follow Jesus's way to do something: it is the mission.

It is true Christian prayer to hear the Lord with his Word of comfort, peace, and promise, to have the courage to strip ourselves of what prevents us from rushing to follow him and join the mission. This does not mean that then there are no temptations. There will be many! But, look, Peter sinned gravely, denying Jesus, but then the Lord forgave him. James and John ... sinned by wanting to go higher, but the Lord forgave them.

Even Today Jesus Passes by (4:18–25)[5]

The Lord is calling today too! The Lord passes through the paths of our daily life. Even today at this moment, here, the Lord is passing through the square. He is calling us to go with him, to work with him for the kingdom of God, in the "Galilee" of our times. May each one of you think: the Lord is passing by today, the Lord is watching me, he is looking at me! What is the Lord saying to me? And if one of you feels that the Lord says to you "Follow me," be brave; go with the Lord. The Lord never disappoints. Feel in your heart if the Lord is calling you to follow him. May we let his gaze rest on us; may we hear his voice and follow him! "That the joy of the Gospel may reach to the ends of the earth, illuminating even the fringes of our world."[6]

Even Today Jesus Calls (4:18–22)[7]

All the baptized need to continually break with the remnants of the old Adam, the man of sin, ever ready to rise up again at the prompting of the devil. How often this happens in our world and in these times of conflict, hate and war! How easy it is to be led into selfishness, distrust, violence, destructiveness, vengeance, indifference to and exploitation of those who are most vulnerable...

And you, dear Central Africans, may you look to the future and, strengthened by the distance you have already come, resolutely determine to begin a new chapter in the Christian history of your country, to set out towards new horizons, to put out into the deep. The apostle Andrew, with his brother Peter, did not hesitate to leave everything at Christ's call: "Immediately they left their nets and followed him" (Matt 4:20). Once again, we are amazed at the great enthusiasm of the apostles. Christ drew them so closely to himself that they felt able to do everything and to risk everything with him.

Jesus calls everyone...

Each of us, in his or her heart, can ask the crucial question of where we stand with Jesus, asking what we have already accepted—or refused to accept—in responding to his call to follow him more closely. The cry of "those who bring good news" resounds all the more in our ears precisely when times are difficult—that cry which "goes out through all the earth... to the ends of the earth" (Rom 10:18; cf. Ps 19:4). And it resounds here, today, in this land of Central Africa. It resounds in our hearts, our families, our parishes, wherever we live. It invites us to persevere in enthusiasm for mission, for that mission which needs new "bearers of good news," ever more numerous, generous, joyful, and holy. We are all called to be, each of us, these messengers whom our brothers and sisters of every ethnic group, religion, and culture await, often without knowing it. For how can our brothers and sisters believe in Christ—Saint Paul asks—if the Word is neither proclaimed nor heard?

...and we answer full of hope

We too, like the apostles, need to be full of hope and enthusiasm for the future. The *other shore* is at hand, and Jesus is crossing the river with us. He is risen from the dead. Henceforth the trials and sufferings that we experience are always opportunities opening up to a new future, provided we are willing to follow him. Christians of Central Africa, each of you is called to be, through perseverance in faith and missionary commitment, an artisan of the human and spiritual renewal of your country. I say again, [you are all called to be] artisans of human and spiritual renewal.

5

The Sermon on the Mount

THE BEATITUDES: THE WAY OF HAPPINESS, OF HOLINESS (5:1–12)[1]

The Word of the risen and living Lord also shows us, today, the way to reach true beatitude, the way that leads to heaven. It is difficult to understand the path because it goes against the current, but the Lord tells us that those who go on this path are happy; they have happiness now or will have it in the future.

"Blessed are the poor in spirit, for theirs is the kingdom of heaven." We might ask ourselves how a person who is poor of heart, one whose only treasure is the kingdom of heaven, can be happy. The reason is exactly this: that having the heart stripped and free of so many worldly things, this person is "awaited" in the kingdom of heaven.

"Blessed are those who mourn, for they shall be comforted." How can those who weep be happy? Yet, those who in life have never felt sadness, angst, sorrow, will never know the power of comfort. Instead, happy are those with the capacity to be moved, the capacity to feel in their heart the sorrow that exists in their life and in the lives of others. They will be happy! Because the tender hand of God the Father will comfort them and will caress them.

"Blessed are the meek." How often are we instead impatient, irritable, always ready to complain! We have many demands regarding others, but when our turn comes, we react by raising our voice, as if we were masters of the world, when in reality we are all children of God. Let us think instead of those mothers and fathers who are so patient with their children who "drive them mad." This is the way of the Lord: the way of meekness and of patience. Jesus traveled this path: as a child he endured persecution and exile; then, as an adult, slander, snares, false accusations in court; and he endured it all with meekness. Out of love for us he endured even the cross.

"Blessed are those who hunger and thirst for righteousness, for they shall be satisfied." Yes, those who have a strong sense of justice, and not only toward others, but first of all toward themselves, will be satisfied, because they are ready to receive the greatest justice—that which only God can give.

Then, *"blessed are the merciful, for they shall obtain mercy."* Happy are those who know how to forgive, who have mercy on others, who do not judge everything and everyone, but try to put themselves in the place of others. Forgiveness is the thing that all of us—without exception—need. This is why at the beginning of Mass we recognize ourselves for what we are, namely, sinners. It isn't an expression or a formality: it is an act of truth. "Lord, here I am; have mercy on me." If we are able to give others the forgiveness we ask for ourselves, we are blessed. As we say in the "Our Father": "Forgive us our trespasses as we forgive those who trespass against us."

"Blessed are the peacemakers, for they shall be called children of God." Let us look at the faces of those who go around sowing discord. Are they happy? Those who are always seeking occasions to mislead, to take advantage of others, are they happy? No, they cannot be happy. Instead, those who patiently try to sow peace each day, who are artisans of peace, of reconciliation, yes, they are blessed, because they are true children of

our heavenly Father, who sows always and only peace, to the point that he sent his Son into the world as the seed of peace for humanity.

This is the way of holiness, and it is the very way of happiness. It is the way that Jesus traveled. Indeed, he himself is the Way. Those who walk with him and proceed through him enter into life, into eternal life. Let us ask the Lord for the grace to be simple and humble people, the grace to be able to weep, the grace to be meek, the grace to work for justice and peace, and above all the grace to let ourselves be forgiven by God so as to become instruments of his mercy.

This is what the saints did, those who have preceded us to our heavenly home. They accompany us on our earthly pilgrimage; they encourage us to go forward. May their intercession help us to walk on Jesus's path and to obtain eternal happiness for our deceased brothers and sisters, for whom we offer this Mass.

The Beatitudes: A Revolutionary Force (5:1–12)[2]

Jesus incarnated the beatitudes . . .

Throughout his life, from his birth in the stable in Bethlehem until his death on the cross and his resurrection, Jesus embodied the beatitudes. All the promises of God's kingdom were fulfilled in him.

In proclaiming the beatitudes, Jesus asks us to follow him and to travel with him along the path of love, the path that alone leads to eternal life. It is not an easy journey, yet the Lord promises us his grace and never abandons us. We face so many challenges in life: poverty, distress, humiliation, the struggle for justice, persecutions, the difficulty of daily conversion, the effort to remain faithful to our call to holiness, and many others. But if we open the door to Jesus and allow him to be part of our lives, if we share our joys and sorrows with him, then we will experience the peace and joy that only God, who is infinite love, can give.

. . . new and revolutionary

The beatitudes of Jesus are new and revolutionary. They present a model of happiness contrary to what is usually communicated by the media and by prevailing wisdom. A worldly way of thinking finds it scandalous that God became one of us and died on a cross! According to the logic of this world, those whom Jesus proclaimed blessed are regarded as useless "losers." What is glorified is success at any cost, affluence, the arrogance of power and self-affirmation at the expense of others.

Jesus challenges us to follow him

Jesus challenges us, young friends, to take seriously his approach to life and to decide which path is right for us and leads to true joy. This is the great challenge of faith. Jesus was not afraid to ask his disciples if they truly wanted to follow him or if they preferred to take another path (cf. John 6:67). Simon Peter had the courage to reply: "Lord, to whom shall we go? You have the words of eternal life" (John 6:68). If you too are able to say "yes" to Jesus, your lives will be both meaningful and fruitful.

The courage to go against the tide

Saint John, writing to young people, told them: "You are strong, and the word of God abides in you, and you have overcome the evil one" (1 John 2:14). Young people who choose Christ are strong; they are fed by his word and they do not need to "stuff themselves" with other things! Have the courage to swim against the tide. Have the courage to be truly happy! Say no to an ephemeral, superficial, and throwaway culture, a culture that assumes that you are incapable of taking on responsibility and facing the great challenges of life!

Jesus Teaches Us to Become Saints (5:1–12)[3]

Being holy is not a privilege for the few, as in the case of someone with a large inheritance; in baptism we all have an inheritance; we are endowed with the ability to become saints. Holiness is a vocation for everyone. Thus we are all called to walk on the path of holiness, and this path has a name and a face: the face of Jesus Christ. He teaches us to become saints. In the Gospel, he shows us the way, the way of the beatitudes (cf. Matt 5:1–12). In fact, the kingdom of heaven is for those who do not place their security in material things but in love for God, for those who have a simple, humble heart that does not presume to be just and does not judge others, for those who know how to suffer with those who suffer and how to rejoice when others rejoice. They are not violent but merciful and strive to be instruments for reconciliation and peace. Saints are instruments for reconciliation and peace; they are always helping people to become reconciled, helping to bring about peace. Thus holiness is beautiful. It is a beautiful path!

The Christian Path of Holiness (5:1–12)[4]

This is the life plan that Jesus proposes to us, a plan that is really simple but really difficult at the same time. And if we want something more, Jesus gives us even further instructions. In particular is the standard by which we will be judged, found in the Gospel of Matthew: "I was hungry and you gave me food; I was thirsty and you gave me drink; I was sick and you visited me; I was in prison and you came to me."

This is the path to live the Christian life in a holy way. The saints did nothing other than live the beatitudes and *that standard for final judgment*. They are few words, simple words, but practical for everyone, because Christianity is a practical religion. It is something to practice, to do, not simply to think about.

Today, if you have a little time at home, pick up the Gospel of Matthew, the fifth chapter: the beatitudes are at the beginning. And then, in chapter 25, there are other words of Jesus. It will do you good to read this plan for holiness once, twice, three times.

The Guide and the Four Woes (5:1–12)[5]

The Guide

We can imagine the context in which Jesus spoke the discourse of the beatitudes (Matt 1–12): Jesus, the crowds, the mountain, the disciples. When Jesus began to speak he taught the new law, which does not erase the old, because he himself said that even the last iota of the ancient law must be fulfilled. In reality, Jesus perfects the ancient law, brings it to its fullness. And this is the new law, that which we call the beatitudes. Yes, it is the new law of the Lord for us. In fact, the beatitudes are a guide for the route, the itinerary. They help us to navigate the Christian life: right here we see, by following this road according to this guide, how we can go forward in our Christian life.

The four woes

In chapter 6 of his Gospel, Luke also has the beatitudes that we find in Matthew, but at the end he adds something else: the woes (Luke 6:24–26). And so, after his list of "blessed, blessed, blessed, blessed, . . ." Luke adds "woe, woe, woe, woe."

There are precisely four woes. That is to say: "Woe to you who are rich, for you have received your consolation. Woe to you who are full now, for you shall hunger. Woe to you who laugh now, for you shall mourn and weep. Woe to you when all speak well of you, for so their fathers did to the false prophets." These woes illuminate the essence of this page, this guide for the Christian journey.

The first woe concerns the wealthy. I have said many times that riches are good and that what hurts and is bad is the attachment to riches, woe! In fact, wealth is idolatry. When I am attached to something, then I am idolatrous. It is certainly not a coincidence that most idols are made of gold. And so there are those who feel happy, who lack nothing; they have a satisfied heart, a closed heart, without horizons; they laugh, they are satiated, and they have no appetite for anything. Then there are those who like incense: they like it when everyone speaks well of them and so they are quiet. But "woe to you" says the Lord. This is the anti-law; it is the wrong guide.

It is important to note that these are the steps that lead to perdition, whereas the beatitudes are the steps that they carry us through life. The first of the steps that lead to perdition is, in fact, *the attachment to riches,* when we feel that we do not need anything.

The second is *vanity,* desiring that everyone say nice things about me, that everyone speak well of me: I feel important ...and in the end I believe that I am right, unlike others. Consider the parable of the Pharisee and the publican: "I thank you that I am not like that." When we are consumed by vanity we can even end up saying—and this happens every day—"Thank you, Lord, because I am such a good Catholic, not like the neighbor, that neighbor."

The third is *the pride of being content,* the laughter that closes the heart. These steps lead to perdition because they are the anti-beatitudes: attachment to riches, vanity, and pride.

The beatitudes

The beatitudes, on the contrary, are the guide for the journey that leads us to the kingdom of God. Among all of them, however, there is one that, though I would not say it is the key, does give us pause for thought: "Blessed are the meek"—specifically, "meekness." Jesus speaks of himself, saying: Learn from me for I am meek of heart, I am humble and meek of heart. Therefore, meekness is a way of being that brings us very close to Jesus, whereas the opposite attitude always leads to enmity, war, and other horrible things. And do not confuse meekness of heart with foolishness. No, it is another thing; meekness is depth in understanding the greatness of God, and adoration.

"Blessed are the poor in spirit..." (5:3)[6]

The first beatitude says that the poor in spirit are blessed, for theirs is the kingdom of heaven. At a time when so many people are suffering as a result of the financial crisis, it might seem strange to link poverty and happiness. How can we consider poverty a blessing?

What does "poor in spirit" mean?

First of all, let us try to understand what it means to be "poor in spirit." When the Son of God became man, he chose the path of poverty and self-emptying. As Saint Paul said in his letter to the Philippians: "Let the same mind be in you that was in Christ Jesus, who, though he was in the form of God, did not count equality with God a thing to be grasped, but emptied himself, taking the form of a servant, being born in human likeness" (Phil 2:5–7). Jesus is God who strips himself of his glory. Here we see God's choice to be poor: he was rich and yet he became poor in order to enrich us through his poverty (cf. 2 Cor 8:9). This is the mystery we contemplate in the crib when we see the Son of God lying in a manger, and later on the cross, where his self-emptying reaches its culmination.

...become "beggars"!

The Greek adjective *ptochós* (poor) does not have a purely material meaning. It means "a beggar," and it should be seen as linked to the Jewish notion of the *anawim*, "God's poor." It suggests lowliness, a sense of one's limitations and existential poverty. The *anawim* trust in the Lord, and they know that they can count on him.

As Saint Therese of the Child Jesus clearly saw, by his incarnation Jesus came among us as a poor beggar, asking for our love. The *Catechism of the Catholic Church* tells us that "man is a beggar before God" (§ 2559) and that prayer is the encounter of God's thirst and our own thirst (§ 2560).

Saint Francis of Assisi understood perfectly the secret of the beatitude of the poor in spirit. Indeed, when Jesus spoke to him through the leper and from the crucifix, Francis recognized both God's grandeur and his own lowliness. In his prayer, the Poor Man of Assisi would spend hours asking the Lord: "Who are you?" "Who am I?" He renounced an affluent and carefree life in order to marry "Lady Poverty," to imitate Jesus and to follow the Gospel to the letter. Francis lived *in imitation of Christ in his poverty* and *in love for the poor*—for him the two were inextricably linked, like two sides of one coin.

Making "poverty of spirit" a way of life

What can we do, specifically, to make *poverty of spirit* a way of life, a real part of our own lives? I will reply by saying three things.

First of all, try to be free with regard to material things. The Lord calls us to a gospel lifestyle marked by sobriety, by a refusal to yield to the culture of consumerism. This means being concerned with the essentials and learning to do without all those unneeded extras that hem us in. Let us learn to be detached from possessiveness and from the idolatry of money and lavish spending. Let us put Jesus first. He can free us from the kinds of idol worship that enslave us.

Put your trust in God, dear young friends! He knows and loves us, and he never forgets us. Just as he provides for the lilies of the field (cf. Matt 6:28), so he will make sure that we lack nothing. If we are to come through the financial crisis, we must be ready to change our lifestyle and avoid so much wastefulness. Just as we need the courage to be happy, we also need the courage to live simply.

Second, if we are to live by this beatitude, all of us need to experience *a conversion in the way we see the poor*. We have to care for them and be sensitive to their spiritual and material needs. To you young people I especially entrust the task of restoring solidarity to the heart of human culture. Faced with old and new forms of poverty—unemployment, migration and addictions of various kinds—we have the duty to be alert and thoughtful, avoiding the temptation to remain indifferent. We have to remember all those who feel unloved, who have no hope for the future, and who have given up on life out of discouragement, disappointment, or fear. We have to learn to be on the side of the poor, and not just indulge in rhetoric about the poor. Let us go out to meet them, look into their eyes, and listen to them. The poor provide us with a concrete opportunity to encounter Christ himself, and to touch his suffering flesh.

However—and this is my third point—the poor are not just people to whom we can give something. They have much to offer us and to teach us. How much we have to learn from the wisdom of the poor! Think about it: several hundred years ago a saint, Benedict Joseph Labre, who lived on the streets of Rome from the alms he received, became a spiritual guide to all sorts of people, including nobles and prelates. In a very real way, the poor are our teachers. They show us that people's value is not measured by their possessions or how much money they have in the bank. A poor person, a person lacking material possessions, always maintains his or her dignity. The poor can teach us much about humility and trust in God. In the parable of the Pharisee and the tax collector (cf. Luke 18:9–14), Jesus holds the tax collector up as a model because of his humility and his acknowledgment that he is a sinner. The widow who gave her last two coins to the temple treasury is an example of the generosity of all those who have next to nothing and yet give away everything they have (Luke 21:1–4).

...for theirs is the kingdom of heaven

The central theme of the Gospel is the kingdom of God. Jesus is the kingdom of God in person; he is Immanuel, God-with-us. And it is in the human heart that the kingdom, God's sovereignty, takes root and grows. The kingdom is at once both gift and promise. It has already been given to us in Jesus, but it has yet to be realized in its fullness. That is why we pray to the Father each day: "Thy kingdom come."

...to be able to evangelize

There is a close connection between poverty and evangelization, between "Go therefore, and make disciples of all nations!" (Matt 28:19) and "Blessed are the poor in spirit, for theirs is the kingdom of heaven" (Matt 5:3). The Lord wants a poor church that evangelizes the poor. When Jesus sent the Twelve out on mission, he said to them: "Take no gold, nor silver, nor copper in your belts, no bag for your journey, nor two tunics, nor sandals, nor a staff; for the laborers deserve their food" (Matt 10:9–10). Evangelical poverty is a basic condition for spreading the kingdom of God. The most beautiful and spontaneous expressions of joy I have seen during my life were those of poor people who had little to hold onto.

Evangelization, in our time, will take place only as the result of contagious joy.

A need for conversion

We have seen, then, that the beatitude of the poor in spirit shapes our relationship with God, with material goods, and with the poor. Having the example and words of Jesus before us, we realize how much we need to be converted, so that the logic of *being more* will prevail over that of *having more*! The saints can best help us to understand the profound meaning of the beatitudes.

In the sign of the cross

John Paul II began the great youth pilgrimage of the cross, which has since crossed the five continents. The pope's words on Easter Sunday in 1984 remain memorable: "My dear young people, at the conclusion of the Holy Year, I entrust to you the sign of this Jubilee Year: the cross of Christ! Carry it throughout the world as a symbol of the love of the Lord Jesus for humanity, and proclaim to everyone that it is only in Christ, who died and rose from the dead, that salvation and redemption are to be found."

The Magnificat is the song of those who live the beatitudes

Dear friends, the Magnificat, the Canticle of Mary, poor in spirit, is also the song of everyone who lives by the beatitudes. The joy of the Gospel arises from a heart that, in its poverty, rejoices and marvels at the works of God, like the heart of Our Lady, whom all generations call "blessed" (cf. Luke 1:48). May Mary, Mother of the poor and Star of the new evangelization, help us to live the Gospel, embody the beatitudes in our lives, and have the courage always to be happy.

Transform Conflict into a New Process (5:9)[7]

When conflict arises, some people simply look at it and go their way as if nothing happened; they wash their hands of it and get on with their lives. Others embrace it in such a way that they become its prisoners; they lose their bearings, project onto institutions their own confusion and dissatisfaction, and thus make unity impossible. But there is a third way, and it is the best way to deal with conflict. It is the willingness to face conflict head on, to resolve it and to make it a link in the chain of a new process. "Blessed are the peacemakers!" (Matt 5:9).

Peace is an art

Commitment to ecumenism is a response to the prayer of the Lord Jesus that "they may all be one" (John 17:21). The credibility of the Christian message would be much greater if Christians could overcome their divisions and the church could realize "the fullness of catholicity proper to her in those of her children who, though joined to her by baptism, are yet separated from full communion with her."[8] We must never forget that we are pilgrims journeying alongside one another. This means that we must have sincere trust in our fellow pilgrims, putting aside all suspicion or mistrust, and turn our gaze to what we are all seeking: the radiant peace of God's face. Trusting others is an art and peace is an art. Jesus told us: "Blessed are the peacemakers" (Matt 5:9). In taking up this task, also among ourselves, we fulfill the ancient prophecy: "They shall beat their swords into ploughshares" (Isa 2:4).

Christian Identity (5:13–16)[9]

To arrive at Christian identity, God, our Father, made us take a long journey in history, over centuries and centuries, with allegorical figures, with promises, covenants, and the like, until the moment of the fullness of time, when he sent his Son, "born of woman." It was a long journey. And we too must make a long journey in our life, so this Christian identity may be strong and bear testimony—a journey that will lead us from ambiguity to our true identity.

Paul: an identity without ambiguity

In the Letter to the Corinthians, Paul writes that "our word to you has not been Yes and No," ambiguous. In fact, Paul adds, "The Son of God, Jesus Christ, whom we preached among you . . . was not Yes and No; but in him it is always Yes" (2 Cor 1:18–22). It is here, then, that our identity is actually found: in imitating, in following this Jesus Christ, who is God's "yes" to us. And this is our life: continuing every day to strengthen this identity and bearing witness to it, step by step, but always toward the "yes," not ambiguously.

Sin is part of our identity

It's true that there is sin and sin makes us fall, but we have the Lord's strength to pick ourselves up and move forward with our identity. I would also say that sin is part of our identity: we are sinners, but sinners with faith in Jesus Christ. Indeed, it is not simply a faith of awareness but a faith that is a gift of God that has entered us from God.

Thus, it is God himself who confirms us in Christ. And he has anointed us, placed the seal on us, and provided us with a guarantee, the pledge of the Spirit in our hearts. Yes, it is God who gives us this gift of identity and the challenge is to be faithful to this Christian identity and allow the Holy Spirit, who is our very guarantee, the pledge in our heart, to lead us forward in life.

The gift of identity through witness

We are people who do not follow a philosopher, because we have a gift, which is our identity: we are anointed, we have had the seal placed on us, and we have the guarantee within us, the guarantee of the Holy Spirit. And heaven begins here. It is a beautiful identity that shows itself in witness. This is why Jesus speaks to us of witness as the language of our Christian identity when he says: "You are the salt of the earth; but if salt has lost its taste, how shall its saltiness be restored?" (Matt 5:13–16).

Surely, Christian identity, because we are sinners, is also tempted—temptations always come—and it can go backwards; it can weaken and become lost. But how can this happen? I think that one can go backwards on two main paths.

Watered-down witness

The first is that of *moving from witness to ideas*, which is a *watering down of witness*. It's like saying, "Yes, I'm a Christian. This is Christianity, a beautiful idea. I pray to God." But by doing this we go from the concrete Christ (because Christian identity is concrete—we find it in the beatitudes as well as in chapter 25 of Matthew) to a somewhat soft and flimsy religion on the path to gnosticism. Christian identity is essentially scandalous. As a result, we are tempted to say, "No, no, we don't want scandal." The cross is a scandal, and the fact that God became human is another scandal, but we ignore this. We would prefer to look for God in a somewhat ethereal, airy Christian spirituality. There are modern gnostics, and they propose this and they propose that. No. The last word of God is Jesus Christ, there is no other!

On this path, there are also those who always need novelty, something new in Christian identity: they have forgotten that they were chosen, anointed, that they have the guarantee of the Spirit, and so they search: "Where are the prophets who will tell us today of the letter that Our Lady will send us at 4:00 this afternoon?" for example. They live by such searching. But this is not Christian identity. The last word of God is called "Jesus" and nothing more.

Worldliness

Another way to go backwards from Christian identity is *worldliness*. And this means expanding the conscience so far that everything can enter: "Yes, we are Christians, but perhaps—morally, humanly—in this case [we should consider other factors]..." Worldliness is human, and it is as a result of worldliness that salt loses its flavor. This is why we see Christian communities, even Christians, who say they are Christian, but who cannot and do not know how to bear witness to Jesus Christ. And this is how identity goes backwards, diminishing and becoming lost. It is this worldly nominalism that we see every day.

God works to bring us from ambiguity to certainty

In salvation history, God, with his fatherly patience, has led us from ambiguity to certainty, to the concreteness of the Incarnation and the redeeming death of his Son: this is our identity. Paul boasts of this: "Jesus Christ, made man: God, the Son of God, became man and died in obedience." Yes, Paul boasts, this is Christian identity and there lies the proof. It is a grace we must ask of the Lord: that he always give us this gift, this gift of an identity that doesn't seek to adapt to things that would make the salt lose its flavor.

The eucharistic celebration

The eucharistic celebration is also a "scandal." Moreover, allow me to say that it is "a twofold scandal." First, because it is the "scandal" of the cross: Jesus, the Son of God, who gives his life for us. And second, it is the "scandal" that, as we Christians celebrate the memorial of the death of the Lord, we know that here this remembrance is renewed. Thus, the very celebration of the Eucharist is a testimony to our Christian identity.

Jesus Brings Jewish Law to Its Fullness (5:17–24)[10]

Jesus brings to completion

The theme of today's reading is Jesus's attitude toward the Jewish Law. He says: "Think not that I have come to abolish the Law and the Prophets; I have come not to abolish them but to fulfill them" (Matt 5:17). Jesus did not want to do away with the commandments that the Lord had given through Moses; rather, he wanted to bring them to fulfillment. He then added that this "fulfillment" of the Law requires a higher kind of justice, a more authentic observance. In fact, he says to his disciples: "Unless your righteousness exceeds that of the scribes and Pharisees, you will never enter the kingdom of heaven" (Matt 5:20).

But what does this "fulfillment" of the Law mean? What is this superior justice? Jesus himself answers this question with a few examples. Jesus was practical, and he always used examples to make himself understood...

...the fifth commandment

He begins with the fifth of the Ten Commandments: "You have heard that it was said to the men of old, 'You shalt not kill'...But I say to you that everyone who is angry with his brother shall be liable to judgment" (Matt 5:21–22). In this way, Jesus reminds us that words can kill! When we say that a person has the tongue of a snake, what does that mean? It means that their words kill! Not only is it wrong to take the life of another, but it is also wrong to spill the poison of anger on him, to strike him with slander, and speak ill of him.

This brings us to gossip. Gossip can also kill, because it destroys the reputation of the person! It is so terrible to gossip! At first it may seem like a nice thing, even amusing, like enjoying a piece of candy. But, in the end, it fills the heart with bitterness and even poisons us. What I am telling you is true. I am convinced that if each one of us decided to avoid gossiping, we would eventually become holy. What a beautiful path that is!

To love without measure

Jesus offers the perfection of love to those who follow him. Love is the only measure that has no measure, that moves past judgments. Love of neighbor is a fundamental attitude that Jesus speaks of, and he tells us that our relationship with God cannot be honest if we are not willing to make peace with our neighbor. He says: "So if you are offering your gift at the altar, and there remember that your brother has something against you, leave your gift there before the altar and go; first be reconciled with your brother, and then come and offer your gift." Therefore we are called to reconcile with our neighbor before showing our devotion to the Lord in prayer.

Protect the Heart (5:38–42)[11]

It is important to protect the heart, to safeguard the heart from our passions. And our passions are many. Even Jesus in the Gospel speaks to us about our passions: "You have heard that it was said, 'An eye for an eye and a tooth for a tooth.' But I say to you, Do not resist an evildoer. But if anyone strikes you on the right cheek, turn the other also; and if anyone wants to sue you and take your coat, give your cloak as well; and if anyone forces you to go one mile, go also the second mile." It is about being free from our passions and having a humble heart, a meek heart. The heart is guarded by humility and meekness, never by fights, by wars. But this is the noise: worldly noise, pagan noise, or the noise of the devil. The heart must be at peace.

The Mercy of God and Men (5:41–45)[12]

Walking on the path of holiness means living in the presence of God, being blameless, turning the other cheek . . . imitating his infinite mercy. "If anyone forces you to go one mile, go also the second mile" (Matt 5:41); "If anyone takes away your coat do not withhold even your shirt" (Luke 6:29); "Give to everyone who asks of you, and do not refuse anyone who wants to borrow from you" (Matt 5:42). And finally: "Love your enemies and pray for those who persecute you" (Matt 5:44). There are so many teachings of the Gospel that help us to understand the overabundance of mercy, the mind of God.

Jesus sends his disciples not as holders of power or as masters of law. He sends them into the world asking them to live a life of love and of generosity. The Christian message is proclaimed by welcoming those in need, accepting the excluded, the marginalized person, and the sinner. In the

Gospels, we read the parable of the king and the guests at the wedding feast of his son (cf. Matt 22:1–14; Luke 14:15–24). It happens that those who had been invited, that is, the best subjects, those who feel content, turn down the invitation because they are too busy with their occupations. So the king orders his servants to go into the streets, to the crossroads, and to gather everyone they meet, good and bad, to bring them to the banquet.

6
Prayer

The Spirituality of Appearance (6:1–4)[1]

Jesus firmly condemned the Pharisees' self-confidence in having fulfilled the law. He condemned their "cosmetic spirituality." They were people who liked to walk in the town square, to be seen while they prayed and to wear a dismal expression while they fasted. The Gospel uses two different but related adjectives for the actions of the Pharisees: greed and malice.

Almsgiving, an expression of justice and faith

In the tradition of the Bible, both in the Old and in the New Testaments, almsgiving has always been a touchstone of justice. A just man or woman is always almsgiving, because in almsgiving we share our own with others, we give what we have within.

Faith is not only reciting the Creed: we all believe in the Father, in the Son, and in the Holy Spirit, in life everlasting... But if our faith is "stagnant" and "inactive," then it is useless. Faith becomes active in charity! It is an almsgiving understood in the broadest sense of the word, or rather, one that is detached from the dictatorship or the idolatry of money, because greed takes us away from Jesus Christ.

Almsgiving without fanfare

Throughout the Bible there is much talk of almsgiving, whether the small everyday alms or the more important ones. It is necessary, however, to pay attention to two things: we must not sound the trumpet when we give alms, and we must not limit ourselves to donating from our surplus. It is necessary to strip oneself, and not give only "the leftovers." It is important to do as the poor widow, who gave all she had to live on.

One who gives alms and "sounds the trumpet" so that everyone knows about it is not a Christian. This is a pharisaic act. It is hypocritical. Once, while Father Pedro Arrupe, the superior general of the Society of Jesus from 1965 to 1983, was a missionary in Japan, he received an invitation from an important lady who wanted to make a donation. The woman did not receive him in private, but wanted to deliver her envelope in front of the journalists who took pictures. In other words, she "sounded the trumpet." Father Arrupe said that he had suffered great humiliation and had endured it only for the sake of the poor of Japan, for the mission. After returning home, he opened the envelope and discovered ten dollars in it. If the heart does not change, appearance does not count.

A Christian life of appearance?

Today, we would do well to consider our faith, our Christian life. Is it a Christian life of cosmetics, of appearance, or is it a Christian life with an active faith lived in charity? Everyone can, before God, make an examination of conscience. And it will do us good to do it.

Weakness, Prayer, Forgiveness (6:5–15)[2]

"Weakness, prayer, forgiveness." These three words remind us that without God's help we cannot move forward in life.

Weakness

"In our weakness, we can do nothing without your help." These words express our awareness that we are weak. We all have this weakness as a result of original sin. We are weak, we slide into sin, and we cannot go forward without the Lord's help.

This is why recognizing and confessing our weakness is truly indispensable. Indeed, one who thinks he is strong, who thinks he can do it on his own, is naïve and, in the end, is a person defeated by the many weaknesses that he carries within himself. Instead, recognition of our weakness leads us to ask the Lord for help, since, as recited in the collect prayer, "in our weakness we can do nothing without your help."

Thus, we cannot take one step in the Christian life without the Lord's help, because we are weak. And a person who is standing must take care not to fall, because she is weak, and also weak in faith. Remember the father who, after the Transfiguration, brought his son to Jesus for healing? Jesus responded by saying that all is possible for those who have faith. The father then said: "I have faith, but make it grow, Lord, for I am weak!"

We all have faith and we all want to move forward in the Christian life. But if we are not conscious of our weakness, we will all end up defeated. This is why this prayer is beautiful: "Lord, I know that in my weakness I can do nothing without your help."

And this is today's first word: *weakness*.

Prayer

The second word is *prayer*. The apostles asked Jesus: "Teach us to pray as John did with his disciples." Jesus teaches the disciples how to pray and advises them not to be like pagans who waste words. "They think that they will be heard for their many words." Jesus tells the disciples: "Do not be like them, for your Father knows what you need before you ask him."

On Mount Carmel, the four hundred prophets of the idol Baal prayed by shouting and crying aloud; and the prophet

Elijah mocked them a little, saying, "Perhaps your god is asleep and doesn't hear you" (1 Kings 18:25–38). But this is how pagans pray. Jesus recommends: "Don't do this! Pray simply. The Father knows what you need. Open your heart before the Father." Do precisely as that woman who was in the temple of Jerusalem, the mother of Samuel: she asked the Lord for the grace to have a son, and she moved only her lips. The priest who was there watched her and, convinced that she was drunk, scolded her and pushed her away.

However, that was her way of expressing sorrow before God. She moved only her lips because in her sorrow she couldn't manage to speak. She was asking for a son. This is how to pray before the Lord. And, since we know that he is good and knows everything about us and knows what we need, we begin speaking that word, "Father," which is a human word, of course... but only in prayer are we able to say it with the strength of the Holy Spirit.

Saint Paul in the Letter to the Romans (8:15), reminds us: "You have received the spirit of sonship, whereby we cry, 'Abba! Father!'" And thus, we begin to pray with the strength of the Spirit who prays in us. We need to pray this way, simply, with our hearts open in the presence of God who is Father and knows the things we need before we ask for them. And this is the second word for today: *prayer*.

Forgiveness

There is a condition for praying well, a condition that Jesus refers to in the very prayer he teaches to his disciples. And this is the third word: *forgiveness*. The prayer that Jesus teaches us says: "forgive us our trespasses as we forgive those who trespass against us." And then Jesus takes up this idea, saying: "For if you forgive others their trespasses, your heavenly Father also will forgive you; but if you do not forgive others their trespasses, neither will your Father forgive your trespasses."

For this reason, we can pray well and say "Father" to God only if our heart is at peace with others, with our brothers and sisters. To one who justifies oneself saying: "This person did this to me, that one did that to me..." there is only one response: "Forgive, forgive as he will forgive you!" And thus the weakness we have—with the help of God in prayer—becomes strength, for forgiveness is a great strength. One needs to be strong in order to forgive, but this strength is a grace that we have to receive from the Lord because we are weak.

In the celebration of the Eucharist, he too makes himself weak for us. He becomes bread: there is the strength. He prays for us. He forgives us. Let us learn from him the strength of trust in God, the strength of prayer, and the strength of forgiveness.

How We Are to Pray (6:7–15)[3]

The disciples had asked Jesus a few times: "Master, teach us to pray." In fact, they did not know how to pray, and they had seen how John had taught his disciples to pray. For his part, the Lord is clear and simple in his teaching: "First," he says, "when praying, do not waste words as the pagans do: they believe that they are heard because of their many words."

Perhaps Jesus had in mind the prophets of Baal, on Mount Carmel, who cried out in prayer to their idol, to their god. The priests of Baal prayed by jumping from side to side, gesticulating and shouting. No, this is a waste, a waste of words. No, this is not prayer. The pagans, Jesus says, think that they will be heard for their many words, as if they were "magic words." This is why Jesus advises: "Do not be like them, God does not need words," because "your Father knows what you need even before you ask him."

The form of prayer: "Father"

Jesus sets aside this prayer of words, of only words, and says: "Pray then like this." Thus, in a word—"Father"—Jesus sums up how we are to pray. Indeed, God knows what we need before we ask. This Father who listens to us in secret... [so] Jesus recommends that we pray in secret. A father is someone who gives us our identity as children. Therefore, when I say, "Father," I am going to the roots of my identity. My Christian identity is being a child, and this is a grace of the Spirit. In fact, no one can say, "Father" without the grace of the Spirit.

The context of prayer: "Our"

But, there is a curious aspect; Jesus recites the "Our Father," the prayer that we all know, and teaches us to pray in this way: "Lead us not into temptation, but deliver us from evil." He quickly adds: "If you forgive others their faults, your Father in heaven will forgive you too. But if you do not forgive others, neither will your Father forgive your faults." It almost seems as if Jesus had forgotten to underline what was in the prayer. He had just said—"and forgive us our trespasses, as we forgive those who trespass against us"—and continued with "Lead us not..." and then—"But no, I have to emphasize this!"

Therefore, if the form of prayer is to say. "Father," the context of prayer is to say "our": we are brothers and sisters, we are family. If, however, we are angry with one another, we are at war, or we hate each other, then we hinder the love of the Father. And this is the atmosphere: the family. We are all children of the same Father: How can I hate my Father's son? Cain did that! I would become Cain!

In short, to say, "Our Father," means to say: "You who give me identity and you who give me a family." This is why it is so important to forgive, to forget offenses, to have that healthy habit of "letting it go," allowing the Lord to handle it, without harboring bitterness, resentment, or the desire for revenge. So, if you go to pray and say only "Father," thinking of the One who gave you life, who gives you identity, and who loves you, and you say "our," forgiving everyone, forgetting offenses, this is the best prayer. In this context... the cornerstone of prayer is "Our Father."

An examination of conscience

Sometimes an examination of conscience on this prayer is good. Do I see God as Father? Do I feel that he is my Father? And if I do not feel that he is, do I ask the Holy Spirit to teach me to know this? Am I capable of forgetting offenses, of forgiving, of letting things go and saying to the Father: "They also are your children, and they treated me badly; please help me to forgive"? This is an examination of conscience that will serve us well. Let us always keep in mind that the words "Father" and "our" give us "the identity of children" and give us "a family" with which to walk together through life.

Heaven's Stock Exchange (6:19–23)[4]

Jesus's advice is very clear here: "Do not accumulate for yourselves treasures on earth." Jesus explains why: This is "where moth and rust consume and where thieves break in and steal." In other words, Jesus tells us that it is dangerous to have an attitude of wanting to store up treasures on earth. It's true that perhaps such an attitude is rooted in the desire for security, as if to say, "I want to be secure and, for this reason, I have these savings."

However, riches are not like a statue. They are not stationary. Riches have a tendency to grow, to move, to take their place in life and in a person's heart. And the person who stores up treasures so as not to become a slave to poverty ends up a slave to treasures. Therefore, this is Jesus's advice: "Do not accumulate for yourselves treasures on earth." After all, wealth invades even the heart, takes over the heart, and corrupts the heart. And that person ends up corrupt because of having an attitude of wanting to accumulate treasures.

Jesus, in another teaching on the same topic, speaks of the man who has a large harvest of grain and thinks: "What shall I do now? I will pull down my barns, and build larger ones." But the Lord says: "Fool, this night you will die." And here is a second feature of this attitude: the man who lays up treasure doesn't realize that he will have to leave it.

Moths and rust: the destruction of the heart

Jesus speaks of moths and rust: but what are they? They are the destruction of the heart, the corruption of the heart, and even the destruction of families. Think of the man who goes to Jesus and says to him: "Please, tell my brother to share the inheritance with me!" And again comes the Lord's counsel: "Be careful not to become attached to treasures!"

Serve two masters?

The passage following this one is very clear: "No one can serve two masters; for either he will hate the one and love the other, or he will be devoted to the one and despise the other." In other words, the Lord says, "You cannot serve God and the treasures."

The statement is extremely clear. And it's true. People who have an attitude of wanting to store up treasures will "stockpile" so many excuses to justify themselves, so many! However, in the end, such treasures do not provide lasting security. Instead, they diminish one's dignity. And this also applies to families; so many families become divided over treasures.

Furthermore, even at the root of war there is this ambition that destroys, corrupts. In fact, in this world, at this moment, there are so many wars waged out of greed for power, for wealth. But we can think too about the war in our own heart:

"Beware of all covetousness," the Lord says. Greed continues on, and on, and on: it's a step, it opens the door, then turns into vanity—believing you are important, believing you are powerful—and, at the end, pride. And that leads to all vices. The process has steps, and the first is greed, the desire to accumulate treasures.

There is a very beautiful saying: "The devil enters through the pocketbook" or "through the pockets." This is how the devil and all the vices enter, adding to our insecure securities. This is actually corruption—the moth and the rust that lead us on.

What to accumulate

After all, accumulating is really a human quality: to make things and to dominate the world—it's even a mission. But what do I have to store up? Jesus's response in today's Gospel is clear: "Accumulate instead your treasures in heaven, where neither moth nor rust consumes and where thieves do not break in and steal." This is truly the daily struggle: how to manage well the treasures of earth so they are directed to heaven and become the treasures of heaven.

When the Lord blesses a person with treasures, he makes him the steward of those treasures for the common good and for the good of all, not for his own good. But it isn't easy to be an honest steward, for there is always the temptation of greed, the temptation to become important: the world teaches us this and leads us down this road.

Rather, one must think of others, considering that what I have is for the service of others and remembering that I won't be able to take anything I have with me. Indeed, if I use what the Lord has given me for the common good, as a steward, this sanctifies me; it will make me holy. However, it isn't easy. Thus, every day we must ask ourselves: Where is my treasure? Is it in wealth or is it in this stewardship, in this service for the common good?

When a wealthy person sees to it that his treasure is administered for the common good, and in his heart and in his life he lives simply, as if he were poor, that person is holy, that person is on the road of sainthood, because his treasures are for everyone. But it's difficult; it's like playing with fire. This is why so many appease their conscience with charity and hand out their leftovers. However, that is not being a steward: a steward takes for oneself what is needed and gives everything in service to others. Indeed, administering riches is a continuous divesting of our own interests, knowing that these riches will not give us salvation. Therefore, accumulate, yes; build a treasure, yes, but one that has real value, so to speak, in "heaven's stock exchange." Store up there!

After all, the Lord in his life lived as a poor man, but such treasures! Paul, himself (cf. 2 Cor 11:18, 21–30), lived as a poor man, and what did he boast of? His weakness. He had opportunities, he had power—but always in service, always in service. Thus, "in service" is really the key phrase. Baptism makes us brothers and sisters of one another through serving, through stripping ourselves: not stripping the other, but stripping myself and giving to the other.

Accumulate to have a bright heart

Let us think about our heart: Is our heart light? How simple is the vision of our heart? The Lord says, again in the Gospel according to Matthew, that the whole body shall be luminous. However, if one is bad—if one is attached to his or her own interests and not to those of others—this will darken the heart. This person, who makes treasures through vices and corruption, darkens the heart when one becomes attached to them.

In the celebration of the Eucharist, the Lord who is so rich—so rich!—made himself poor to enrich us. It is precisely through his poverty that he teaches us this way of not accumulating treasures on the earth, for they corrupt. And, when we have them, we must use them, as stewards, in service to others.

Serene Attentiveness (6:26)[5]

We are speaking of an attitude of the heart, one that approaches life with serene attentiveness, that is capable of being fully present to someone without thinking of what comes next, that accepts each moment as a gift from God to be lived to the full. Jesus taught us this attitude when he invited us to contemplate the lilies of the field and the birds of the air, or when, in seeing the rich young man and knowing his restlessness, "he looked at him with love" (Mark 10:21). Jesus was completely present to everyone and to everything, and in this way he showed us the way to overcome that unhealthy anxiety which makes us superficial, aggressive, and compulsive consumers.

Trust in Providence (6:26, 28–29)[6]

God does not forget

At the center of this Sunday's liturgy we find one of the most reassuring truths: Divine Providence. The prophet Isaiah speaks of this by using the image of maternal love full of tenderness: "Can a woman forget her nursing child, that she should have no compassion on the son of her womb? Even these may forget, yet I will not forget you" (Isa 49:15). How beautiful this is! God does not forget us, not one of us! He knows everyone by name and surname. He loves us and doesn't forget. What a beautiful thought... The invitation to trust in God finds a parallel on a page of Matthew's Gospel: "Look at the birds of the air," Jesus says. "They neither sow nor reap nor gather into barns, and yet your heavenly Father feeds them... Consider the lilies of the field, how they grow: they neither toil nor spin; yet I tell you, even Solomon in all his glory was not arrayed like one of these" (Matt 6:26, 28–29).

Abstract words

However, when we think of the many people who live in precarious conditions, or even in a poverty that demeans their dignity, these words of Jesus could seem abstract, if not illusory. But actually they are relevant, now more than ever! They remind us that one cannot serve two masters: God and wealth. As long as everyone seeks to accumulate for himself or herself, there will never be justice. We must take heed of this! While all seek to accumulate for themselves, there will be no justice. If, however, we entrust ourselves to God's providence and seek his kingdom together, no one will lack the necessary means to live with dignity.

Full heart, empty heart

A heart troubled by the desire for possessions is a heart full of desire for possessions but empty of God. That is why Jesus frequently warned the rich, because they risk placing their security in the goods of this world, while security, the final security, is in God. In a heart possessed by wealth, there isn't much room for faith; everything is caught up in concern for wealth, so there is no room for faith. If, however, one gives God his rightful place, that is, first place, then his love leads one to share even one's wealth, to set it at the service of projects of solidarity and development, as so many examples (even recent ones) in the history of the church demonstrate.

Similarly, God's Providence comes through our service to others, our sharing with others. If each of us accumulates not for ourselves alone but for the service of others, in this act of solidarity, the Providence of God is made visible. If, however, we accumulate only for ourselves, what will happen when we are called by God [at the end of our lives]? No one can take his riches with him, because, as we know, the shroud has no pockets! It is better to share, for we can take with us to heaven only what we have shared with others.

Jesus leads us to the right scale of values

The road that Jesus points out can seem a little unrealistic with respect to common attitudes and to the problems due to the economic crisis, but, if we think about it, this road leads us back to the right scale of values. Jesus says: "Is not life more than food, and the body more than clothing?" (Matt 6:25). In order to ensure that no one lacks bread, water, clothing, a home, work, health, we need to recognize that all people are children of the Father who is in heaven and, therefore, brothers and sisters among us, and that we must act accordingly. I recalled this in the Message for Peace of January 1: the way to peace is fraternity—this journey together, sharing things with one another.

Mary, mother of providence

In the light of this Sunday's Word of God, let us invoke the Virgin Mary as Mother of Divine Providence. To her we entrust our lives, the journey of the church, and all humanity. In particular, let us invoke her intercession that we may all strive to live in a simple and focused manner, always keeping in mind care for those who are most in need.

7
A True Christian

No One Can Judge (7:1–5)[1]

Judging makes us hypocrites

Judging others leads us to hypocrisy. And Jesus defines hypocrites as those who act as judges. A person who judges gets it wrong, becomes confused, and is defeated.

One who judges always gets it wrong, because he takes the place of God, who is the only judge. Taking that place is taking the wrong place! Believing that he has the authority to judge everything—people, life, everything—a person also assumes he has the capacity to condemn.

Judging others was one of the acts of the legal experts called "hypocrites" by Jesus. These are the people who "judge everything." However, the worst thing is that, in doing this, they put themselves in the place of God, who is the only judge. In judging, God takes time; he waits. These people instead act hastily. This is why whoever judges gets it wrong, simply because he assumes a place that isn't his.

Whoever judges lives in confusion and becomes a loser

The person who judges doesn't only get it wrong; he also gets confused. And he often becomes obsessed with the one he wants to judge—so very obsessed!—sometimes losing sleep over the speck he sees in that person's eye. Meanwhile, he isn't aware of the log he has in his own eye. In this sense, he gets confused, and he thinks the log is a speck. And so, one who judges another is a person who is confused about reality; he is deluded.

Not only this. One who judges becomes defeated and cannot help but finish badly, because the same measure will be used to judge him, as Jesus says in the Gospel of Matthew. Therefore, the arrogant and condescending judge who assumes the wrong place, because he is taking God's place, is betting on a loser. And who is that loser? He is, because he will be judged by the same measure with which he judges. The only one with the right to judge is God and those to whom God grants the authority to do so. Others have no right to judge: that's why there's confusion, that's why there's defeat.

Switching from accusers to defenders

Furthermore, defeat goes even further, because one who judges always makes accusations. In judging others—Jesus gives the example of "the speck in your eye"—there's always an accusation. This is exactly the opposite of what Jesus does before the Father. In fact, Jesus never accuses but, on the contrary, he defends. He is the first Paraclete. Then he invites the second, the Holy Spirit, to us. Jesus is "the defender": he is before the Father to defend us against accusations.

But when there's a defender, there's also an accuser. In the Bible, the accuser is called devil, Satan. Jesus will judge at the end of the world, but in the meantime he intercedes, he defends. John says it so well in his Gospel: don't sin, please, but if someone sins, remember that we have an advocate who defends us before the Father.

Thus, if we want to go on Jesus's path, instead of accusers we must be defenders of others before the Father. Jesus advises us to come to the defense of a person who has done something bad. Without thinking too much about it, we should pray for that person and, like Jesus, defend him before the Father. Pray for him.

But most of all, we must not judge, because if we do, then when we do something bad, we will be judged! It is worth remembering this truth whenever we want to judge others—or to speak ill of others, which is also a form of judging.

Thus, a person who judges takes the wrong place, becomes confused, and is defeated. And in doing this, he isn't imitating Jesus, who always defends before the Father: he's a defense lawyer. One who judges is instead an imitator of the prince of this world, who always goes against people to accuse them before the Father.

May the Lord grant us the grace to imitate Jesus the intercessor, defender, and lawyer for every one of us. And to not imitate the other one, who will destroy us in the end.

Accompanying Others (7:1)[2]

One who accompanies others has to realize that each person's situation before God and his or her life in grace are mysteries that no one can else can fully know. The Gospel tells us to correct others and to help them to grow on the basis of a recognition of the objective evil of their actions (cf. Matt 18:15), but without making judgments about their responsibility and culpability (cf. Matt 7:1; Luke 6:37). Someone good at such accompaniment does not give in to frustrations or fears. He or she invites others to let themselves be healed, to take up their mat, embrace the cross, leave all behind and go forth ever anew to proclaim the Gospel. Our personal experience of being accompanied and assisted, and of openness to those who accompany us, will teach us to be patient and compassionate with others, and to find ways of fostering their trust, their openness, and their readiness to grow.

An Extension of the Incarnation (7:2)[3]

The inseparable bond between our acceptance of the message of salvation and genuine fraternal love appears in several scriptural texts on which we would do well to meditate in order to appreciate all their implications. The message is one that we often take for granted and can repeat almost mechanically, without necessarily taking steps to ensure that it has a real effect on our lives and in our communities. How dangerous and harmful this is, for it makes us lose our amazement, our excitement, and our zeal for living the Gospel of fraternity and justice! God's word teaches that our brothers and sisters are the prolongation of the Incarnation for each of us: "As you did it to one of these, the least of my brethren, you did it to me" (Matt 25:40). The way we treat others has a transcendent dimension: "The measure you give will be the measure you get" (Matt 7:2). It corresponds to the mercy that God has shown us: "Be merciful, just as your Father is merciful. Do not judge, and you will not be judged; do not condemn, and you will not be condemned. Forgive, and you will be forgiven; give, and it will be given to you . . . For the measure you give will be the measure you get back" (Luke 6:36–38). What these passages make clear is the absolute priority of "going forth from ourselves toward our brothers and sisters" as one of the two great commandments which ground every moral norm and as the clearest sign for discerning spiritual growth in response to God's completely free gift.

Listen First! (7:21–29)[4]

The false prophets

The people following the Lord were "astonished," because "he taught them as one with authority, and not like their scribes."

People know when a priest, a bishop, a catechist, a Christian has that consistency which gives him or her authority...

In an earlier passage, Jesus himself admonishes his disciples, the people, everyone: "Beware of false prophets." The correct word—although it is a neologism—would be "pseudo-prophets." These pseudo-prophets resemble little sheep, good sheep, but they are predatory wolves. And the gospel reading recalls precisely the verse in which Jesus explains how to discern where the true preachers of the Gospel are, and where are those who preach a gospel that is not the Gospel.

Three key words

There are three key words to understanding this: speak, do, and listen. Regarding *speaking,* Jesus states: "Not everyone who says to me, 'Lord, Lord,' shall enter the kingdom of heaven." He continues: "On that day many will say to me, 'Lord, Lord, did we not prophesy in your name, and cast out demons in your name, and do many mighty works in your name?" However, he will respond to them: "I never knew you; depart from me, you evildoers."

Why is this? Because these people speak, they do, but they lack another attitude, which is very basic, which is actually the foundation of speaking, of doing: they don't *listen.* Jesus continues: "Everyone who hears these words of mine and does them...." Therefore, the "speak-act" binary standard isn't enough—in fact, it can even be deceiving. The correct binary standard is another one: it is *"listening and doing, putting into practice."* Indeed, Jesus tells us: "Everyone who hears these words of mine and does them will be like a wise man who built his house on rock. Then the rain falls and the winds blow, but the house remains firm, because it is a house of stone, built on rock." However, one who hears the words but does not make them his own, who lets them go, that is, who doesn't take them seriously and doesn't put them into practice, will be like a man who builds on sand.

Here then is the key to recognizing false prophets: "You will know them by their fruits"—in other words, by their attitude. They speak so many words, so many words. They are prodigious, they do great things, but their heart is not open to hear the Word of God; they are afraid of the silence of the Word of God. These are "pseudo-Christians, pseudo-pastors," who do good things but have not built on rock.

Listening to the rock of love

The prayer of the day states: "You never abandon those who trust in the rock of your love." But "pseudo-Christians," instead, are not founded on the rock of God's love, the rock of the Word of God. Without this rock they cannot build: they are pretending, because in the end it will all come to nothing.

These are "pseudo-pastors," worldly pastors, the pastors or Christians who talk too much. Perhaps it is because they are afraid of silence, and perhaps they do too much. They are incapable of acting from the standpoint of listening; they operate starting from themselves, not from God.

Thus, one who only speaks and acts is not a true prophet, is not a true Christian, and in the end all his efforts will fail, because they are not built on the rock of God's love, not founded on rock. However, one who knows how to listen and, having listened, acts, does so with the strength of the word of another, not of one's own, and remains firm, like a rock. Although he or she may be a humble person who doesn't seem important, that person is great. And how many of these great ones are there in the church? How many great bishops, how many great priests, how many great faithful who know how to listen and, from listening, act?

Teresa of Calcutta heard the Lord's voice. She didn't speak, and in the silence she knew how to listen, and therefore, how to act. She did so much. And like the house built on rock, both she and her work endure. From her witness we understand that the great ones know how to listen and from listening, they act. Their faith and their strength stand on the rock of the love of Jesus Christ.

On the rock of the Eucharist
The liturgy uses the strong, firm altar of stone as a symbol of Jesus. Upon this altar Jesus becomes weak; he is a piece of bread given to all. The Lord became weak to make us strong.

Rock Christians versus Sand Christians (7:24–27)[5]

Christians "with makeup"
The Gospel speaks of Christian strength and weakness, of rock and sand. Indeed, a Christian is strong when he not only declares that he is a Christian but when he lives his life as a Christian, when he puts Christian doctrine, the Word of God, the commandments, the beatitudes, into practice. The key point is "putting into practice."

However, there are those who are Christians only in appearance, people who present themselves as Christians and look like Christians but at the moment of truth it becomes clear that they are only wearing makeup. And we all know what happens when a woman, all made up, gets caught in the rain without an umbrella: the makeup melts, and appearances wind up on the ground. That makeup is a temptation. Thus, in order to truly be a Christian it isn't enough to say, "I'm a Christian, Lord." Jesus himself says that it doesn't suffice to simply repeat, "Lord! Lord!" in order to enter his kingdom. We must do the Father's will and put his Word into practice. This is the difference between living "a Christian in life" and being a Christian in appearance only.

Foundation of a Christian life
It is clear that a Christian life must be founded on rock. In fact, Paul clearly says so when he speaks about the water from the

rock in the desert: the rock was Christ, the rock is Christ. Therefore, the only thing that counts is being founded on the person of Jesus, following Jesus on the path of Jesus. I have so often met not bad people but people who are good yet are victims of the "Christianity of appearances." They are people who say, "I'm from a very Catholic family" or "I'm a member of that association and also a benefactor of another one." But the real questions to ask these people are: "Is your life founded on Jesus? Where is your hope? Is it in that rock or in these appearances?"

This is the importance of being founded on rock. After all, we have seen so many apparent Christians whose Christianity washes away with the first temptation, that is, with the rain. Indeed, when the rivers overflow, when the winds blow—when faced with life's temptations and trials—a Christian of appearance only falls away, because there is no substance there; there is no rock, there is no Christ.

Christian saints

On the other hand, there are so many saints among the People of God—not necessarily canonized, but saints! There are so many men and women who lead their life in Christ, who put the commandments into practice, who put Jesus's love into practice. So many!

Consider the sick who offer their suffering for the church, for others, and the many lonely elderly people who pray for others. Consider also the many mothers and fathers who struggle so hard for their families, their children's education, working every day, confronting problems, always with hope in Jesus; they don't strut about, but they quietly do whatever they can.

Truly, there are saints in everyday life. Think of the many priests who stay behind the scenes but who work with such love in their parishes providing catechesis for the children, care for the elderly and the sick, and preparation for newlyweds. And every day it's the same, the same, the same. They don't tire because the rock is their foundation, as it is for all those who live in Jesus. This is what gives holiness to the church; this is what gives hope. This is why we have to take great care of the hidden holiness that there is in the church, that of people who are Christians not in appearance only but who are founded on rock, on Jesus. Look to those Christians who follow Jesus's advice at the Last Supper: "Abide in me." Yes, to the Christians who abide in Christ, because we are certainly all sinners, but when any of these Christians commit a grave sin, they repent, they ask forgiveness: this is a great thing. It means having the capacity to ask for forgiveness, not confusing sin with virtue, knowing well where virtue is and where sin is. These Christians are founded on rock, and the rock is Christ. They follow the path of Jesus, they follow him.

Let us ask the Lord that we may be firmly founded on the rock that is Christ: he is our hope. It's true, we are all sinners, we are all weak, but if we place our hope in him, we can all carry on. And this is Christian joy: to know that in him there is hope, there is forgiveness, there is peace, there is joy. This is why it makes no sense to put our hope in things that are here today and gone tomorrow.

Family Founded on the Rock (7:24–27)[6]

The Bible is full of families, births, love stories and family crises. This is true from its very first page, where we meet the family of Adam and Eve with all its burden of violence but also its enduring strength (cf. Gen 4), to its very last page, where we behold the wedding feast of the Bride and the Lamb (Rev 21:2, 9). Jesus's description of the two houses, one built on rock and the other on sand (cf. Matt 7:24–27), symbolizes any number of family situations shaped by the exercise of their members' freedom, for, as the poet says, "every home is a lampstand." Let us now enter one of those houses, led by the Psalmist with a song that even today resounds in both Jewish and Christian wedding liturgies:

> Blessed is everyone who fears the Lord, who walks in his ways!
> You shall eat the fruit of the labor of your hands; you shall be happy, and it shall go well with you.
> Your wife will be like a fruitful vine within your house;
> your children will be like olive shoots round your table.
> Thus shall the man be blessed who fears the Lord.
> The Lord bless you from Zion!
> May you see the prosperity of Jerusalem all the days of your life!
> May you see your children's children!
> Peace be upon Israel! (Ps 128:1–6)

Christ Is the Rock (7:24–27)[7]

All of us are familiar with Jesus's parable about the man who built his house on sand, rather than rock. When the winds came, it fell with a mighty crash. God is the rock on which we are called to build. He tells us this in the first reading, and he asks us: "Is there a God besides me?" (cf. Isa 44:8).

When the Risen Jesus says, in today's Gospel, "All authority in heaven and on earth has been given to me" (Matt 28:18), he is telling us that he, the Son of God, is himself the rock. There is none besides him. As the one Savior of mankind, he wishes to draw men and women of every time and place to himself, so that he can bring them to the Father. He wants all of us to build our lives on the firm foundation of his word.

This is the charge the Lord gives to each of us. He asks us to be missionary disciples, men and women who radiate the truth, beauty, and life-changing power of the Gospel; men and women who are channels of God's grace, who enable his mercy, kindness, and truth to become the building blocks of a house that stands firm, a house that is a home, where brothers and sisters at last live in harmony and mutual respect, in obedience to the will of the true God who has shown us, in Jesus, the way to that freedom and peace for which all hearts long.

May Jesus, the Good Shepherd, the rock on whom we build our lives, guide you and your families in the way of goodness and mercy all the days of your lives. May he bless all Kenyans with his peace. "Stand strong in faith! Do not be afraid!" For you belong to the Lord.

Called to Be Rock Disciples (7:28–29)[8]

So many people follow Jesus. Consider that more than five thousand were present on the day of the multiplication of the loaves. There were people who followed Jesus closely, along the way. And the Gospel explains that they followed Jesus because his words astonished their hearts. It was the astonishment of finding something good, great. Jesus indeed taught them as one with authority, not like the scribes.

The people needed teachers, preachers, experts with authority. Those who had no authority spoke, but their words failed to reach the people; they were far removed from the people. Jesus, however, spoke in a way that touched the hearts of the people, that was an answer to their questions.

Messengers who do not speak to the heart

At that time, various groups of leaders spoke to the people but their message didn't reach the heart of the people. The people heard them and left.

Surely the best known were the *Pharisees*. There were also good Pharisees. But when Jesus referred to the Pharisees, he was speaking about those who were bad, not the good ones. The bad ones were those who practiced religious rituals of God and emphasized the following of rules: out of ten commandments they made more than three hundred! Then they loaded this weight on the people's shoulders: "You must do this! You have to!" They reduced faith in the living God to legalism, ending in contradictions based on cruel casuistry. And the people, for their part, respected these Pharisees, because people are respectful, but they didn't listen to them.

Those in another group were the *Sadducees*. This group had no faith; they had lost the faith. And thus, they carried out their religious duties by making deals with the powerful, those who were politically powerful, economically powerful. In short, they were men of power, and they bargained with everyone. However, the people didn't follow them either.

A third group consisted of revolutionaries. In that era, they were often called *zealots*. They were the ones who wanted a revolution to free the people of Israel from Roman occupation. Some of them were guerrillas. The people, however, had common sense and knew how to tell when the fruit is ripe and when it isn't. And so, they didn't follow them.

Finally, the fourth group was made up of good people: the Essenes. They were monks, good people who consecrated their life to God: they practiced contemplation and prayer in the monasteries. But they were far from the people and the people couldn't follow them.

Jesus had authority

Jesus was different. That is why the crowds were astonished. Their hearts were warmed when they heard Jesus, because his message touched their hearts and he taught as a person with authority. In fact, Jesus drew close to the people. Jesus healed the hearts of the people. He understood the problems of the people. Jesus wasn't ashamed to talk to the sinners but went to visit them. Jesus felt joy. He was pleased to go and be with his people. And Jesus himself explains why: "I am the good shepherd. My sheep hear my voice and they follow me."

And this is precisely why the people followed Jesus: because he was the good shepherd. Certainly, he wasn't a legalistic and moralistic Pharisee, or a Sadducee who made political deals with the powerful, or a guerilla who sought the political freedom of his people, or a contemplative from a monastery. He was a shepherd. He spoke the language of his people; he made himself understood; he spoke the truth, the matters of God; he never negotiated on matters of God. But he spoke of them in such a way that the people loved the matters of God. This is why they followed him.

Jesus never distances himself from the people, and he never distances himself from his Father: he is one with the Father. And he thus had this authority and this is why the people followed him.

An examination of conscience

While we are contemplating Jesus the Good Shepherd, we should ask oursleves: Whom do I want to follow? Someone who speaks to me about abstractions and over-subtle moral platitudes? Is it those who call themselves people of God but who have no faith and who negotiate everything with the politically and economically powerful? Those who always want to do strange things, destructive things, who engage in so-called wars of liberation, but who in the end aren't on the path of the Lord? Do I want to follow a faraway contemplative?

This, then, is the key question we need to ask ourselves: Whom do I want to follow?...It is a question that leads us to ask God, the Father, to inspire us to draw closer to Jesus, to follow Jesus, to be astonished by what Jesus tells us.

8
The Miracles of Jesus

Who Is This Man? (8:1–4)[1]

The people who follow Jesus

"When Jesus came down from the mountain, a great crowd followed him." All of those people following him heard his teaching. They were astonished because he spoke to them "with authority," not like the doctors of the law whom they were used to hearing.

These people were following Jesus without getting tired of listening to him. Many of them stayed all day and, in the end, the apostles realized that they must have been hungry. But hearing Jesus was a joy for them. And so, when Jesus finished speaking, he came down from the mountain and the people followed him and gathered round him. They followed him, traveling with him on the road.

The curious and the unclean

However, there were other people who didn't follow Jesus. They watched him from afar, wondering, "Who is this man?" After all, never had they heard such astonishing teachings. There were people who were watching from the sidewalk and there were other people who couldn't approach: the law forbade it, for they were "unclean." The leper referred to in Matthew's Gospel was from this group.

The courage to approach Jesus

In his heart, this leper felt a longing to draw close to Jesus: he took courage and approached. But he was a marginalized person and therefore had to keep his distance, stay apart. However, he had faith in Jesus, took courage and drew near, and simply prayed: "Lord, if you will, you can make me clean." He said this because he was unclean. Indeed, leprosy was a life sentence. And healing a leper was as difficult as bringing a dead man back to life: this is why lepers were marginalized... They could not mix with the people.

There were, however, also some who were self-marginalized, like the doctors of the law who were always watching with a longing to put Jesus to the test, to make him slip up, and then condemn him. The leper, however, knew he was unclean and sick, and he approached. So, what did Jesus do? He didn't stand still or try to avoid touching him, but instead drew even closer, stretched out his hand, and healed him.

The mystery of closeness

"Closeness" is such an important word. You can't build a community without closeness; you can't make peace without closeness; you can't do good without drawing near. Jesus could have said to the leper: "Be healed!" But instead he drew close and touched him. What's more, at the moment when Jesus touched the unclean man, he himself became unclean. And this is the mystery of Jesus: he takes upon himself our uncleanliness, our impurities.

It is a reality Saint Paul describes well when he writes that Jesus, "though he was in the form of God, did not regard equality with God as something to be exploited, but emptied himself" (Phil 2:6–7). Paul goes even further, confirming that "Jesus became sin": Jesus became excluded, took impurity upon himself to draw close to man. He did not count equality with God a thing to be grasped, but instead *he emptied himself, became sin, became unclean, drew near*.

So often I think that it may be not necessarily impossible, but very difficult to do good without getting our hands dirty. And Jesus got dirty with his closeness. But then, Matthew recounts, he went even further, saying to the man who had been freed from his illness: "Go to the priests, and do what must be done when a leper is healed."

Essentially, that man who has been excluded from social life, Jesus includes: includes in the church, includes in society. He advises: "Go, so that all things shall be as they must be." Thus, Jesus never marginalizes anyone, ever! Moreover, Jesus marginalizes himself in order to include the marginalized, to include us, sinners, marginalized people! And this is beautiful.

How many people followed Jesus at that time and have followed Jesus throughout history because they have been astonished by the way he speaks? And how many people are watching from afar and do not understand, are not interested? How many people watch from afar but with a wicked heart, to put Jesus to the test, to criticize him, to condemn him? How many people watch from afar because, while they don't have the courage of that leper, they still have a longing to draw near? Jesus stretches out his hand first. By his very being he reaches out his hand to everyone, because he has become one of us, like us; although without sin, he has taken on our sins, been soiled by our sins. And this is Christian closeness.

Do we know how to get closer?

"Closeness" is a beautiful word. But do I know how to draw near? Do I have the strength, do I have the courage to touch those who are marginalized? The church, parishes, communities, consecrated men and women, bishops, priests, everyone should also answer this question: Do I have the courage to draw near or do I always keep my distance? Do I have the courage to close the distance, as Jesus did?

The Eucharist, the mystery of closeness

On the altar, Jesus draws near to us: "Lord, may I not be afraid to draw close to the needy, to the needy who are visible or to those who have hidden wounds."

Jesus and the Family (8:14–15)[2]

"The example of Jesus is a paradigm for the church... He began his public ministry with the miracle at the wedding feast of Cana (cf. John 2:1–11). He shared in everyday moments of friendship with the family of Lazarus and his sisters (cf. Luke 10:38) and with the family of Peter (cf. Mark 8:14). He sympathized with grieving parents and restored their children to life (cf. Mark 5:41; Luke 7:14–15). In this way he demonstrated the true meaning of mercy, which entails the restoration of the covenant (cf. John Paul II, *Dives in Misericordia,* 4). This is clear from his conversations with the Samaritan woman (cf. John 1:4–30) and with the woman found in adultery (cf. John 8:1–11), where the consciousness of sin is awakened by an encounter with Jesus's gratuitous love."[3]

Following Jesus (8:18–22)[4]

Follow Jesus by bearing witness...

Jesus explains in a parable that the kingdom of heaven is just like a man who has sown the seed, then goes home, relaxes, works, keeps watch by night and by day, and the seed grows, it sprouts, without his knowing how. The central question to ask oneself, therefore, is how is it that this seed of God's word grows and becomes the kingdom of God, grows and becomes the church? There are two great forces at work: the Holy Spirit—the power of the Holy Spirit—and Christian testimony.

First of all, we know that there is no growth without the Spirit: it is he who builds the church; it is he who makes the church grow; it is he who summons the community of the church. However, Christian witness is also necessary. And in the end, when historical circumstances call for the strongest testimony of all, there are martyrs: the greatest witnesses! And it is here that the church is watered by the blood of martyrs. This is truly the beauty of martyrdom: it begins with day-to-day testimony and it may end with blood, as in the case if Jesus, the first martyr, the first witness, the faithful witness.

. . . without conditions

However, to be true, the testimony must be unconditional. The gospel reading of the day's liturgy (Matt 8:18–22) is clear on this point. We heard what the Lord said when a disciple made an excuse after being called to follow Jesus: "Lord, let me first go and bury my father." But the Lord stopped him: "No!" In fact, testimony must be unconditional. It must be firm, it must be decisive, it must use the language—so powerful—of Jesus: "Yes, yes! No, no!" And this is precisely the language of testimony.

Jesus Lived in Full Harmony with Creation (8:27)[5]

Jesus lived in full harmony with creation, and others were amazed: "What sort of man is this, that even the winds and the sea obey him?" (Matt 8:27). His appearance was not that of an ascetic set apart from the world, nor someone opposed to the pleasing things of life. Of himself he said: "The Son of Man came eating and drinking and they say, 'Look, a glutton and a drunkard!'" (Matt 11:19). He was far removed from philosophies that despised the body, matter, and the things of the world. Such unhealthy dualisms nevertheless left a mark on certain Christian thinkers in the course of history and disfigured the Gospel. Jesus worked with his hands, in daily contact with the matter created by God, to which he gave form by his craftsmanship. It is striking that most of his life was dedicated to this task in a simple life that awakened no admiration at all: "Is not this the carpenter, the son of Mary?" (Mark 6:3). In this way he sanctified human labor and endowed it with a special significance for our development. As Saint John Paul II taught, "By enduring the toil of work in union with Christ crucified for us, man in a way collaborates with the Son of God for the redemption of humanity."[6]

9

Compassion

Loving-Kindness (9:2)[1]

To be open to a genuine encounter with others, "a kind look" is essential. This is incompatible with a negative attitude that readily points out other people's shortcomings while overlooking one's own. A kind look helps us to see beyond our own limitations, to be patient, and to cooperate with others, despite our differences. Loving-kindness builds bonds, cultivates relationships, creates new networks of integration, and knits a firm social fabric. In this way, it grows ever stronger, for without a sense of belonging we cannot sustain a commitment to others; we end up seeking our convenience alone and life in common becomes impossible.

Antisocial persons think that others exist only for the satisfaction of their own needs. Consequently, there is no room for the gentleness of love and its expression. Those who love are capable of speaking words of comfort, strength, consolation, and encouragement. These were the words that Jesus himself spoke: "Take heart, my son!" (Matt 9:2); "Great is your faith!" (Matt 15:28); "Arise!" (Mark 5:41); "Go in peace" (Luke 7:50); "Be not afraid" (Matt 14:27). These are not words that demean, sadden, anger, or show scorn. In our families, we must learn to imitate Jesus's own gentleness in our way of speaking to one another.

An Exchange of Glances (9:9–10)[2]

We are celebrating the feast of the apostle and evangelist Saint Matthew. We are celebrating the story of a conversion. Matthew himself, in his Gospel, tell us what it was like, this encounter that changed his life. He shows us an "exchange of glances" that was capable of changing history.

On a day like any other, as Matthew, the tax collector, was seated at his table, Jesus passed by, saw him, came up to him, and said: "Follow me." Matthew got up and followed him.

Jesus looked at him. How strong was the love in that look of Jesus that moved Matthew to do what he did! What power must have been in Jesus's eyes to make Matthew get up from his table! We know that Matthew was a publican: he collected taxes from the Jews to give to the Romans. Publicans were looked down upon and considered sinners. This is why they lived apart and were despised by others. One could hardly eat, speak, or pray with the likes of these. In the eyes of the people, publicans were traitors: they extorted from their own to give to others. They belonged to their own separate social class.

When he saw Matthew, Jesus stopped. He did not quickly turn away. He looked at Matthew calmly, peacefully. He looked at him with eyes of mercy. He looked at him as no one had ever looked at him before. And that look unlocked Matthew's heart. It set him free, it healed him, it gave him hope and a new life, as it did to Zacchaeus, to Bartimaeus, to Mary Magdalene, to Peter, and to each of us.

Jesus also glances at us

Even if we dare not raise our eyes to the Lord, he always looks at us first. This is our story, and it is like that of so many others. Each of us can say: "I, too, am a sinner, whom Jesus has looked upon." I ask you today, in your homes or at church, when you are alone and at peace, to take a moment to recall with gratitude and happiness those situations, that moment, when you felt the merciful gaze of God in your life.

Jesus's love goes before us; his look anticipates our needs. He can see beyond appearances, beyond sin, beyond failures and unworthiness. He sees beyond our position in society. He sees beyond all of this. He sees our dignity as sons and daughters, a dignity at times sullied by sin, but one that endures in the depth of our soul. It is our dignity as sons and daughters. He came precisely to seek out all those who feel unworthy of God, unworthy of others.

Let us allow Jesus to look at us. Let us allow his gaze . . . to become our joy, our hope, our happiness in life.

The mission

After the Lord looked upon him with mercy, he said to Matthew: "Follow me." Matthew got up and followed him. After that look, a word. After love, the mission. Matthew is no longer the same; he is changed inside. The encounter with Jesus and his loving mercy transformed him. His table, his money, his exclusion—were all left behind. Before, he had sat waiting to collect his taxes, to take from others. Now, with Jesus, he must get up and give, give himself to others. Jesus looks at him, and Matthew experiences the joy of service. For Matthew and for all who have felt the gaze of Jesus, other people are no longer to be "lived off," used and abused. The gaze of Jesus gives rise to missionary activity, service, self-giving. Other people are those whom Jesus serves. His love heals our shortsightedness and pushes us to look beyond, not to be satisfied with appearances or with what is politically correct.

Let us look and learn to see

Jesus goes before us, he precedes us. He opens the way and invites us to follow him. He invites us slowly to overcome our preconceptions and our reluctance to think that others, much less ourselves, can change. He challenges us daily, asking: Do you believe? Do you believe it is possible that a tax collector can become a servant? Do you believe it is possible that a traitor can become a friend? Do you believe it is possible that the son of a carpenter can be the Son of God? His gaze transforms our way of seeing things. His heart transforms our hearts. God is a Father who seeks the salvation of each of his sons and daughters.

Let us gaze upon the Lord in prayer, in the Eucharist, in confession, in our brothers and sisters, especially those who feel excluded or abandoned. May we learn to see them as Jesus sees us. Let us share his tenderness and mercy with the sick, prisoners, the elderly, and families in difficulty. Again and again we are called to learn from Jesus, who always sees what is most authentic in every person, which is the image of his Father.

Mercy, Feast, and Memory (9:9–13)[3]

Mercy received and accepted

Jesus passes between those who received the tax money and those who took it to the Romans. These men were not considered very commendable, because they were double sinners—attached to money and even traitors to the country. Among them was Matthew, the man sitting at the tax table. Jesus looks at Matthew and awakens something new within him, something he had never experienced. The gaze of Jesus makes him feel an interior wonder, and then he hears the call of Jesus: "Follow me." It takes only a moment for him to understand that that look has changed his life forever. And it is in this moment that Matthew says yes, leaves everything, and goes with the Lord.

The feast

The first moment of the encounter, which consists of "a deep spiritual experience," is followed by a second experience: that of celebration. The Gospel continues with Jesus sitting at table with publicans and sinners, people who have been rejected by society. But this is how God celebrates: the Lord feasts with sinners. Luke's Gospel (15) clearly says that there will be more rejoicing in heaven over one sinner who repents than over ninety-nine righteous people who have no need of repentance. This is why celebration is very important, because the encounter with Jesus and the mercy of God should be celebrated.

The memory

But life is not one big party. There is a time for celebration, but then there must be daily work, fueled by the memory of that first encounter. It is the memory of mercy and of that celebration that gives Matthew—and everyone who has chosen to follow Christ—the strength to go forward. This must be remembered forever.

THE GHOST OF HYPOCRISY (9:14–15)[4]

The Word of the Lord today speaks of fasting, which is the penance that we are invited to do in this season of Lent: penance so as to draw near to the Lord.

The first reading, taken from the prophet Isaiah (58:1–9), is a discussion between God and those who lament that God does not listen to their prayers, their penance, their fasting. The Lord tells them: "Your fasting is an artificial fast; it is not a true fast; it is a fast to fulfill a formality." They fasted only to comply with certain laws. They lament because their fast is not effective, and they ask: "Why fast, if you do not see it; humble ourselves, if you do not know?" But, "Behold"—the Lord responds—"you fast only to quarrel and to fight and to hit with wicked fist." In other words, on the one hand you fast, you repent, and on the other hand, you carry out injustices. In the end, they believed that fasting was somewhat like "dressing up" the heart: "I am just because I fast." And it is the lament that John's disciples—who were good—and the Pharisees make to Jesus: "I am just; I dress up my heart but then I argue, I exploit people."

In response to these people who are complaining, the Lord explains what true fasting is: "This, rather, is the fasting that I wish: releasing those bound unjustly, untying the thongs of the yoke; setting free the oppressed, breaking every yoke; sharing your bread with the hungry, sheltering the poor and the homeless; clothing the naked when you see them, and not turning your back on your own. I want this. This is the fasting that I wish."

The other kind of fasting is "hypocritical" (a word that Jesus used often), fasting in order to be seen or to feel just. But even as I am doing it, I am committing injustices; I am not just, I exploit people. There is no point in saying, "I am generous; I give a nice offering to the church." Instead, tell me: Do you pay your domestic workers fairly? Do you pay your employees "under the table" or do you pay them as the law requires so they can feed their children?

Show Mercy (9:35–38)[5]

It is good to reflect together as priests on mercy. We all need it. The faithful also need it, and as pastors we must extend great, great mercy!

Jesus is on the streets

The passage from the Gospel of Matthew makes us turn our gaze to Jesus as he goes about the cities and villages. And this is curious. Where was Jesus most often, where could he most easily be found? On the road. He might have seemed to be homeless, because he was always on the road. Jesus's life was on the road. He especially invites us to be aware of what is in the depths of his heart, what he feels for the crowds, for the people he encounters, that interior attitude of compassion: seeing the crowds, he felt compassion for them. He saw the people were "harassed and helpless, like sheep without a shepherd." We have heard these words so many times that perhaps they do not strike us powerfully. But they are powerful! Those crowds are a little like the many people whom you meet today on the streets of your own neighborhoods... Then the horizon broadens, and we see that these towns and villages are not only Rome and Italy; they are the world... and those helpless crowds are the peoples of many nations who are suffering through even more difficult situations...

The good shepherd

Let us ask ourselves what mercy means for a priest—allow me to say for us priests. For us, for all of us! Priests are moved to compassion before the sheep, like Jesus, when he saw the people harassed and helpless, like sheep without a shepherd. Jesus has the "bowels" of God, about which Isaiah often speaks. Jesus is full of tenderness for people, especially for those who are excluded, that is, for sinners, for the sick whom no one takes care of... Reflecting the image of the Good Shepherd, the priest is a man of mercy and compassion, close to his people and a servant to all. This is a pastoral criterion that I would like to strongly emphasize—closeness. Closeness and service, but [especially] closeness, nearness... Whoever is wounded in life, in whatever way, can find in the priest attention and a sympathetic ear... The priest reveals a heart filled with mercy especially in administering the sacrament of reconciliation; he reveals it by his entire attitude, by the manner in which he welcomes, listens, counsels and absolves... But this comes from how he experiences the sacrament firsthand, from how he allows himself to be embraced by God the Father in confession and remains in this embrace...If one experiences this in one's own regard, in his own heart, he can also give it to others in his ministry. And I leave you with these questions: How do I confess? Do I allow myself to be embraced?

The "field hospital"

The priest is called to learn this, to have a heart that is moved. Priests who are—allow me to say the word—"aseptic," those "from the laboratory," all clean and tidy, do not help the church. Today, we can think of the church as a "field hospital." Forgive me for repeating it, but this is how I see it, how I feel it: a "field hospital." Wounds need to be treated, so many wounds! So many wounds! There are so many people who are wounded by material problems, by scandals, also in the church...People wounded by the world's illusions...We priests must be there, close to these people. Mercy first means treating the wounds. When someone is wounded, he needs immediate treatment, not tests for such things as cholesterol level and glucose tolerance...There is a wound. That wound needs to be attended to, and then we can look at test results. Then specialized treatments can be done, but first we need to treat the open wound. That is what is most important at this time. And there are also hidden wounds, because there are people who distance themselves in order to avoid exposing their wounds... What comes to mind is the custom in the Mosaic Law regarding the lepers. In Jesus's time they were always kept at a distance in order not to spread the contagion...There are people who distance themselves through shame—through shame, so as not to let their wounds be seen...And perhaps they distance themselves with some bitterness against the church, but deep down inside, there is a wound...They want a hug! And you, dear brothers—I ask you—do you know the wounds of your parishioners? Do you perceive them? Are you close to them? It's the only question...

Care for the person

True mercy takes the person into one's care, listens to him attentively, approaches the situation with respect and truth, and accompanies him on the journey of reconciliation. And this is demanding, yes, certainly. The truly merciful priest behaves like the Good Samaritan... And why does he do it? Because his heart is capable of having compassion; it is the heart of Christ!

Knowing how to cry

In the old missals, those of another age, there is a most beautiful prayer asking for the gift of tears. The prayer began like this: "Lord, who commanded Moses to strike the rock so that water might gush forth, strike the stone of my heart so that tears..." This is very beautiful. But how many of us weep before the suffering of a child, before the breakup of a family, before so many people who do not find the path?... The weeping of a priest... Do you weep? Or in the priesthood have we lost all tears? Do you weep for your people?

Knowing how to fight with God

Tell me, do you offer intercessory prayer before the tabernacle? Do you struggle with the Lord for your people, as Abraham struggled? "Suppose they were fewer? Suppose there were twenty-five? And suppose there were twenty?" (cf. Gen 18:22–33). This courageous prayer of intercession... We talk of speaking the truth to power and of apostolic courage, and we think about creating effective pastoral plans. All this this is good. However, the same boldness is also needed in prayer. Do you struggle with the Lord? Do you argue with the Lord as Moses did? When the Lord was annoyed, tired of his people, he said to Moses: "Don't worry... I will destroy everything, and I will make you the head of another people." "No. No." Moses replied. "If you destroy the people, destroy me too." This required guts! Do we have the guts to struggle with God for our people?

Don't be ashamed of your brother's flesh

Do not be ashamed of the flesh of your brother. In the end, we will be judged on our ability to draw close to "all flesh"—this from Isaiah. Do not be ashamed of the flesh of your brother. "Making ourselves close": closeness, nearness, being close to the flesh of one's brother.

The priest and the Levite who passed by the man who had been beaten up and left in a ditch did not know how to draw near to him. Their hearts were closed. Perhaps the priest looked at his watch and said: "I have to go to Mass, I cannot be late for Mass," and he left. Excuses! How often we justify ourselves to get around the problem, the person. The other, the Levite, or the doctor of the law, the lawyer, said: "No, I cannot, because I have to go and testify tomorrow, and if I do this I will lose time . . ." Excuses! Their hearts were closed. A closed heart always justifies itself for what it has not done. Finally the Samaritan comes along. He opens his heart and allows his heart to be moved. This interior movement translates into practical action, a concrete and effective intervention to assist another.

At the end of time, only those who have not been ashamed of the flesh of their brother who is injured and excluded will be permitted to contemplate the glorified flesh of Christ.

A Church that Lives Compassion (9:36)[6]

To have the heart of Jesus

We must have the heart of Jesus, who "when he saw the crowds, he had compassion for them, because they were harassed and helpless, like sheep without a shepherd" (Matt 9:36). Seeing the crowds, he feels compassion for them. I like to dream of a church that lives the compassion of Jesus, a church that can "suffer with," feel what others feel, and accompany them emotionally. A Mother Church that caresses her children with compassion like a mother. A church that has a heart without borders, but not just a heart—also a gaze that has the sweetness of Jesus's gaze, which is often much more eloquent than many words. People expect to find in us the gaze of Jesus, sometimes without even knowing it, that serene gaze, a happiness that seeps into the heart. But—as your representatives said—it takes a whole parish to be a welcoming community, not just the priests and the catechists. The whole parish! Welcome...

Welcoming parishes

We must give some thought to how welcoming our parishes are: whether the hours of activities encourage the participation of young people; whether we are capable of speaking their language, of reaching out by other means (as for example sports, new technologies) for opportunities to proclaim the Gospel. Let us be bold in exploring new ways in which our communities can be homes where the door is always open. An open door! It is important that the welcome be followed by a clear proposal of the faith; many times a *proposal of the faith* may not be explicit, but is conveyed by attitude, by witness. In this institution called the church, in this institution called the parish, one breathes the air of faith, because one believes in the Lord Jesus.

An orphan to care for

I will ask you to study carefully these things that I have said, and to consider how we can recover the memory of the family, how we can make the parish warmer and more generous, so that it will not be an institution tied solely to the conditions of the moment. No, let it have a history, let it be on a journey of pastoral conversion. Let it know how to welcome with tenderness in the present, and how to send forth its children with hope and patience.

Having the Gaze of Jesus (9:37–38)[7]

Considering the fact that the number of priests and religious is not yet sufficient, the Lord Jesus repeats to you today: "The harvest is plentiful, but the laborers are few; pray, therefore, the Lord of the harvest to send out laborers into his harvest" (Matt 9:37–38). We must not forget that this prayer begins with a gaze: the gaze of Jesus, who sees the great harvest. Do we also have this gaze? Do we know how to recognize the abundant fruits that the grace of God has produced and the work that there is to be done in the field of the Lord? It is by gazing with faith on the field of God that prayer springs forth, namely, the daily and pressing invocation to the Lord for priestly and religious vocations. Dear seminarians, postulants and novices, you are the fruit of this prayer of the people of God, which always precedes and accompanies your personal response.

10

The Mission of the Disciples

Key Words (10:7–13)[1]

Jesus sends his disciples to proclaim the Gospel, the Good News, the Gospel of salvation. There are three key words that will give us a clear understanding of what Jesus wanted from his disciples and from all of us who follow him. The three words are: journey, service, and gratuitousness.

Journey

First of all, Jesus sends the disciples on a journey. It is a journey, not just a simple "stroll." It has a purpose: to proclaim the Gospel, to go out to bring salvation, the Gospel of salvation. And this is the task that Jesus gives to his disciples. Therefore, one who stands still and doesn't go out, doesn't give to others what he or she received in baptism, is not a true disciple of Jesus. Such persons lack the missionary spirit, the ability to go out of themselves to bring something good to others.

There is also another path of the disciple of Jesus, and that is the inner journey of the disciple who seeks the Lord every day, in prayer, in meditation. And this is not secondary: disciples must also take this journey because if they do not always seek God, the Gospel that they bring to others will be a weak, watered down Gospel, without strength.

So there is a twofold journey that Jesus wants from his disciples. This sums up the first word highlighted by today's Gospel: *journey*.

Service

Then comes the second word, "service," which is closely linked to the first. In fact, one has to walk in order to serve others. The Gospel says: "Preach as you go, saying: 'The kingdom of heaven is at hand.' Heal the sick, raise the dead, cleanse lepers, cast out demons." Here we find again the disciple's duty: to serve. A disciple who doesn't serve others is not a Christian.

Every disciple's point of reference should be what Jesus preached, his words about those two pillars of Christianity: the beatitudes and the standard by which we will be judged, namely that found in Matthew 25. This is the "framework" of evangelical service. There are no "loopholes." If a disciple does not walk in order to serve, his walking is of no use. If his life is not in service, his life as a Christian is of no use.

With regard to this we find, in many, the "temptation to selfishness." There are indeed those who say: "Yes, I'm a Christian; I'm at peace, I confess, I go to Mass, I follow the commandments." But where is the service to others? Where is the service to Jesus in the sick, in the imprisoned, in the hungry, in the naked? This is precisely what Jesus told us we must do, because he is present in them. Therefore, the second key is *service* to Christ in others.

Gratuitousness

The third word, gratuitousness, is also important. Walk, in service, without pay. Indeed, the passage reads: "You received without pay; give back without pay." This is something so fundamental that the Lord stated it clearly, to make sure the disciples would understand. He went on to explain: "Take no gold, nor silver, nor copper in your belts, no bag for your journey, nor two tunics." In other words, the journey of service is gratuitous because we received salvation gratuitously. None of us bought salvation, none of us earned it: it is ours purely by the grace of the Father in Jesus Christ, in the sacrifice of Jesus Christ.

Therefore, it is sad when we see Christians who forget these words of Jesus: "You received without pay; give back without pay." And it's sad when those who forget this gratuitousness are Christian communities, parishes, religious congregations, or dioceses. When this happens, it is because in the background there is the mistake of assuming that salvation comes from riches, from human power.

In summary

Three words. Walk: but walk in order to proclaim. Service: the life of a Christian is not for oneself; it is for others, as Jesus's life was. And third, gratuitousness: this is how we place our hope back in Jesus, who offers us a hope that never disappoints. However, when hope is directed to being comfortable on the journey, or when hope is aimed at selfishly seeking things for oneself and not at serving others, or when hope lies in riches or in small worldly assurances, it all caves in. The Lord himself crushes it.

Let us make this journey toward God with Jesus on the altar, so that we can then walk toward others in service and in poverty, with only the riches of the Holy Spirit that Jesus himself gives us.

The Kingdom Is Near (10:7)[2]

Reading the scriptures makes it clear that the Gospel is not merely about our personal relationship with God. Nor should our loving response to God be seen simply as an accumulation of small personal gestures to individuals in need, a kind of "charity à la carte" or a series of acts aimed solely at easing our conscience. The Gospel is about the kingdom of God (cf. Luke

4:43); it is about loving God, who reigns in our world. To the extent that he reigns within us, the life of society will be a setting for universal fraternity, justice, peace, and dignity. Both Christian preaching and life, then, are meant to have an impact on society. We are seeking God's kingdom: "Seek first God's kingdom and his righteousness, and all these things will be given to you as well" (Matt 6:33). Jesus's mission is to inaugurate the kingdom of his Father; he commands his disciples to proclaim the Good News that "the kingdom of heaven is at hand" (10:7).

The Spirituality of Evangelization (10:8)[3]

Go out and give for free

The phrase "to go out" is very important, as it expresses the movement of evangelization, which is to go out. To go out as Jesus went out from the bosom of the Father to proclaim the word of love to all, even to the gift of his whole self on the wood of the cross. We must learn from him, from Jesus, this "drive to go forth and give, to go out from ourselves, to keep pressing forward in our sowing of the good seed,"[4] to generously communicate God's love to all, with respect and as the Gospel teaches us: "You received without pay; give without pay" (Matt 10:8), in the sense of giving freely. Because redemption was given to us freely, forgiveness of sins cannot be "paid for." It was Christ who "paid for" it once and for all! We must share the gratuitousness of redemption with our brothers and sisters, giving freely, without payment, of what we have received. And gratuitousness goes along with creativity: the two go together.

Dialogue

In order to go out and give freely, we must become experts in that art which is called "dialogue," something that is not easily learned. We cannot be content with half measures. We cannot hesitate. With God's help we must aim high and broaden our gaze! And to do this we must go out with courage "to him outside the camp, bearing abuse for him" (Heb 13:13). He is there in the trials and in the moans of our brothers, in the hurts of society and in the questions of the culture of our time. It hurts the heart when, in light of a church, in light of a humanity with so many wounds, moral wounds, existential wounds, wounds of war that we all hear of every day, we see Christians begin to do philosophical, theological, spiritual "introspection," when what is needed is a spirituality of going-out. Go out with this spirituality: do not remain securely locked inside. That is not good... Today we have no right to introspective reflection. We must go out! Because—and I have said this many times—the Church is like a field hospital. And when one goes to a field hospital, the first task is to heal the wounded, not to run tests... this will come later... Is this clear?

Is It Possible to Give for Free? (10:8)[5]

We have repeatedly said that to love another we must first love ourselves. Paul's hymn to love, however, states that love "does not seek its own interest," nor "seek what is its own." This same idea is expressed in another text: "Let each of you look not only to his own interests, but also to the interests of others" (Phil 2:4). The Bible makes it clear that generously serving others is far more noble than loving ourselves. Loving ourselves is only important as a psychological prerequisite for being able to love others: "If a man is mean to himself, to whom will he be generous? No one is meaner than the man who is grudging to himself" (Sir 14:5–6).

Saint Thomas Aquinas explains that "it is more proper to charity to desire to love than to desire to be loved."[6] Indeed, "mothers, who are those who love the most, seek to love more than to be loved."[7] Consequently, love can transcend and overflow the demands of justice, "expecting nothing in return" (Luke 6:35), and the greatest of loves can lead to "laying down one's life" for another (cf. John 15:13). Can such generosity, which enables us to give freely and fully, really be possible? Yes, because it is demanded by the Gospel: "You received without pay; give without pay" (Matt 10:8).

Prudent and Simple (10:16)[8]

For this reason, dear friends, I ask you to not let yourselves be excluded; do not allow yourselves to be devalued, do not let them treat you like a commodity. For this Jesus gave us good advice, so that we would not be left excluded, left without value, treated as a commodity: "Be wise as serpents and innocent as doves" (Matt 10:16). These two virtues go together. Young people do not lack a lively mind but they do sometimes lack that wisdom that would prevent them from being naive. The two things: wisdom, but with simplicity and goodness. Of course, on this journey, you may perhaps not be able to have the latest model car parked outside your door, you will not have pockets filled with money, but you will have something that no one can take away from you, which is the experience of being loved, embraced, and accompanied. It is the delight of enjoying an encounter, the delight of dreaming and desiring encounter between everyone. It is the experience of being family, of feeling oneself part of a community. It is the experience of being able to look the world in the face, with your head held high, without the car, without the money, but with your head held high: that is dignity!

Three [important words]: value, because you have been made valuable; hope, because we want to be open to hope; and dignity...It is the value, the worth that God has given you. You are the wealth of Mexico. The hope and dignity that Jesus

Christ gives you means not allowing yourselves to succumb to flattery, not allowing yourselves to be used as commodities to fill the pockets of others.

Live Christmas to the Full (10:22)[9]

Today the liturgy recalls the witness of Saint Stephen ... Through his martyrdom, Stephen honors the coming of the King of Kings into the world. He bears witness to him and offers up his very life, as he did in his service to the most needy. And he thereby shows us how to live the mystery of Christmas in its fullness.

On this feast day, the Gospel recounts part of Jesus's discourse to his disciples when he sends them on mission. He says, among other things: "you will be hated by all because of my name. But he who endures to the end will be saved" (Matt 10:22). These words of the Lord do not disturb the celebration of Christmas, but they do remove that artificial sugary coating which does not appertain to it. They enable us to understand that in the trials accepted as the result of faith, *violence is conquered by love, death by life*. And to truly welcome Jesus into our life and to prolong the joy of the Holy Night, the path is the very one indicated by this Gospel, that is, to bear witness to Jesus in humility, in silent service, without fear of going against the current and of paying a price. And if not all are called, like Saint Stephen, to shed their blood, each Christian is, however, asked to be consistent in every circumstance with the faith that he or she professes. And Christian consistency is a grace that we must ask of the Lord. To be consistent, to live as Christians—not to say, "I am a Christian" but live as a pagan. *Consistency is a grace we must ask for today.*

Following the Gospel is certainly a demanding but beautiful, very beautiful, journey. Those who follow the Gospel with faithfulness and courage receive the reward promised by the

Lord to men and women of good will. As the angels sang on Christmas Day: "Peace! Peace!" This peace granted by God is capable of calming the conscience of those who, through the trials of life, are able to receive the Word of God and commit themselves to observing it with perseverance to the end (cf. Matt 10:22).

The Demands of the Christian Vocation (10:34–37)[10]

The Gospel goes on to remind us that children are not the property of a family, but have their own lives to lead. Jesus is a model of obedience to his earthly parents, placing himself under their charge (cf. Luke 2:51), but he also shows that children's life decisions and their Christian vocation may demand a parting for the sake of the kingdom of God (cf. Matt 10:34–37; Luke 9:59–62). Jesus himself, at twelve years of age, tells Mary and Joseph that he has a greater mission to accomplish apart from his earthly family (cf. Luke 2:48–50). In this way, he shows the need for other, deeper bonds even within the family: "My mother and my brethren are those who hear the word of God and do it" (Luke 8:21). All the same, in the concern he shows for children—whom the societies of the ancient Near East viewed as subjects without particular rights and even as family property—Jesus goes so far as to present them as teachers, on account of their simple trust and spontaneity toward others. "Truly I tell you, unless you change and become like children, you will never enter the kingdom of heaven. Whoever becomes humble like this child is the greatest in the kingdom of heaven" (Matt 18:3–4).

11
Jesus's Way

The Sign of God (11:3)[1]

The need for a sign

In prison, Saint John the Baptist, suffering, had heard of the preaching of Christ, but he was confused. In the solitude of the cell, he fell prey to doubts and sent the disciples to ask Jesus: "Are you the one who is to come, or are we to wait for another?" (Matt 11:3). He asked for the "great sign," that of the manifestation of God, which had been proclaimed by the prophets and which the people of Israel had been expecting for hundreds of years.

The sign of the Child

When the angels announced to the shepherds the birth of the Redeemer, they did it with these words: "This is the sign for you: you will find a child wrapped in swaddling clothes, lying in a manger" (Luke 2:12). The sign, therefore, is the humility of God taken to the extreme, the love with which, that night, he looked at our fragility, our suffering, our anguish, our desires, and our limits. The message that awaited all the bewildered people, and even his enemies, what everyone was searching for in the depths of his soul, was nothing but the tenderness of

God; God who watches us with eyes full of affection, who caresses us in our misery. A God in love with our smallness.

The sign of tenderness

Today the sweetness of the Lord is announced to us. The world goes on. We continue to look for a sign, but the sign always remains the same. Contemplating the Child born in a manger, I invite you to reflect on how you welcome God's tenderness in your life. Do you allow God to embrace you, or do you prevent God from approaching? No, I look for God, you could argue. However, the most important thing is not to look for God, but to let God find and caress you lovingly. This is the first question that the Child asks us with only his presence: Do we allow God to love us? And again: Do we have the courage to accept the difficult situations and problems of those around us or do we prefer impersonal and efficient solutions that have little to do with gospel values? We must not be afraid of the sweetness that God shows toward us...

The Christian sign of God's tenderness

Finally: Through our behavior, are we able to express the love that must accompany us throughout life, both in moments of joy and those of sadness and difficulty?

The Christian's response cannot be different from God's response to us. This is the implicit message of Christmas night. God falls in love with our littleness. He himself becomes sweetness to better caress us. When we recognize this emblem of God's meekness and closeness, we cannot help but open our hearts to him and beg him: "Lord, help us to be like you; give us the grace of tenderness in the harshest circumstances of life, of 'closeness' in the face of every human need, of meekness in any conflict..."

Do a brief examination of conscience: Is God tender toward me? Am I tender toward others? How do I behave in difficult situations? Do I maintain a gentle attitude at work and when am I involved in disputes? Pray that Jesus will answer you, and he will do it.

The People and their Leaders (11:15)[2]

God, the Lord, complains. He complains that he has not been heard throughout history... And the same happened with the Lord, with Jesus. Some said: "This is the Son of God. He is a great prophet!" Others, those of whom the Gospel speaks today, said: "No, he is a sorcerer who heals with the power of Satan." The people of God were alone, and this ruling class—the doctors of the law, the Sadducees, the Pharisees—was closed in its ideas, in its pastoral care, in its ideology. And this is the class that did not listen to the Word of the Lord, and they tried to justify themselves by saying what we heard in the Gospel: "This man, Jesus, casts out demons with the power of Beelzebul" (Matt 11:15). It is the same as saying: "He is a soldier of Beelzebul or of Satan or of the Satan clique." They justified themselves for not having listened to the call of the Lord. They could not hear it: they were so, so closed, far from the people...

Jesus looked at the people and was moved, because he saw them as "sheep without shepherds," says the Gospel. And he went to the poor, to the sick, to everyone—from widows to lepers—to heal them. He spoke to them with words that evoked admiration among the people: "But he speaks as one who has authority!" He spoke differently from those of the ruling class who had moved away from the people... They had abandoned the flock. Were these people sinners? Yes. Yes, we are all sinners, everyone. All of us who are here are sinners. But these were more than sinners: the hearts of these people, of this little group, had hardened so much over time that it was impossible for them to hear the voice of the Lord. And they slipped from sinfulness into corruption. It is so difficult for a corrupt man to turn back. The sinner, yes, because the Lord is merciful and awaits us all. But the corrupt person is set in his ways, and these people were corrupt... Step by step, they ended up convincing themselves that they had to kill Jesus, and one of them said: "It is better that one man die for the people."

Slipping from a theology of faith to a theology of duty

These men took the wrong path. They resisted the salvation of the Lord's love and so they slipped from faith, from a theology of faith to a theology of duty: "You have to do this, and this, and this..." And Jesus used a very ugly word for them: "Hypocrites! You lay so many heavy burdens on the backs of the people. And you? You don't even lift a finger to help them! Hypocrites!" They refused the love of the Lord, and this refusal set them on a path that was out of line with the dialectic of freedom that the Lord offered, [a path determined by] the logic of necessity, where there was no room for the Lord. In the dialectic of freedom there is room for the good Lord who loves us, loves us so much! Instead, in the logic of necessity there is no place for God: one must do, one must do, one must... These men became conventional, men of good manners, but of bad habits. Jesus called them "whitewashed tombs." This is the Lord's sorrow, the sorrow of God, the lament of God.

"Come, let us worship the Lord because he loves us." "Come back to me with all your heart," he tells us, "because I am compassionate and merciful." These who justify themselves do not understand mercy or pity.

The Divine Way (11:16–17)[3]

In scripture we meet a discontented people, and criticizing is a way out of this discontent (cf. Num 21:4–9). In their discontent the people vented, but they didn't realize that the soul becomes poisoned with this attitude. Jesus also speaks of this kind of attitude, this way of not being content, not satisfied (cf. Matt 11:16–18; Luke 7:32). When Jesus speaks of it, he says: "How are you to be understood? Are you like those youths in the square: we played for you and you did not dance; we wailed and you did not mourn. Does nothing satisfy you?" The problem wasn't salvation but rather liberation, because everyone wanted this. The problem had to do with God's way: they didn't like dancing to God's song; they didn't like mourning to God's lamentations. So what did they want? They wanted to act according to their own thoughts, to choose their own path to salvation. But that path didn't lead anywhere.

Rejecting the way

This is an attitude that we still encounter today. Among Christians, how many are somewhat poisoned by discontent? We hear: "Yes, truly, God is good. Christians, yes, but..." They are the ones who end up not opening their hearts to God's salvation, those who always ask for conditions, who say, "Yes, yes, yes, I want to be saved"—but on the path of their own choosing. This is how the heart becomes poisoned. This is the heart of "lukewarm Christians" who always have something to complain about: "Why has the Lord done this to me?"—But he saved you, he opened the door for you, he forgave you so many sins—"Yes, yes, it's true, but..." Thus the Israelites in the desert said: "I would like water, and bread, but the kind I like, not this worthless food. I loathe it." And we, too, so often say that we loathe the divine way.

Not accepting the gift of God in his way, that is the sin; that is the venom that poisons the soul. It takes away your joy; it doesn't let you go.

Jesus's solution

So, how does the Lord resolve this? With the same poison, with the same sin: that is, he himself takes poison, sin, and is raised up. Thus this lukewarmness of soul, this being halfway Christians, this being "Christians, yes, but..." becomes healed. Healing comes only by looking to the cross, by looking to God who takes on our sins: "my sin is there." However, how many Christians in the desert die of their sorrow, of their lamenting, of their not wanting God's way? This is something for every Christian to reflect on. While God saves us and shows us what salvation is like, I am not really able to tolerate a path that I don't like much. This is the selfishness that Jesus rebukes in his generation, which said of John the Baptist: "He has a demon." And when the Son of Man came, he was defined as a glutton and a drunkard...

Look at the serpent, the venom there in the Body of Christ, the poison of all the sins of the world. Let us ask for the grace to accept the divine way of salvation, and to accept also this food—so wretched that the Hebrews complained about it—the grace, that is, to accept the ways by which the Lord leads us forth.

Jesus, the Model of Evangelization (11:19)[4]

Jesus himself is the model of this method of evangelization which brings us to the very heart of his people. How good it is for us to contemplate the closeness that he shows to everyone! If he speaks to someone, he looks into their eyes with deep love and concern: "Jesus, looking upon him, loved him" (Mark 10:21). We see how accessible he is as he draws near the blind man (cf. Mark 10:46–52) and eats and drinks with sinners (cf. Mark 2:16) without worrying about being thought a glutton and a drunkard himself (cf. Matt 11:19). We see his sensitivity in allowing a sinful woman to anoint his feet (cf. Luke 7:36–50) and in receiving Nicodemus by night (cf. John 3:1–15). Jesus's sacrifice on the cross is nothing else than the culmination of the way he lived his entire life. Moved by his example, we want to enter fully into the fabric of society, sharing the lives of all, listening to their concerns, helping them materially and spiritually in their needs, rejoicing with those who rejoice, weeping with those who weep. Arm in arm with others, we are committed to building a new world. But we do so not from a sense of obligation, not as a burdensome duty, but as the result of a personal decision that brings us joy and gives meaning to our lives.

Father of All Creation (11:25)[5]

Jesus took up the biblical faith in God the Creator, emphasizing a fundamental truth: God is Father (cf. Matt 11:25). In talking with his disciples, Jesus would invite them to recognize the paternal relationship God has with all his creatures. With moving tenderness he would remind them that each one of them is important in God's eyes: "Are not five sparrows sold for two pennies? And not one of them is forgotten before God" (Luke 12:6). "Look at the birds of the air: they neither sow nor reap nor gather into barns, and yet your heavenly Father feeds them" (Matt 6:26).

Come to Me: Your Joy will be Full (11:28)[6]

I have felt the pain of families living in situations of poverty and war. I have listened to young people who want to be married even though they face numerous difficulties. And so, let us ask ourselves: How is it possible to live the joy that comes from faith, in the family, today? But I ask you also: Is it possible or not to live this joy?

A saying of Jesus in the Gospel of Matthew speaks to us: "Come to me, all who labor and are heavy laden, and I will give you rest" (Matt 11:28). Life is often wearisome, and many times tragically so. We have heard this recently... Work is tiring; looking for work is exhausting. And finding work today requires much effort. But what is most burdensome in life is not this. What weighs more than all of these things is a lack of love. It weighs upon us never to receive a smile, to be unwanted. Certain silences are oppressive, even at times within families, between husbands and wives, between parents and children, among siblings. Without love, the burden becomes even heavier, unbearable. I think of elderly people living alone, and families who receive no help in caring for someone at home with special needs. "Come to me, all who labor and are heavy laden," Jesus says.

Dear families, the Lord knows our struggles: he knows them. He knows the burdens we have in our lives. But the Lord also knows our great desire to find joy and rest! Do you remember? Jesus said, ". . . that your joy may be complete" (cf. John 15:11). Jesus wants our joy to be complete! He said this to the apostles and today he says it to us. Here, then, is the first thing I would like to share with you this evening, and it is a saying of Jesus: Come to me, families from around the world—Jesus says—and I will give you rest, so that your joy may be complete. Take home this Word of Jesus, carry it in your hearts, and share it with the family. It invites us to come to Jesus so that he may give this joy to us and to everyone.

A Merciful Heart (11:28–29)[7]

In the Gospels we find various references to the Heart of Jesus. For example, there is a passage in which Christ himself says: "Come to me, all who labor and are heavy laden, and I will give you rest. Take my yoke upon you, and learn from me; for I am gentle and lowly of heart" (Matt 11:28–29). Most significant is the key account of Christ's death according to John. Indeed, this evangelist bears witness to what he saw on Calvary, that is, that when Jesus was already dead a soldier pierced his side with a spear and blood and water came out of the wound (cf. John 19:33–34). In that apparently incidental sign, John recognizes the fulfillment of the prophecies: from the Heart of Jesus, the Lamb sacrificed on the cross, flow forgiveness and life for all people.

The mercy of Jesus is not simply an emotion; it is a force that gives life that raises man! Today's Gospel also tells us this in the episode of the widow of Nain (Luke 7:11–17). With his disciples, Jesus arrives in Nain, a village in Galilee, right at the moment when a funeral is taking place. A boy, the only son of a widow, is being carried out for burial. Jesus immediately fixes his gaze on the weeping mother. The Evangelist Luke says: "And when the Lord saw her, he had compassion on her" (Matt 11:13). This "compassion" is God's love for people, it is mercy, the attitude of God in contact with human misery, with our destitution, our suffering, our anguish. The biblical term "compassion" recalls a mother's womb. A mother in fact reacts in a way all her own in confronting the pain of her children. It is in this way, according to Scripture, that God loves us.

A heart that gives life

What is the fruit of this love and mercy? It is life! Jesus says to the widow of Nain: "Do not weep" and then he calls out to the dead boy and awakens him as if from sleep (cf. Matt 11:13–15). Let us think about this. It is beautiful: God's mercy gives life, raises a person from the dead. Let us not forget that the Lord always watches over us with mercy; he always watches over us with mercy. Let us not be afraid of approaching him! He has a merciful heart! If we show him our inner wounds, our inner sins, he will always forgive us. It is all mercy. Let us go to Jesus!

Meek and Humble of Heart (11:28–29)[8]

When they think of Saint Francis, many people think of peace. Very few people, however, go deeper. What is the peace that

Francis received, experienced, and lived, and which he passes on to us? It is the peace of Christ, which is born of the greatest love of all, the love of the cross. It is the peace that the Risen Jesus gave to his disciples when he stood in their midst (cf. John 20:19–20).

Franciscan peace is not something saccharine. Hardly! That is not the real Saint Francis! Nor is it a kind of pantheistic harmony with forces of the cosmos... That is not Franciscan either! It is not Franciscan, but a notion that some people have invented! The peace of Saint Francis is the peace of Christ, and it is found by those who "take up" their "yoke." namely, Christ's commandment: Love one another as I have loved you (cf. John 13:34; 15:12). This yoke cannot be borne with arrogance, presumption, or pride, but only with meekness and humbleness of heart.

We turn to you, Francis, and we ask you: Teach us to be "instruments of peace," of that peace which has its source in God, the peace which Jesus has brought us.

12

Jesus and the Pharisees

The Conspiracy (12:14)[1]

The corrupt person

It is so difficult for prophecy to melt a corrupt heart! Such a heart is so entrenched in the satisfaction of self-sufficiency that it cannot be challenged. "So it is with those who store up treasures for themselves but are not rich toward God" (Luke 12:21). Such a person feels at ease and happy, like the man who planned the construction of new barns (cf. Luke 12:16–21), thinking that if things went wrong he would be all right. He knew all the excuses for getting away with things, as the corrupt administrator did (cf. Luke 16:1–8)...

The corrupt person has built a self-esteem based exactly on this type of fraudulent behavior. He spends his life navigating shortcuts of opportunism at the price of his own dignity and that of others. The corrupt person says, "I didn't do it," and puts on a "holier-than-thou face," as my grandmother used to say. He deserves a doctorate in social cosmetics. And the worst thing is that the person ends up believing the fiction that he has created. This is why it is so difficult for prophecy to enter such a person's heart!

The persecutor

One of the characteristics of the corrupt person in the face of prophecy is his dislike of being questioned. The person becomes offended by any criticism, discredits its source—whether individual or institution—resorts to a nominalistic-ideological sophistry and balancing act to justify himself while belittling others, and attacks and insults those who think differently (cf. John 9:34). The corrupt person usually imagines that he is being persecuted, and the irritation caused by this assumption drives him to persecute his neighbor. Saint Luke shows the fury of such men before the prophetic truth of Jesus: "They were full of anger and they discussed among themselves what they could do to Jesus" (Luke 6:11). They impose a regime of terror on all who contradict them (cf. John 9:22) and take revenge by casting them out (cf. John 9:34–35). They fear the light because their souls have acquired the characteristics of earthworms: living in darkness and under the earth.

The conspirator

The corrupt appear in the Gospel as people playing with the truth: deceiving Jesus (cf. John 8:1–11; Matt 22:15–22; Luke 20:1–8), conspiring to get him out of the way (cf. John 11:45–57, Matt 12:14), corrupting those who could betray them (cf. Matt 26:14–16) or officials on duty (cf. Matt 28:11–15). Saint John sums them up in one sentence: "The light shone in the darkness, and the darkness did not overcome it" (John 1:5). They are men who do not welcome the light. We can re-read the Gospels to discover more of the typical traits of these characters and their reactions to the light that the Lord brings.

Familiarity with the Word (12:34)[2]

The preacher "ought first of all to develop a great personal familiarity with the word of God. Knowledge of its linguistic or exegetical aspects, though certainly necessary, is not enough. He needs to approach the word with a docile and prayerful heart so that it may deeply penetrate his thoughts and feelings and bring about a new outlook in him."[3] It is good for us to renew our fervor each day and every Sunday as we prepare the homily, examining ourselves to see if we have grown in love for the word that we preach. Nor should we forget that "the greater or lesser degree of the holiness of the minister has a real effect on the proclamation of the word."[4] As Saint Paul says, "We speak, not to please men, but to please God who tests our hearts" (1 Thess 2:4). If we have a lively desire to be the first to hear the word which we must preach, this will surely be communicated to God's faithful people, for "out of the abundance of the heart, the mouth speaks" (Matt 12:34). The Sunday readings will resonate in all their brilliance in the hearts of the faithful if they have first done so in the heart of their pastor.

THE WILL OF GOD: AN EXPRESSION OF LOVE AND HOPE (12:50)[5]

The supreme law

Let us contemplate the one who knew and loved Jesus like no other creature. The Gospel that we heard reveals the fundamental way Mary expressed her love for Jesus: by doing the will of God. "For whoever does the will of my Father in heaven is my brother, and sister, and mother" (Matt 12:50). With these words, Jesus leaves us with an important message: the will of God is the supreme law that establishes true belonging to him. This is how Mary established a bond of kinship with Jesus even before giving birth to him. She becomes both disciple and mother to the Son at the moment she receives the words of the angel and says: "Behold, I am the handmaid of the Lord; let it be done to me according to your word" (Luke 1:38). This "let it be" is not only acceptance, but also a trustful openness to the future. This "let it be" is hope!

Icon of hope

Mary is the mother of hope, the icon that most fully expresses Christian hope. The whole of her life is a series of episodes of hope, beginning with her "yes" at the moment of the Annunciation. Mary did not know how she could become a mother, but she entrusted herself totally to the mystery that was about to be fulfilled, and she became the woman of expectation and of hope. Then we see her in Bethlehem, where the One proclaimed to her as the Savior of Israel and as the Messiah is born into poverty. Later, while she was in Jerusalem to present him in the temple amid the joy of the elderly Simeon and Anna, a promise is made that a sword will pierce her heart and a prophecy foretells that he will be a sign of contradiction. She realizes that the mission and the very identity of this Son surpasses her own motherhood. Then we come to the episode of Jesus being lost in Jerusalem. When he is found, his mother asks, "Son, why have you treated us so?" (Luke 2:48). Jesus's reply puts aside her maternal anxiety and turns to the things of the Heavenly Father.

Yet in the face of all these difficulties and surprises in God's plan, the Virgin's hope is never shaken! She is the woman of hope. This tells us that hope is nourished by listening, contemplation, and patience until the time of the Lord has come.

Mother of hope

Again at the wedding in Cana, Mary is the mother of hope, which makes her attentive to and solicitous of human affairs. With the start of his public ministry, Jesus becomes the Teacher and the Messiah. Our Lady looks upon the mission of the Son with joy but also with apprehension, because Jesus becomes ever more that sign of contradiction foretold by Simeon in the temple. At the foot of the cross, she is at once the woman of sorrow and the woman of watchful expectation of a mystery far greater than sorrow, a mystery that is about to be fulfilled. It seemed that everything had come to an end; every hope could be said to have been extinguished. She too, at that moment, remembering the promises of the Annunciation, could have said: Those promises did not come true, I was deceived. But she did not say this. And so she who was blessed because she believed saw a new future blossoming from her faith and awaited God's tomorrow with expectation.

Knowing how to wait for God's tomorrow

At times I think: Do we know how to wait for God's tomorrow? Or do we want it today? For Mary, the tomorrow of God is the dawn of Easter morning, the dawn of the first day of the week. It would do us good to think, in contemplation, of the embrace of mother and son. The single lamp lit at the tomb of Jesus is the hope of the mother, which in that moment is the hope of all humanity. I ask myself and I ask you: Is this lamp still alight in monasteries? In your monasteries are you waiting for God's tomorrow?

We owe so much to this Mother! She is present at every moment in the history of salvation, and in her we see a firm witness to hope. She, the mother of hope, sustains us in times of darkness, difficulty, discouragement—in times of seeming or actual human defeat. May Mary, our hope, help us to make of our lives a pleasing offering to the Heavenly Father and a joyful gift to our brothers and sisters, with an attitude that always looks forward to tomorrow.

13

The Parables

The Need for Prayer (13:1–23)[1]

Let us not heed the call of the sirens bidding us to perform pastoral care in a disjointed series of initiatives without managing to grasp the essential commitment of evangelization. At times, it seems that we are more concerned with redoubling activities than with being attentive to the people and their encounter with God. Pastoral care that does not pay attention to this becomes, little by little, sterile. Let us not forget to do as Jesus did with his disciples: after they had gone into the villages to spread the message of the Gospel, they returned happy about their success; but Jesus took them aside to a lonely place to stay with them for a while (cf. Mark 6:31). Pastoral care without prayer and contemplation can never reach the heart of the people. It will stop at the surface without allowing the Word of God to take root, to sprout, to grow and bear fruit (cf. Matt 13:1–23).

The Weeds among the Wheat (13:24–30)[2]

This criterion also applies to evangelization, which calls for attention to the bigger picture, openness to suitable processes, and concern for the long run. The Lord himself, during his earthly life, often warned his disciples that there were things they could not yet understand and that they would have to wait for the Holy Spirit (cf. John 16:12–13). The parable of the weeds among the wheat (cf. Matt 13:24–30) graphically illustrates an important aspect of evangelization: the enemy can intrude upon the kingdom and sow harm, but ultimately he is defeated by the goodness of the wheat.

Bearing Fruit (13:24–30)[3]

An evangelizing community is also supportive, standing by people at every step of the way, no matter how difficult or lengthy this may prove to be. It is familiar with patient expectation and apostolic endurance. Evangelization consists mostly of patience and disregard for constraints of time. Faithful to the Lord's gift, it also bears fruit. An evangelizing community is always concerned with fruit, because the Lord wants it to be fruitful. It cares for the grain and does not grow impatient at the weeds. The sower, when he sees weeds sprouting among the grain, does not grumble or overreact. He or she finds a way to let the word take flesh in a particular situation and bear fruits of new life, however imperfect or incomplete these may appear. The disciple is ready to put his or her whole life on the line, even to accepting martyrdom, in bearing witness to Jesus Christ, yet the goal is not to make enemies but to see God's word accepted and its capacity for liberation and renewal revealed.

The Seed that Grows (13:24–30, 33)[4]

Faith also means believing in God, believing that he truly loves us, that he is alive, that he is mysteriously capable of intervening, that he does not abandon us, and that he brings good out of evil by his power and his infinite creativity. It means believing that he marches triumphantly in history with those who "are called and chosen and faithful" (Rev 17:14). Let us believe the Gospel when it tells us that the kingdom of God is already present in this world and is growing, here and there, and in different ways: like the small seed which grows into a great tree (cf. Matt 13:31–32), like the measure of leaven that makes the dough rise (cf. Matt 13:33) and like the good seed that grows amid the weeds (cf. Matt 13:24–30) and can always pleasantly surprise us. The kingdom is here, it returns, it struggles to flourish anew. Christ's resurrection everywhere calls forth seeds of that new world; even if they are cut back, they grow again, for the resurrection is already secretly woven into the fabric of this history, for Jesus did not rise in vain. May we never remain on the sidelines of this march of living hope!

The mystery

Because we do not always see these seeds growing, we need an interior certainty, a conviction that God is able to act in every situation, even amid apparent setbacks: "We have this treasure in earthen vessels" (2 Cor 4:7). This certainty is often called "a sense of mystery." It involves knowing with certitude that all those who entrust themselves to God in love will bear good fruit (cf. John 15:5). This fruitfulness is often invisible, elusive, and unquantifiable. We can know quite well that our lives will be fruitful, without claiming to know how, or where, or when. We may be sure that none of our acts of love will be lost, nor any of our acts of sincere concern for others. No single act of love for God will be lost; no generous effort will have been meaningless, no painful endurance wasted. All of these encircle our world like a vital force. Sometimes it seems that our work is fruitless, but mission is not like a business transaction or investment, or even a humanitarian activity. It is not a show where we count how many people come as a result of our publicity; it is something much deeper, which escapes all measurement. It may be that the Lord uses our sacrifices to shower blessings in another part of the world which we will never visit. The Holy Spirit works as he wills, when he wills, and where he wills; we entrust ourselves without pretending to see striking results. We know only that our commitment is necessary. Let us learn to rest in the tenderness of the arms of the Father amid our creative and generous commitment. Let us keep marching forward; let us give him everything, allowing him to make our efforts bear fruit in his good time.

God's Patience (13:24–30, 36–43)[5]

The liturgy proposes several Gospel *parables*, that is, short stories that Jesus used to announce the kingdom of heaven to the crowds. Among those in today's Gospel, there is a rather complex one which Jesus explained to the disciples: it is that of *the good grain and the weed*, which deals with the *problem of evil* in the world and calls attention to God's patience. The story takes place in a field where the owner sows grain, but during the night his enemy comes and sows weeds, a term which in Hebrew derives from the same root as the name "Satan" and which alludes to the concept of division. We all know that the demon is a "sower of weeds," one who always seeks to sow division between individuals, families, nations and peoples. The servants wanted to uproot the weeds immediately, but the field owner stops them, explaining that "in gathering the weeds you root up the wheat along with them" (Matt 13:29), because, as we all know, a weed, when it grows, looks very much like good grain, and there is the risk of confusing them.

Evil does not come from God

The teaching of the parable [of the wheat and the weeds] is twofold. First of all, it tells us that the evil in the world comes not from God but from his enemy, the evil one. It is curious that the evil one goes at night to sow the weeds, in the dark, in confusion; he goes where there is no light to sow weeds. This enemy is astute: he sows evil in the midst of good, and thus it is impossible for us to distinctly separate them; but God, in the end, will be able to do so.

God is patient

And here we arrive at the second theme: the juxtaposition of the impatience of the servants and the patient waiting of the field owner, who represents God. At times we are in a great hurry to judge, to categorize, to put the good here, the bad there... But remember the prayer of that self-righteous man: "God, I thank you that I am good, that I am not like other men, malicious" (cf. Luke 18:11–12). God knows how to wait. With patience and mercy he gazes into the "field" of life of every person; he sees much better than we do the filth and the evil, but he also sees the seeds of good and waits with trust for them to grow. God is patient, he knows how to wait. This is so beautiful: our God is a patient father, who always waits for us and waits with his heart in hand to welcome us, to forgive us. He always forgives us if we go to him.

The field owner's attitude is that of hope grounded in the certainty that evil does not have the first or the last word. And it is thanks to this patient hope of God that the same weed that is the malicious heart with so many sins can in the end can become good grain. But be careful: evangelical patience is not indifference to evil; one must not confuse good and evil! In facing weeds in the world, the Lord's disciple is called to imitate the patience of God, to nourish hope with the support of indestructible trust in the final victory of good, that is, of God.

In the end, in fact, evil will be removed and eliminated. At the time of harvest, that is, of judgment, the harvesters will follow the orders of the field owner, separating the weed to burn it (cf. Matt 13:30). On the day of the final harvest, the judge will be Jesus, he who has sown good seed in the world and who himself became the "grain of wheat" that died and rose. In the end, we will all be judged by the same measure with which we have judged: the mercy we have shown to others will also be shown to us. Let us ask Our Lady, our Mother, to help us to grow in patience, in hope and in mercy with all our brothers and sisters.

Handing on the Faith (13:31–32)[6]

Raising children calls for an orderly process of handing on the faith. This is made difficult by current lifestyles, work schedules, and the complexity of today's world, where many people keep up a frenetic pace just to survive.[7] Even so, the home must continue to be the place where we learn to appreciate the meaning and beauty of the faith, to pray and to serve our neighbor. This begins with baptism, in which, as Saint Augustine said, mothers who bring their children "cooperate in the sacred birthing."[8] Thus begins the journey of growth in that new life. Faith is God's gift, received in baptism, and not our own work, yet parents are the means God uses for it to grow and develop. Hence "it is beautiful when mothers teach their little children to blow a kiss to Jesus or to Our Lady. How much love there is in that! At that moment the child's heart becomes a place of prayer."[9]

Handing on the faith presumes that parents themselves genuinely trust God, seek him, and sense their need for him, for only in this way does "one generation laud your works to another, and declare your mighty acts" (Ps 144:4) and "fathers make known to children your faithfulness" (Isa 38:19). This means that we need to ask God to act in their hearts, in places where we ourselves cannot reach. A mustard seed, small as it is, becomes a great tree (cf. Matt 13:31–32); this teaches us to see the disproportion between our actions and their effects. We know that we do not own the gift, but that its care is entrusted to us. Yet our creative commitment is itself an offering that enables us to cooperate with God's plan. For this reason, "couples and parents should be properly appreciated as active agents in catechesis . . . Family catechesis is of great assistance as an effective method in training young parents to be aware of their mission as the evangelizers of their own family."[10]

The Vocation (13:44)[11]

I like comparing the vocation to the ordained ministry to the "treasure hidden in a field" (Matt 13:44). It is truly a treasure that God places from the beginning in the hearts of some men, those whom he has chosen and called to follow him in this special state of life. This treasure, which needs to be discovered and brought to light, is not meant to "enrich" just one person. The one called to the ministry is not the "master" of his vocation, but the administrator of a gift that God has entrusted to him for the good of all people, of all men and women, including those who have distanced themselves from religious practice or do not profess faith in Christ. At the same time, the whole of the Christian community is the guardian of the treasure of these vocations, destined for his service, and it must be ever more conscious of the duty to promote them, welcome them, and accompany them with affection.

Search and Find (13:44–52)[12]

Among the parables of the kingdom of God (Matt 13:44–52) are two small masterpieces: the parables of the treasure hidden in the field and of the pearl of great value. They tell us that the discovery of the kingdom of God can happen suddenly, as in the case of the farmer who, plowing, finds an unexpected treasure; or of the pearl merchant who, after a long search, eventually finds the most precious pearl, so long dreamt of. In each case, the point is that the treasure and the pearl are worth more than all other possessions, and therefore when the farmer and the merchant discover them, they give up everything else in order to obtain them. They do not need to rationalize or think or reflect: they immediately perceive the incomparable value of what they have found and they are prepared to lose everything in order to keep it.

Jesus is the treasure

This is how it is with the kingdom of God: those who find it have no doubts. They sense that this is what they have been seeking and waiting for, and this is what fulfills their most authentic aspirations. And it really is like this: those who know Jesus, encounter Him personally, are captivated, attracted by so much goodness, so much truth, so much beauty, and all with great humility and simplicity. To seek Jesus, to find Jesus: this is the great treasure!

Many people, many saints, reading the Gospel with an open heart, have been so struck by Jesus that they convert to him. Consider Saint Francis of Assisi: he was already a Christian, though a somewhat indifferent one. When in a decisive moment of his youth he read the Gospel, he encountered Jesus and discovered the kingdom of God. With this, all his dreams of worldly glory vanished. The Gospel allows you to know the real Jesus; it lets you know the living Jesus; it speaks to your heart and changes your life. And then yes, you leave it all. You can change lifestyles or continue to do what you did before, but you are someone else, you are reborn. You have found what gives meaning, what gives flavor, what gives light to all things, even to toil, even to suffering, and even to death.

God's love shines through

Read the Gospel. Read the Gospel. We have spoken about it, do you remember? To read a passage of the Gospel every day, and to carry a little copy of the Gospel with us, in a pocket or in a purse, in some way, to keep it at hand. In reading the Gospel we will find Jesus. Everything takes on meaning when we find our treasure there, in the Gospel. Jesus calls [this treasure] "the kingdom of God," that is to say, God who reigns in your life, in our life; God who is love, peace and joy in every person and in all people. This is what God wants and it is why Jesus gave himself up to death on the cross, to free us from the power of darkness and to move us to the kingdom of life, of beauty, of goodness, and of joy. To read the Gospel is to find Jesus and to have this Christian joy, which is a gift of the Holy Spirit.

Dear brothers and sisters, the joy of finding the treasure of the kingdom of God shines through; it's visible. The Christian cannot keep his or her faith hidden, because it shines through in every word, in every deed, even in what is most simple and mundane. The love that God has given through Jesus shines through. Let us pray, through the intercession of the Virgin Mary, that his kingdom of love, justice, and peace may reign in us and in the whole world.

THE FAMILY OF JESUS (13:55)[13]

No family can be fruitful if it sees itself as overly different or "set apart." To avoid this risk, we should remember that Jesus's own family, so full of grace and wisdom, did not appear unusual or different from others. That is why people found it hard to acknowledge Jesus's wisdom: "Where did this man get all this? Is not this the carpenter, the son of Mary?" (Mark 6:2–3). "Is this not the carpenter's son?" (Matt 13:55). These questions make it clear that theirs was an ordinary family, close to others, a normal part of the community. Jesus did not grow up in a narrow and stifling relationship with Mary and Joseph, but readily interacted with the wider family, the relatives of his parents and their friends. This explains how, on returning from Jerusalem, Mary and Joseph could imagine for a whole day that the twelve-year-old Jesus was somewhere in the caravan, listening to people's stories and sharing their concerns: "Supposing him to be in the group of travelers, they went a day's journey" (Luke 2:44). Still, some Christian families, whether because of the language they use, the way they act or treat others, or their constant harping on the same two or three issues, end up being seen as remote and not really a part of the community. Even their relatives feel that they are looked down upon or judged by them.

14
Faith

The Death of John the Baptist (14:1–12)[1]

Precursor in life and in death

John was aware that his duty was only to proclaim: to proclaim the coming of the Messiah. He was aware, in the words of Saint Augustine, "that he was only the voice; the Word was another." And when he was tempted to "steal" this truth, he remained steadfast: "The one who is more powerful than I is coming after me" (Mark 1:7).

John is the forerunner, not only of the Lord's entry into public life but of the entire life of the Lord. The Baptist goes forth on the Lord's path. He bears witness to the Lord not only by indicating—"He is the one!"—but also by leading life to the end as the Lord did. Through his martyrdom, John became the forerunner of the life and death of Jesus Christ...John, like Jesus, humbles himself; he knows the way of humility. John, with all that authority, thinking of his life, comparing it with that of Jesus, tells the people who Jesus is, how Jesus's life will be: "It is fitting that he grow; however, I must diminish." And this is John's life: to become small before Christ, so that Christ may grow. It is the life of the servant who makes room, makes way for the Lord to come.

On the same road

When I read this passage, I am moved. I think of two things: first, I think of our martyrs, of the martyrs of our day, those men, women, children who are persecuted, hated, driven from their homes, tortured, and massacred. And this is not a thing of the past; it is happening today.

This passage also urges us to reflect on our own life: I too will meet my end . . . No one can "buy" life. We too, willingly or unwillingly, are traveling the road of the existential ending of life. And this impels us to pray that our death will resemble that of Jesus Christ, his death, as much as possible.

Three Messages (14:13–21)[2]

The Gospel presents the miracle of the multiplication of loaves and fish (Matt 13:13–21). Jesus performed it along the Lake of Galilee, in a deserted place where he had withdrawn with his disciples after learning of the death of John the Baptist. But many people followed them and joined them there. Upon seeing them, Jesus felt compassion and healed their sick until evening. And seeing the late hour, the disciples became concerned and suggested that Jesus send the crowd away so they could go into the villages and buy food to eat. But Jesus calmly replied: "You give them something to eat" (Matt 14:16). Then he asked them to bring five loaves and two fish, blessed them, began to break them and gave them to the disciples, who distributed them to the people. They all ate and were satisfied, and there were even leftovers!

Compassion

There are three messages in this event. The first is *compassion*. In facing the crowd who follows him and—so to speak—"won't leave him alone," Jesus does not react with irritation. He does not say: "These people are bothering me." No, no. He reacts with compassion, because he knows they are not seeking him out of curiosity but out of need. But we must be careful: compassion—which Jesus feels—is not simply feeling pity; it's more! It means *to suffer with,* in other words to empathize with the suffering of another, to the point of taking it upon oneself. Jesus is like this: he suffers together with us, he suffers with us, and he suffers for us. And the sign of this compassion is his healing of countless people. Jesus teaches us to place the needs of the poor before our own. Our needs, even if legitimate, are not as urgent as those of the poor who lack the basic necessities of life. We often speak of the poor. But when we speak of the poor, do we sense that this man or that woman or those children lack the bare necessities of life? That they have no food, they have no clothing, they cannot afford medicine ...their children do not have the means to attend school? Our needs, although legitimate, are not as urgent as those of the poor who lack life's basic necessities.

Sharing

The second message is *sharing*... It's helpful to compare the reaction of the disciples to the tired and hungry people with that of Jesus. They are different. The disciples think it would be better to send the people away so they can go and buy food. Jesus, instead, says: "You give them something to eat." Two different reactions, which reflect two contrasting outlooks: on the one hand, the disciples, reasoning with worldly logic by which each person must think of himself, reason as if to say, "Sort it out for yourselves." Jesus, on the other hand, reasons with God's logic, which is that of sharing. How many times do we turn away so as not to see our brothers and sisters in need? And this looking away is a polite way of saying..."Sort it out for yourselves." But this is not Jesus's way: this is selfishness. Had he sent away the crowds, many people would have been left with nothing to eat. Instead, those few loaves and fish, shared and blessed by God, were enough for everyone. And pay heed! It isn't magic, it's a "sign": a sign that calls for faith in God, provident Father, who does not let us go without "our daily bread," if we know how to share it with one another.

The Eucharist

And the third message: the miracle of the loaves foreshadows the *Eucharist*. It is seen in the gesture of Jesus who, before breaking and distributing the loaves, "blessed" them (Matt 14:19). It is the same gesture that Jesus was to make at the Last Supper, when he established the perpetual memorial of his redeeming sacrifice. In the Eucharist, Jesus gives not just any bread, but the bread of eternal life. He gives himself, offering himself to the Father out of love for us. But we must go to the Eucharist with the sentiments of Jesus, which are compassion and the will to share. One who goes to the Eucharist without having compassion for the needy and without sharing is not at ease with Jesus.

Compassion, sharing, Eucharist. This is the path that Jesus points out to us in this gospel passage. A path that leads us to face the needs of this world with fraternity, but that also leads us beyond this world, because it comes from God the Father and returns to him. May the Virgin Mary, Mother of Divine Providence, accompany us on this journey.

The Scandal of Hunger (14:20–21)[3]

I was hungry and you gave me food

Hunger today is a matter of truly "scandalous" dimensions, one that threaten the life and dignity of many people—men, women, children, and the elderly. Every day, we must address this injustice—I would go even further—this sin, in a world rich in food resources, thanks also to enormous technological progress, for there are too many who lack the basic necessities for survival. And this is true not only in poor countries, but also in rich and developed societies. The situation is aggravated by the increase in migratory flows bringing to Europe thousands of refugees fleeing from their countries and in need of everything. Jesus's words resound in the face of such a huge problem: "I was hungry and you gave me food" (Matt 25:35). We see in the Gospel that, when the Lord realizes that the crowds that have come to listen to him are hungry, he does not ignore the problem, nor does he give a good discourse on the fight against poverty. Instead, he does something that leaves everyone astonished; he takes the little that the disciples had brought with them, blesses it, and multiplies the loaves and fishes, so much so that at the end "they took up twelve baskets full of the broken pieces left over" (Matt 14:20).

Educating ourselves

We cannot work a miracle as Jesus did; however, we can do something in the face of this hunger emergency, something that is humble, but that also has the force of a miracle. First of all, we should learn more about humanity, learn to recognize the humanity in every person who is in need...

It is Jesus himself who invites us to make room in our hearts for the urgent need to "feed the hungry," and the church has made it one of the corporal works of mercy. To share what we have with those who lack the means to satisfy such a primary need educates us in that charity that is an overflowing gift of passion for the life of the poor whom the Lord has us encounter.

See in them the flesh of Christ

In sharing the need for daily bread, you meet hundreds of people every day. Do not forget that they are people, not numbers, each one with his or her burden of pain that at times seems impossible to bear. By always keeping this in mind, you will be able to look them in the face, to look them in the eye, to shake their hand, to see the flesh of Christ in them, to help them win back their dignity and get back on their feet. I encourage you to be brothers and sisters, friends to the poor, and to make them feel that they are important in the eyes of God. May the difficulties that you will surely meet not discourage you. Rather, may they induce you to increasingly support one another as you strive together in active charity.

Jesus Walks on the Water (14:22–33)[4]

In today's gospel reading, we are presented with the account of Jesus walking on the water. After the multiplication of loaves and fish, he asks the disciples to get into the boat and go before him to the other side of the lake while he dismisses the crowds. He then goes up into the hills by himself to pray until late at night. Meanwhile, a strong storm blows up on the lake. Right in the middle of the storm Jesus reaches the disciples' boat, walking upon the water of the lake. When they see him, the disciples are terrified, but he calms them: "Take heart, it is I; have no fear!" (Matt 14:27). Peter, with his usual passion, almost demands proof: "Lord, if it is you, bid me come to you on the water." Jesus answers, "Come!" (Matt 14:28–29). Peter gets out of the boat and walks on the water; but a strong wind hits him and he begins to sink. And so he shouts out: "Lord, save me!" (Matt 14:30), and Jesus reaches out his hand and catches him.

Peter, an icon of faith

This story presents a beautiful image of the faith of the apostle Peter. In the voice of Jesus who tells him: "Come!" he recognizes the echo of the first encounter on the shore of that very lake and, right away, once again, he leaves the boat and goes toward the Teacher. And Peter walks on the water! A faithful and ready response to the Lord's call always enables one to achieve extraordinary things. But Jesus himself told us that we are capable of performing miracles with our faith, faith in him, faith in his word, faith in his voice. Peter, however, begins to sink the moment he looks away from Jesus and allows himself to be overwhelmed by the hardships around him. But the Lord is always there, and when Peter calls him, Jesus saves him from danger. Peter's character, with his passion and his weaknesses, can describe our faith: ever fragile and impoverished, anxious yet victorious, Christian faith walks in the midst of the world's storms and dangers to meet the Risen Lord.

All the disciples in the same boat

The final scene is also very important. "And when they got into the boat, the wind ceased. And those in the boat worshiped him, saying, 'Truly you are the Son of God'!" (Matt 14:32–33). All the disciples are on the boat, united in the experience of weakness, doubt, fear and "little faith." But when Jesus climbs into that boat again, the weather suddenly changes: they all feel united in their faith in him. All the little and frightened ones become great at the moment in which they fall on their knees and recognize the Son of God in their Teacher. How many times the same thing happens to us! Without Jesus, far from Jesus, we feel frightened and inadequate to the point of thinking we cannot succeed. Faith is lacking! But Jesus is always with us, hidden perhaps, but present and ready to support us.

The boat of the church

This is an effective image of the church: a boat that must brave the storms and sometimes seems on the point of capsizing. What saves her is not the skill and courage of her crew members but faith, which allows her to walk amid hardships, even in the dark. Faith gives us the certainty of Jesus's presence always beside us, of his hand that grasps us to pull us back from danger. We are all on this boat, and we feel secure here despite our limitations and our weaknesses. We are safe, especially when we are ready to kneel and worship Jesus, the only Lord of our life. This is what our Mother, Our Lady always reminds us. We turn to her trustingly.

Faith Is Touching Jesus (14:34–36)[5]

This is faith: to touch Jesus is to draw from him the grace that saves. It saves us, it saves our spiritual life, it saves us from so many problems. Jesus notices that someone has touched his cloak and, in the midst of the people, he searches for the woman's face. She steps forward trembling and he says to her: "Daughter, your faith has healed you" (Matt 9:22). It is the voice of the heavenly Father who speaks in Jesus: "Daughter, you are not cursed, you are not excluded, you are my child!" And every time Jesus approaches us, when we go forth from him with faith, we feel this from the Father: "Child, you are my son, you are my daughter! You are healed. I forgive everyone for everything. I heal all people and all things."

15
Encountering Jesus

FAITH IN JESUS (15:21–28)[1]

Today's gospel reading about Jesus's encounter with a Canaanite woman, a foreigner to the Jews, presents us a with unique example of faith The scene unfolds while he is on the way to the cities of Tyre and Sidon, northwest of Galilee. It is here that the woman implores Jesus to heal her daughter who "is tormented by a demon" (Matt 15:22). Initially, the Lord seems not to listen to this cry of grief... Jesus's apparent detachment does not discourage this mother, who insists on her plea.

Unwavering faith

The inner strength of this woman, which enables her to overcome every obstacle, is found in her maternal love and in her confidence that Jesus can hear her request. And this makes me think of the strength of women. With their fortitude they are able to obtain great things. We have known so many women like this one! We can say that it is love that moves faith, and faith in turn becomes the reward of love. Her heartrending love for her daughter induces her to cry out: "Have mercy on me, O Lord, Son of David!" (Matt 15:22). And her steadfast faith in Jesus enables her not to be discouraged, even when she is faced with his initial refusal. So the woman kneels before him, saying, "Lord, help me!" (Matt 15:25).

At the end, seeing such perseverance, Jesus is filled with admiration, almost astonished by the faith of the pagan woman. He responds to her plea, saying: "'O woman, great is your faith! Be it done for you as you desire.' And her daughter was healed instantly" (Matt 15:28). Jesus holds up this humble woman as an example of unwavering faith. Her insistence on invoking Christ's intervention encourages us not to lose heart, not to despair when we are oppressed by life's harsh trials. The Lord does not turn away in face of our needs, and if at times he seems deaf to our cries for help, it is to test and strengthen our faith. We must continue to call out like this woman: "Lord, help me! Lord, help me!" with perseverance and courage. This is the courage we must have in prayer.

This evangelical episode helps us to understand that we all need to grow in faith and to strengthen our trust in Jesus. When we have lost our bearings he can help us to rediscover the way; when the way no longer seems smooth but rough and arduous, when it is hard to be faithful to our commitments. It is important to nurture our faith every day, listening attentively to the Word of God, celebrating the sacraments, with personal prayer as a "cry" to him—"Lord, help me!"—and with concrete attitudes of charity to our neighbor.

We entrust ourselves to the Holy Spirit so that he will help us to persevere in faith. The Spirit infuses boldness into the hearts of believers. He gives our life and our Christian witness the strength of conviction and persuasion; he encourages us to overcome disbelief toward God and indifference toward our brothers and sisters.

May the Virgin Mary make us increasingly aware of our need of the Lord and of his Spirit; may she obtain for us a strong faith, full of love, a love that is able to become an entreaty, a courageous entreaty to God.

Encountering Jesus (15:21–28)[2]

The Gospel narrates many scenes of search and encounter with Jesus and, in each of them, there is some element that can help us in prayer. An encounter with Jesus always brings with it a call, large or small (Matt 4:19; 9:9; 10:1–4); it happens at any time and is pure gratuitousness (Matt 20:5–6); it must be sought and wanted (Matt 8:2–3; 9:9), sometimes with heroic constancy (Matt 15:21), sometimes with cries of dismay (Matt 8:25), and in searching one can experience the pain of perplexity and doubt (Luke 7:18–24; Matt 11:2–7). An encounter with Jesus Christ leads us ever more toward humility (Luke 5:9); sometimes the search can be refused, sometimes accepted (Matt 13:1–23). The former is a source of great sorrow for the heart of Christ (Matt 20:30, 23:37–39). It is not a matter of research and an aseptic, Pelagian encounter, but of a path that also has to do with sin and repentance (Matt 21:28–32). The encounter with Jesus Christ takes place in everyday life, in the assiduous practice of prayer, in the wise reading of the signs of the times (Matt 24:32; Luke 21:29) and in our brothers and sisters (Matt 25:31–46; Luke 10:25–37).

Compassion (15:22)[3]

Among the many aspects of mercy, there is one that consists of feeling *compassion* for those who need love. *Pietas*—piety—is a concept that comes to us from the Greco-Roman world, where it meant a kind of submission to superiors, especially devotion due to the gods and then filial respect for one's parents, the elderly in particular. Today, however, we must be careful not to identify piety with pietism, which is only a superficial emotion that disregards the dignity of others. Similarly, it should not be confused with the compassion we feel for our pets; indeed, it happens that at times we feel deeply for animals and are indifferent to the suffering of our brothers and sisters. How often we see people who are so attached to their cats or dogs that they leave their neighbor—a neighbor in need—without help. . . This is not right.

A manifestation of mercy

The piety we wish to talk about is a manifestation of God's mercy. It is one of the seven gifts of the Holy Spirit given by the Lord to his disciples to render them "docile in readily obeying divine inspirations" (*Catechism of the Catholic Church*, §1831). Many times the Gospel refers to the spontaneous cry that the sick, those who are possessed, poor or afflicted people addressed to Jesus: "Have mercy" (cf. Mark 10:47–48; Matt 15:22; 17:15). Jesus responded to all with his gaze of mercy and the comfort of his presence. In those invocations for help or requests for mercy, these persons also expressed their faith in Jesus, calling him "Teacher," "Son of David," and "Lord." They perceived that there was something extraordinary about him, something that could help them in their state of distress. They perceived in him the love of God himself.

Even when people were crowding around him, Jesus was aware of those cries for mercy and he was moved to compassion, especially when he saw people suffering and wounded in their dignity, as in the case of the hemorrhaging woman (cf. Mark 5:32). He called her to trust in him and in his Word . . . For Jesus, feeling compassion is the same as sharing in the distress of those he meets, but at the same time, it also means getting involved in a personal way so that it might be transformed into joy.

Cultivating compassion

We too are called to cultivate within ourselves attitudes of compassion, to shake off the indifference that impedes us from recognizing the needs of the brothers and sisters who surround us and to free ourselves from slavery to material things (cf. 1 Tim 6:3–8).

Let us look to the example of the Virgin Mary, who takes care of each one of her children and is for us believers the image of compassion. In the words of Dante Alighieri's prayer to Our Lady in *Paradiso*: "In you compassion is, in you is pity…in you is every goodness found in any creature" (XXXIII, 19–21).

Walking with Those on the Margins (15:30)[4]

One could say that today we are living an epoch of not so much of change as of epochal change. The situations in which we are living today pose new challenges that are sometimes difficult to understand. Our times require us to live problems as challenges and not as obstacles; the Lord is active and at work in our world. Thus, we must go out into the streets and go out to the crossroads and call all those we find, excluding no one (cf. Matt 22:9), and accompany especially those who are on the roadside, "the lame, the maimed, the blind, the dumb" (Matt 15:30). Wherever we may be, we must build neither walls nor borders but village squares and field hospitals.

16
Who Is Jesus?

The Two Questions (16:13–20)[1]

Today's Gospel recounts a narrative that is fundamental to our journey of faith. It concerns the dialogue in which Jesus asks his disciples the question about his identity. He first asks them: "Who do men say that the Son of Man is?" (Matt 16:13). And then he asks them directly: "Who do you say that I am?" (Matt 16:15). With these two questions, Jesus seems to say that it is one thing to follow the prevailing opinion, and another to encounter him and open oneself to his mystery: there it is that one discovers the truth. Prevailing opinion contains a true but partial response; Peter, and with him the church of the past, present, and always, by the grace of God, responds with the truth: "You are the Christ, the Son of the living God" (Matt 16:16).

Throughout the centuries, the world has defined Jesus in different ways: a great prophet of justice and love; a wise teacher of life; a revolutionary; a dreamer of God's dreams ...and so on. Many beautiful things. In the confusion of these and other statements, even today, a simple and clear one stands out, the confession of Simon, called Peter, a humble man full of faith: "You are the Christ, the Son of the living God" (Matt 16:16). Jesus is the Son of God. Hence, he is perennially alive as his Father is eternally alive. This is the novelty that grace ignites in the heart of those who are open to the mystery of Jesus: not a mathematical certainty, but one that is even stronger—the inner certainty of having encountered the Wellspring of Life, Life itself made flesh, visible, and tangible in our midst. This is the experience of Christians, and it is not something they have merited. Rather, it the free gift of God, the grace of God, the Father and Son and Holy Spirit. All this is contained in the seed of Peter's response: "You are the Christ, the Son of the living God."

Jesus's response

Jesus's response is full of light: "You are Peter, and on this rock I will build my church, and the powers of death shall not prevail against it" (Matt 16:18). It is the first time that Jesus says the word "church": and he does so expressing all his love for her, defining it as "my church." It is the new community of the covenant, no longer based on lineage and on the Law, but on faith in him, Jesus, the Face of God...

Through the intercession of the Virgin Mary, Queen of the Apostles, may the Lord grant that the church, in Rome and throughout the entire world, may be ever faithful to the Gospel, to the service of which Saints Peter and Paul consecrated their lives.

Who Is Jesus? (16:13–20)[2]

In today's gospel passage Jesus asks his disciples two questions. The first, "Who do men say that the Son of Man is?" (Matt 16:13), is a question that shows that Jesus's heart and gaze are open to everyone. Jesus is concerned with what the people think—not to please them, but to be able to communicate with them. Without knowing what the people think, a disciple would be isolated and judge people according to his or her own thoughts and convictions. Maintaining healthy contact with reality, with what people experience, with their tears and their joys, is the only way to be able to help, to be able to teach and communicate with them. It is the only way to speak to the hearts of people, by being in touch with their daily experiences of such things as work, family, health problems, traffic, school, health services, and so forth…It is the only way to open their hearts to the call of God. In reality, when God wanted to speak with us he became flesh. Disciples of Jesus must never forget from where they were chosen, namely, from among the people, and they must never give in to the temptation of taking on an attitude of detachment, as if what the people think and experience does not concern them or is not important to them.

…The church, like Jesus, lives in the midst of the people and for the people. For this reason the church, throughout her history, has always faced the same question: *Who is Jesus for the men and women of today?*

Saint Pope Leo the Great, originally from Tuscany…also carried in his heart this question, this apostolic concern that everyone might come to know Jesus, and know him for what he truly is, not an image distorted by the philosophies and ideologies of the time. This is why it is important to develop a *personal faith in him.*

Identity and mission

Here then is the second question that Jesus asks his disciples: *"But who do you say that I am?"* (Matt 16:15). Even today the question echoes in our conscience, because we are his disciples, an answer to that question is decisive for our identity and our mission. Only if we recognize Jesus in his truth will we be able to see the truth in our human condition, and will we be able to make our contribution to the *full humanization of society.*

To safeguard and proclaim steadfast faith in Jesus Christ is the heart of our Christian identity, because in recognizing the mystery of the Son of God made man, we are able to comprehend the mystery of God in *the mystery of humanity.*

Simon answers Jesus's question: *"You are the Christ, the Son of the living God"* (Matt 16:16). This response encompasses Peter's entire mission and sums up what will become for the church the petrine ministry, that is, safeguarding and proclaiming the truth of the faith; defending and promoting communion among all the churches; preserving the discipline of the church. In this mission, Pope Leo was and still is an exemplary model, both in his luminous teaching, and in his actions filled with the meekness, compassion, and the strength of God.

Recognizing Christ today

Today, too, our joy is to share this faith and to respond together to the Lord Jesus: *"You are for us the Christ, the Son of the Living God."* Our joy lies also in going against the tide and in moving away from the prevailing opinion that is now, as it was at that time, unable to see more than a prophet or teacher in Jesus. Our joy is recognizing the presence of God in him, God's Emissary, the Son who came to make himself the instrument of salvation for humanity. The profession of faith that Simon Peter proclaimed also holds true for us. It represents not only the foundation of our salvation but also *the path* on which it is fulfilled and *the goal* to which it is directed.

At the root of the mystery of salvation, in fact, lies the will of a *merciful God* who does not want to surrender to the misunderstandings, failures, and misery of man, but gives himself to the point of *becoming a man himself* in order to meet each person in his or her actual condition. This merciful love of God is what Simon Peter recognizes in Jesus's face—the same face that we are called to recognize in the forms in which the Lord has assured us of his presence in our midst: in his Word, which illuminates the darkness of our mind and of our heart; in his sacraments, which regenerate in us new life from every death; in fraternal communion, which the Holy Spirit engenders among his disciples; in the boundless love placed at the generous and caring service of all; in the poor who remind us that Jesus wanted the supreme revelation of himself and of the Father to bear the image of the humbled, crucified Christ.

This *truth of the faith* is a *truth that scandalizes,* because it asks one to believe in Jesus, who, despite being in the form of God, emptied himself, humbled himself, taking on the form of a servant, even unto death on the cross, and because of this God made him Lord of the Universe (cf. Phil 2:6–11). It is the truth that still today scandalizes those who cannot bear the mystery of God imprinted on the face of Christ. It is the truth that we cannot touch and embrace, as Saint Paul says, without entering into the mystery of Jesus Christ and without making his feelings our own (cf. Phil 2:5). Only by beginning from the heart of Christ can we understand, profess, and live his truth.

Divine and human

In reality, *the communion between the divine and human, fully realized in Jesus, is our destination,* the culmination of human history according to the Father's design. It is the blessedness of the encounter between our weakness and his greatness, between our smallness and his mercy, which will compensate for every one of our limitations. Not only do we move toward the horizon that illuminates our path, but we are drawn by his gentle strength; it is what offers a foretaste and lives here and is built day after day with all the good that we sow around us. These are the seeds that help to create a *new, renewed humanity,* where no one is left on the margins or discarded; where those who serve are greatest; where the small and the poor are accepted and helped.

God and man are not at two opposite extremes: they have always sought each other, because God recognizes in man his own image and man recognizes himself only by looking at God. This is true wisdom, which as the Book of Sirach states, is the trait of the one who follows the Lord. It is the wisdom of Saint Leo the Great, the fruit of the convergence of various elements: word, intelligence, prayer, teaching, memory. But Saint Leo also reminds us that there can be no true wisdom except in the bond with Christ and in service to the church. This is the path on which we intersect with humanity and we encounter it with the spirit of the Good Samaritan. It is not in vain that *humanism . . . has always had the face of charity*. May this legacy bear the fruit of a new humanism.

Finding Freedom (16:13–20)[3]

The Gospel account of Peter's confession of faith and the mission entrusted to him by Jesus shows us that the life of Simon, the fishermen of Galilee—like the life of each of us—opens, opens up fully, when it receives from God the Father the grace of faith. Simon sets out on the journey—a long and difficult journey—that will lead him to go out of himself, leaving all his human supports behind, especially his pride tinged with courage and generous selflessness. In this, his process of liberation, *the prayer* of Jesus is decisive: "I have prayed for you [Simon], that your own faith may not fail" (Luke 22:32). Likewise, decisive is the *compassionate gaze* of the Lord after Peter had denied him three times: a gaze that pierces the heart and brings tears of repentance (cf. Luke 22:61–62). At that moment, Simon Peter *was set free from the prison of his selfish pride* and of his fear, and overcame the temptation of closing his heart to Jesus's call to follow him along the way of the cross.

You Are Peter (16:13–20)[4]

This Sunday's Gospel is a well-known passage, central to Matthew's account, in which Simon, on behalf of the Twelve, professes his faith in Jesus as "the Christ, the Son of the living God"; and Jesus calls Simon "blessed" for this faith, recognizing in him a special gift of the Father, and telling him: "You are Peter, and on this rock I will build my church."

Let us pause at this point and consider the fact that Jesus gives Simon this name, "Peter," which in Jesus's language is pronounced *"Kefa,"* a word that means "rock." In the Bible, this term, "rock," refers to God. Jesus gives it to Simon not because of his character or for his merits as a human being but because of his *genuine and steadfast faith*, which comes to him from above.

Jesus feels great joy in his heart, recognizing in Simon the hand of the Father, the work of the Holy Spirit. He recognizes that God the Father has given Simon "steadfast" faith on which he, Jesus, can build his church, meaning his community, that is, all of us. Jesus intends to give life to "his" church, a people founded no longer on heritage, but on faith, which means on a relationship with him, a relationship of love and trust. The church is built on our relationship with Jesus. And to begin his church, Jesus needs to find in his disciples a solid faith, "steadfast" faith. It is this that he must verify at this point of the journey. The Lord has in mind a picture of a community-like structure. This is why, when he hears Simon's candid profession of faith, he calls him a "rock," and declares his intention to build his church upon this faith.

We are living stones

What happened in a unique way in Saint Peter also happens in every Christian who develops a sincere faith in Jesus the Christ, the Son of the Living God. Today's Gospel passage also asks each of us: Is your faith good? We each need to ask in our heart. Is my faith good? What does the Lord see when he looks at my heart? A heart that is firm as a rock or a heart like sand, one that is doubtful, diffident, disbelieving? It will do us good to think about this throughout the day today. If the Lord finds in our heart—I don't say a perfect—but a sincere, genuine faith, then he also sees us as living stones with which to build his community. This community's foundation stone is Christ, the unique cornerstone. At his side, Peter is the rock, the visible foundation of the church's unity. Yet every baptized person is called to offer Jesus his or her lowly but sincere faith, so that he may continue to build his church, today, in every part of the world.

Even now, so many people think Jesus may be a great prophet, a knowledgeable teacher, a model of justice...And even now, Jesus asks his disciples, that is, all of us: "Who do you say that I am?" What do we answer? Let us think about this. But above all, let us pray to God the Father, through the intercession of the Virgin Mary. Let us pray that he grant us the grace to respond with a sincere heart: "You are the Christ, the Son of the living God." This is a confession of faith. This is really "the Creed."

17
The Transfiguration

The Mystery of the Transfiguration (17:1–9)[1]

I invite you to be educators, spiritual guides, and catechists for those who are from your home, who are members of your communities, and who approach the Eucharist. Take them by the hand and lead them to Mount Tabor (cf. Luke 9:28–36), guiding them to knowledge of the mystery they profess, to the splendor of the divine face hidden in the Word which perhaps they are used to hearing without perceiving its power. For those who already walk with you, find places and prepare tents in which the Risen Christ can reveal his splendor. Spare no energy in accompanying them on the climb. Do not let them resign themselves to the ordinary. Gently and carefully remove the wax that slowly collects in their ears and prevents them from hearing God who attests: "This is my beloved Son, with whom I am well pleased" (cf. Matt 17:5).

It is joy that attracts, enchants, and enraptures. Without joy, Christianity deteriorates into fatigue, pure fatigue. Take care of your priests, so that they can awaken enchantment with God in people, so that they always want to remain in his presence, feel nostalgia for his company, and desire nothing other than to return to his presence.

There are too many empty words that take men far from themselves, relegating them to the ephemeral and limiting them to the provisional. Make sure that it is Jesus, God's beloved, who is the solid nourishment that is continually savored and incorporated.

The Purpose of the Transfiguration (17:1–9)[2]

Taking aside three of the apostles, Peter, James and John, Jesus led them up a high mountain. And that is where this unique occurrence took place: Jesus's face "shone like the sun, and his garments became white as light" (Matt 17:2). The Lord allowed the divine glory that could be understood through faith in his preaching and his miraculous gestures, to shine forth from within Him. The Transfiguration was accompanied by the appearance of Moses and Elijah who were "talking with him" (Matt 17:3).

The "brightness" that characterizes this extraordinary event symbolizes its purpose: to enlighten the minds and hearts of the disciples so that they may clearly understand who their Teacher is. It is a flash of light that suddenly opens onto the mystery of Jesus and illuminates his whole person and his whole story.

By now decisively headed toward Jerusalem, where he will be sentenced to death by crucifixion, Jesus wanted to prepare his own for this scandal—the scandal of the cross—this scandal too intense for their faith and, at the same time, to foretell his resurrection by manifesting himself as the Messiah, the Son of God. Jesus was preparing them for that sad and very painful moment. In fact, Jesus was already revealing himself as a Messiah different from their expectations, from how they imagined the Messiah, how the Messiah would be: not a powerful and glorious king, but a humble and unarmed servant; not a lord of great wealth, a sign of blessing, but a poor man

...not a patriarch with many descendants, but a celibate man without a home. It is truly an overturned revelation of God, and the most bewildering sign of this scandalous overturning is the cross. But it is through the cross that Jesus will reach the glorious Resurrection, which will be definitive, not like this Transfiguration, which lasted a moment, an instant.

Transfigured on Mount Tabor, Jesus wanted to show his disciples his glory, not for them to circumvent the cross, but to see where the cross would lead. Those who die with Jesus shall rise again with Jesus. The cross is the door to Resurrection. Whoever struggles alongside Jesus will triumph with him. This is the message of hope contained in Jesus's cross, urging us to be strong in our existence. The Christian cross is not something hanging on a wall or an adornment to be worn. Rather, the Christian cross is a call to the love with which Jesus sacrificed himself to save humanity from evil and sin. In this Lenten season, we contemplate with devotion the image of the crucifix, Jesus on the cross. This is the symbol of Christian faith, the emblem of Jesus, who died and rose for us. Let us ensure that the cross marks the stages of our Lenten journey so that we may better understand the seriousness of sin and the value of the sacrifice by which the Savior has redeemed us all.

The Blessed Virgin was able to contemplate the glory of Jesus hidden in his humanness. May she help us remain with him in silent prayer and allow ourselves to be enlightened by his presence so that, even through our darkest nights, we may carry in our hearts a reflection of his glory.

Ascent and Descent (17:1–9)[3]

In the Transfiguration there are two significant elements that can be summed up in two words: ascent and descent. We all need to go apart, to ascend the mountain in silence, in order to find ourselves and better perceive the voice of the Lord. This we do in prayer. But we cannot stay there! Encounter with God in prayer inspires us to then "descend the mountain" and return to the plain where we meet many brothers and sisters weighed down by fatigue, sickness, injustice, ignorance, and poverty, both material and spiritual. To these brothers and sisters in difficulty we are called to bear the fruit of that experience with God by sharing the grace we have received. And this is curious. When we hear the Word of Jesus, when we listen to the Word of Jesus and carry it in our heart, this Word grows. Do you know how it grows? By giving it to others! The Word of Christ grows in us when we proclaim it, when we give it to others! And this is what Christian life is. It is a mission for the whole church, for all the baptized, for all of us: listen to Jesus and offer him to others.

18

Who Is the Greatest?

The Angel and the Child (18:1–11)[1]

God does not abandon us

In Eucharistic Prayer IV there is a phrase that gives us pause. What we say to the Lord in that prayer is: "When, because of his disobedience, man lost your friendship, you did not abandon him." Let us think about what happened when Adam was thrown out of Eden: the Lord did not say, "Survive as best you can!" He did not leave man alone. God has always sent help. Today we talk about the help of angels. In fact, we read in the biblical passage: "Behold, I send an angel before you, to guard you on the way and to make you enter the place that I have prepared" (Exod 23:20–23). The Lord, therefore, did not abandon but walked with his people, walked with the man who had lost friendship with him The heart of God is a heart of a father who never abandons his children.

Today the liturgy leads us to reflect on this, and also on a particular type of companionship, of help, that the Lord has given us all: the guardian angels. Each of us has one, an angel to accompany us. And in the prayer at the beginning of the Mass we asked for the grace of having that angel support us in our journey of life and then be with us in the joy of heaven.

We are supported precisely by the help of the angel who walks with us: "Behold, I send an angel before you to keep you on the path and to let you enter the place I have prepared."

The guardian angel is truly always with us, an ambassador of God with us.

Listen to your angel

Perhaps there are times when we think we can hide certain things. It's true; we can hide them. Yet the Lord tells us that although we can hide many bad things, in the end everything will be known. A wise folk adage says: "The devil makes the pans, not the lids." In the end, therefore, all will be known, and this angel, whom we all have, guides us along the path. Thus our angel is a friend, a friend whom we do not see but we hear, a friend who will be with us in heaven, in eternal joy.

God sends the angel to free us, to ward off fear, to distance us from misfortune. He asks us only to listen to him, to respect him—only this: respect and listening. And respect and listening to our traveling companion is called obedience. The Christian must be open to the Holy Spirit, but openness to the Holy Spirit begins with yielding to the advice of this traveling companion.

Jesus Bears Us on His Shoulders (18:12, 22)[2]

I invite all Christians, everywhere, at this very moment, to a renewed personal encounter with Jesus Christ, or at least an openness to letting him encounter them; I ask all of you to do this unfailingly each day. No one should think that this invitation is not meant for him or her, since "no one is excluded from the joy brought by the Lord."[3] The Lord does not disappoint those who take this risk; whenever we take a step towards Jesus, we come to realize that he is already there, waiting for us with open arms. Now is the time to say to Jesus: "Lord, I have let myself be deceived; in a thousand ways I have shunned your love, yet here I am once more, to renew my covenant with you. I need you. Save me once again, Lord, take me once more into your redeeming embrace." How good it feels to come back to him whenever we are lost! Let me say this once more: God never tires of forgiving us; we are the ones who tire of seeking his mercy. Christ, who told us to forgive one another "seventy times seven" (Matt 18:22), has given us his example: he has forgiven us seventy times seven. Time and time again he bears us on his shoulders. No one can strip us of the dignity bestowed upon us by this boundless and unfailing love. With a tenderness that never disappoints, but is always capable of restoring our joy, he makes it possible for us to lift up our heads and to start anew. Let us not flee from the resurrection of Jesus. Let us never give up, come what will. May nothing inspire more than his life, which impels us onwards!

The Joy of the Church (18:12–14)[4]

The joy of the church is to give birth, to come out of herself in order to give life. In other words, the joy of the church is to go out in search of those sheep who are lost, thus manifesting the tenderness of a shepherd, the tenderness of a mother.

The Gospel of Matthew (18:12–14) presents the shepherd "who goes out," who "goes to look for" the lost and missing sheep. This zealous shepherd can keep count like a prudent businessman. If he loses one of ninety-nine, his balance sheet still shows plenty of assets. However, he has the heart of a shepherd, so he goes out to search and, when he finds that one, he celebrates, he is joyful.

[It is in the example of the shepherd] that the joy of going out in search of faraway brothers and sisters is born. This is the joy of the church. It is precisely in this way that the church becomes mother, becomes fruitful. When the church doesn't do this, she locks herself in; she is closed, even though she might be well organized. And so she becomes a discouraged, anxious, sad church, a church that is more spinster than mother, a church that doesn't work. Such a church is no more than a museum.

Integrating Everyone into the Church (18:17)[5]

It is a matter of reaching out to everyone, of needing to help each person find his or her proper way of participating in the ecclesial community and thus to experience being touched by an "unmerited, unconditional, and gratuitous" mercy. No one can be condemned forever, because that is not the logic of the Gospel! Here I am not speaking only of the divorced and remarried, but of everyone, in whatever situation they find themselves. Naturally, if someone flaunts an objective sin as if it were part of the Christian ideal, or wants to impose something other than what the church teaches, he or she can in no way presume to teach or preach to others; this is a case of something which separates from the community (cf. Matt 18:17). Such a person needs to listen once more to the gospel message and its call to conversion. Yet even for that person there can be some way of taking part in the life of community, whether in social service, prayer meetings, or another way that his or her own initiative, together with the discernment of the parish priest, may suggest. As for the way of dealing with different "irregular" situations, the Synod Fathers reached a general consensus, which I support: "In considering a pastoral approach toward people who have contracted a civil marriage, who are divorced and remarried, or simply living together, the church has the responsibility of helping them understand the divine pedagogy of grace in their lives and offering them assistance so they can reach the fullness of God's plan for them,"[6] something which is always possible by the power of the Holy Spirit.

God Forgives (18:21–22)[7]

God always forgives! He never tires of forgiving. It is we who tire of asking forgiveness. But He never tires of forgiving. Indeed, when Peter asks Jesus: "How often shall I forgive, seven times?" he received an eloquent reply: "Not seven times, but seventy times seven" (cf. Matt 18:21–22). In other words, "always," because this is how God forgives: always. Therefore, if you have lived a life of many sins, many bad things, but at the end, contritely ask for forgiveness, He forgives you straight away. He always forgives."

However, we do not have this certainty in our heart and many times we are doubtful, wondering whether God will forgive. In reality, we need only repent and ask for forgiveness: nothing more! It costs us nothing! Christ paid for us and He always forgives.

...forgives everything

Another important thing is that, not only does God always forgive, but he also forgives all: there is no sin that he would not forgive. Perhaps someone could say: "I don't go to confession because I have done so many bad things, so many things for which I will not be forgiven..." But that isn't true, because if you go contritely, then God forgives all. And many times he doesn't even let you speak: you start asking for forgiveness and he lets you feel the joy of forgiveness before you have even finished what you are saying. It is just like what happened with that son who, after having squandered all his inheritance on an immoral life, repented and decided to return home. He had prepared a speech he would use when he presented himself to his father. However, when he arrived, the father didn't let him speak. Instead, he immediately embraced him: because he forgives all. He embraced him.

. . . celebrates

And then, there is another thing God does when he forgives: he celebrates. And this is not something we just imagine. Jesus says it: "There will be a feast in heaven when a sinner goes to the Father." Truly, God celebrates. Thus, when we feel our heart heavy with sins, we can say: "Let's go to the Lord to give him joy, so that he may forgive us and celebrate." God works in this way: he always celebrates because he reconciles.

. . . forgets

There is something beautiful about the way God forgives: God forgets. Scripture also tells us: "Your sins shall be cast into the sea, and though they are red like blood, they shall become white as a lamb" (cf. Micah 7:19; Isa 1:18).

Hence, God forgets, and if one of us goes to the Lord and says: "Do you remember that year when I did something bad?" He answers: "No, no, no. I don't remember." Because once he forgives, he no longer remembers; he forgets. We, however, so often "keep a record": "This one did this, another one did that . . ." But God doesn't do this: he forgives and forgets. And so, if he then forgets, who am I to remember the sins of others? The Father forgets. He always forgives, forgives all, celebrates when he forgives, and he forgets, because he wants to reconcile, He wants to encounter us.

The priest's mission

When one of us—a priest, a bishop—goes to hear confessions, he must always think: "Am I ready to forgive all? Am I always ready to forgive all? Am I ready to rejoice and celebrate? Am I ready to forget that person's sins?" Because, if you aren't ready, it's better that you don't enter the confessional that day . . . because you don't have the heart of God to forgive. In confession, it's true, there's a judgment, because the priest judges, saying: "You've done harm here, you did . . ." However, it is more than a judgment: it's an encounter, an encounter with the good God who always forgives, who forgives all,...and who forgets our sins when he forgives us. And we priests need to have this attitude of encounter. So often confessions seem to be a formality, a procedure where everything seems mechanical. But then, where is the encounter with the Lord who reconciles, embraces, and celebrates? This is our God, who is so good.

A good confession

It is important to teach children how to make a good confession, reminding them that going to confession isn't like going to the dry cleaner to have a stain removed. Confession is going to encounter the Father who reconciles, who forgives, and who celebrates.

May the Lord give us the grace of being content today to have a Father who always forgives, who forgives all, who celebrates when he forgives, and who forgets our history of sin.

Always Keep the Door Open (18:21–35)[8]

Sin is not simply a mistake. Sin is idolatry...Peter asks Jesus the question: "Lord, if my brother sins against me, how often must I forgive him?" In the Gospel, there aren't many times when a person asks forgiveness. Take, for example, the sinner who cries at Jesus's feet, bathes his feet in her tears, and dries them with her hair. The woman had sinned much, loved much, and asked forgiveness. Recall too the episode in which Peter, after the miraculous catch of fish, says to Jesus: "Stay away from me, for I am a sinner"...And again, we can consider the night of Holy Thursday, when Peter weeps after Jesus turns and looks at him.

In any case, there are few moments when forgiveness is sought. In today's Gospel Peter asks the Lord how great the measure of our forgiveness must be: "Only seven times?" Jesus answers the apostle with a play on words meaning "always": seventy times seven; that is, you must always forgive.

This speaks of forgiveness, not simply tolerating a mistake, but forgiving one who has offended me, who has harmed me, one who through his or her cruelty has injured my life, my heart.

The measure of my forgiveness

And thus the question for each of us today is: "What is the measure of my forgiveness?" The answer can be found in the parable Jesus tells of the man who was forgiven an incredible monetary debt of many, many millions, and who then, quite happy about having been forgiven, goes out and finds a companion who owes him perhaps a debt of ten dollars and sends him to jail. The example is obvious: "If I cannot forgive, I cannot ask forgiveness." This is why Jesus teaches us to pray like this to the Father: "Forgive us our trespasses as we forgive those who trespass against us."

What does this really mean? Imagine the following dialogue:

"Father, I confess, I am going to confess..."

"And what do you do, before confessing?"

"I think about the things I have done wrong."

"Okay."

"Then I ask the Lord's forgiveness and I promise not to do it any more..."

"Good. And then you go to the priest?"

"Yes."

"But wait a minute. You are missing something. Have you forgiven those who have harmed you?"

Since the prayer we were taught is "Forgive us our trespasses as we forgive others," we know that "the forgiveness that God will give you" requires "the forgiveness that you give to others."

Asking forgiveness is not simply apologizing. It requires being aware of the sin, of the idolatry that I have committed, of the many idolatries. And it requires something else too. God always forgives, always, but he also requires that I forgive, because if I don't forgive, it is, in a sense, as if I were closing God's door. This is a door that we need to keep open. Let us allow God's forgiveness to come in so that we may forgive others.

19

From Galilee to Judea

An Image of the Trinity (19:1–12)[1]

Scripture and Tradition give us access to knowledge of the Trinity, which is revealed as having the features of a family. The family is the image of God, who is a communion of persons. At Christ's baptism, the Father's voice was heard, calling Jesus his beloved Son, and in this love we can recognize the Holy Spirit (cf. Mark 1:10–11). Jesus, who reconciled all things in himself and redeemed us from sin, not only returned marriage and the family to their original form but also raised marriage to be the sacramental sign of his love for the church (cf. Matt 19:1–12; Mark 10:1–12; Eph 5:21–32). In the human family, gathered by Christ, "the image and likeness" of the Most Holy Trinity (cf. Gen 1:26) has been restored, the mystery from which all true love flows. Through the church, marriage and the family receive the grace of the Holy Spirit from Christ, in order to bear witness to the Gospel of God's love.[2]

Jesus Fulfills the Divine Project (19:3–9)[3]

The gift of marriage

Contrary to those who rejected marriage as evil, the New Testament teaches that "everything created by God is good and nothing is to be rejected" (1 Tim 4:4). Marriage is "a gift" from the Lord (1 Cor 7:7)...Because of this positive understanding, the New Testament strongly emphasizes the need to safeguard God's gift: "Let marriage be held in honor among all, and let the marriage bed be undefiled" (Heb 13:4). This divine gift includes sexuality: "Do not refuse one another" (1 Cor 7:5).

God's original plan

The Synod Fathers noted that Jesus, in speaking of God's original plan for man and woman, reaffirmed the indissoluble union between them, even stating that "it was for your hardness of heart that Moses allowed you to divorce your wives, but from the beginning it was not so" (Matt 19:8). The indissolubility of marriage—"What God has joined together, let no man put asunder" (Matt 19:6)—should not be viewed as a "yoke" imposed on humanity, but as a "gift" granted to those who are joined in marriage...God's indulgent love always accompanies our human journey; through grace, it heals and transforms hardened hearts, leading them back to the beginning through the way of the cross. The Gospels clearly present the example of Jesus who...proclaimed the meaning of marriage as the fullness of revelation that restores God's original plan (cf. Matt 19:3).[4]

Marriage and family restored

Jesus, who reconciled all things in himself, restored marriage and the family to their original form (cf. Matt 10:1–12). Marriage and the family have been redeemed by Christ (cf. Eph 5:21–32) and restored in the image of the Holy Trinity, the mystery from which all true love flows. The spousal covenant, originating in creation and revealed in the history of salvation, takes on its full meaning in Christ and his church. Through his church, Christ bestows on marriage and the family the grace necessary to bear witness to the love of God and to live the life of communion. The Gospel of the family spans the history of the world, from the creation of man and woman in the image and likeness of God (cf. Gen 1:26–27) to the fulfillment of the mystery of the covenant in Christ at the end of time with the marriage of the Lamb (cf. Rev 19:9).[5]

The example of Jesus

The example of Jesus is a paradigm for the church . . . He began his public ministry with the miracle at the wedding feast of Cana (cf. John 2:1–11). He shared in everyday moments of friendship with the family of Lazarus and his sisters (cf. Luke 10:38) and with the family of Peter (cf. Mark 8:14). He sympathized with grieving parents and restored their children to life (cf. Mark 5:41; Luke 7:14–15). In this way, he demonstrated the true meaning of mercy, which entails the restoration of the covenant (cf. John Paul II, *Dives in Misericordia*, 4). This is clear from his conversations with the Samaritan woman (cf. John 1:4–30) and with the woman found in adultery (cf. John 8:1–11), where the consciousness of sin is awakened by an encounter with Jesus's gratuitous love.[6]

The mystery of the Incarnation

The Incarnation of the Word in a human family, in Nazareth, by its very newness changed the history of the world. We need to enter into the mystery of Jesus's birth, into that "yes" given by Mary to the message of the angel, when the Word was conceived in her womb, as well as the "yes" of Joseph, who gave a name to Jesus and watched over Mary. We need to contemplate the joy of the shepherds before the manger, the adoration of the Magi, and the flight into Egypt, in which Jesus shares his people's experience of exile, persecution, and humiliation. We need to contemplate the religious expectation of Zechariah and his joy at the birth of John the Baptist, the fulfillment of the promise made known to Simeon and Anna in the temple and the marvel of the teachers of the Law who listened to the wisdom of the child Jesus. We then need to peer into those thirty long years when Jesus earned his keep by the work of his hands, reciting the traditional prayers and expressions of his people's faith and coming to know that ancestral faith until he made it bear fruit in the mystery of the kingdom. This is the mystery of Christmas and the secret of Nazareth, exuding the beauty of family life! It was this that so fascinated Francis of Assisi, Therese of the Child Jesus, and Charles de Foucauld and continues to fill Christian families with hope and joy.

The covenant of love and fidelity

The covenant of love and fidelity lived by the Holy Family of Nazareth illuminates the principle that gives shape to every family and enables it better to face the vicissitudes of life and history. On this basis, every family, despite its weaknesses, can become a light in the darkness of the world. "Nazareth teaches us the meaning of family life, its loving communion, its simple and austere beauty, its sacred and inviolable character. May it teach how sweet and irreplaceable is its training, how fundamental and incomparable its role in the social order" (Paul VI, Address in Nazareth, January 5, 1964)."[7]

PAIN AND EVIL (19:3–9)[8]

Blessed are all who fear the LORD,
who walk in obedience to him.
You will eat the fruit of your labor;
blessings and prosperity will be yours.
Your wife will be like a fruitful vine

within your house;
your children will be like olive shoots
around your table.
Yes, this will be the blessing
for the man who fears the Lord.
May the Lord bless you from Zion;
may you see the prosperity of Jerusalem
all the days of your life.
May you live to see your children's children—
peace be on Israel.

The idyllic picture presented in Psalm 128 is not at odds with a bitter truth found throughout sacred scripture, that is, the presence of pain, evil, and violence that breaks up families and their communion of life and love. For good reason, Christ's teaching on marriage (cf. Matt 19:3–9) is inserted within a dispute about divorce. The word of God constantly testifies to that somber dimension already present at the beginning, when, through sin, the relationship of love and purity between man and woman turns into domination: "Your desire shall be for your husband, and he shall rule over you" (Gen 3:16).

Doing the Will of God (19:16–22)[9]

Doing the will of God isn't easy. Recall that good young man, whom the Gospel says that Jesus loved because he was just. Jesus proposed something else to him, but the young man lacked courage. This is why, when the Father, when Jesus asks something of us, we need to ask ourselves: "Is this his will?" It may be something difficult, and we may not feel capable, not feel strong enough to respond to what the Lord is asking of us. But we can find help by praying: "Lord, give me the courage, give me the strength to continue going forward according to the Father's will."

May the Lord give all of us the grace that one day he may say of us what he said of that group, of that crowd who followed him, those who were seated around him: "Here are my mother and my brethren! Whoever does the will of God is my brother and sister and mother." Doing God's will makes us part of Jesus's family. It makes us mother, father, sister, brother to him. May the Lord give us the grace of this familiarity with him, a familiarity that actually means doing God's will.

20
The Margins

Go Out at All Hours (20:1–16)[1]

Jesus tells the story of the vineyard owner who, in need of workers, left the house at various times of the day to call laborers to come to his vineyard (cf. Matt 20:1–16). He did not go out only once. In the parable, Jesus says that he went out at least five times: at dawn, at nine o'clock, at midday, at three o'clock, and at five o'clock in the afternoon—maybe he will still come to us! There was much work to do in the vineyard, and this landlord spent almost all his time going down the streets and to the town squares to seek workers. Think of those of the last hour: no one had called them. Who knows how they must have felt, because at the end of the day they would have nothing to bring home, nothing with which to buy food for their children. All those in charge of pastoral care can take this parable as a good example. We must go out at various times of the day to meet the many who are in search of the Lord; to reach the weakest and the poorest in order to give them the support of feeling useful in the Lord's vineyard, even if only for an hour.

Jesus's Concern (20:3)[2]

In Jesus, his Son, God came down among us. He took flesh and showed his solidarity with humanity in all things but sin. Jesus identified with us; he became "the first-born among many brethren" (Rom 8:29). He was not content merely to teach the crowds but was concerned for their welfare, especially when he saw them hungry (cf. Mark 6:34–44) or without work (cf. Matt 20:3). He was concerned not only for men and women, but also for the fish of the sea, the birds of the air, plants and trees, all things great and small. He saw and embraced all of creation. But he did more than just see. He touched people's lives; he spoke to them, helped them, and showed kindness to those in need . . . He felt strong emotions, he wept (cf. John 11:33–44), and he worked to put an end to suffering, sorrow, misery, and death.

Responding to God's Call (20:7)[3]

The church needs young people capable of giving a response to God who calls them, to return to having stable and fruitful Christian families, to return to having consecrated men and women who exchange their all for the treasure of the kingdom of God, to return to having priests immolated with Christ for their brothers and sisters. We have so many unemployed young people while the kingdom of heaven lacks workers and servants . . . God cannot want this. So what is happening? "No one has hired us today" (cf. Matt 20:7). We must include a vocational dimension in catechesis so that, in their life journey, people of all ages throughout the world can respond to the good God who calls. Even in our mother's womb, he called us to life . . . Once our earthly days have ended, we will have to respond with all our being to this call: "Good and faithful servant . . . enter into the joy of your master" (Matt 25:21).

Unemployment (20:1–16)[4]

We can appreciate the suffering created by unemployment and the lack of steady work as reflected in . . . Jesus's own parable of the laborers forced to stand idly in the town square (Matt 20: 1–16), and in his personal experience of meeting people suffering from poverty and hunger. Sadly, these realities are present in many countries today where the lack of employment opportunities takes its toll on the serenity of family life.

A Place Prepared for Us (20:20–28)[5]

In looking at your faces, the Mexican people have the right to discover the signs of those "who have seen the Lord" (cf. John 20:25), of those who have been with God. This is essential. Do not waste time or energy, then, on secondary things . . . on empty plans for superiority, or in unproductive groups that seek their own interests. Do not allow yourselves to be dragged into gossip and slander. Foster in your priests a correct understanding of sacred ministry. For us ministers of God, it is enough to have the grace to "drink the cup of the Lord," the gift of protecting that portion of the heritage that has been entrusted to us, though we may be unskilled administrators. Let us allow the Father to assign the place he has prepared for us (Matt 20–28). Can we really be concerned with affairs that are not the Father's? Away from the "Father's affairs" (Luke 2:48–49) we lose our identity and, through our own fault, empty his grace of meaning.

At the Service of All Living Beings (20:25–26)[6]

When nature is viewed solely as a source of profit and gain, this has serious consequences for society. This notion of "might makes right" has engendered immense inequality as well as injustice and acts of violence against the majority of humanity, since resources end up in the hands of the first comer or the most powerful; the winner takes all. Completely at odds with this model are the ideals of harmony, justice, fraternity, and peace as proposed by Jesus. As he said of the powers of his own age: "You know that the rulers of the Gentiles lord it over them, and their great men exercise authority over them. It shall not be so among you; but whoever would be great among you must be your servant" (Matt 20:25–26).

A Love Marked by Humility (20:26–28)[7]

The word *perpereúetai* denotes vainglory, the need to be haughty, pedantic, and somewhat pushy. Those who love not only refrain from speaking too much about themselves but are focused on others; they do not need to be the center of attention. The word that comes next [in 1 Corinthians 13:4–7]—*physioútai*—is similar, indicating that love is not arrogant. Literally, it means that we do not become "puffed up" before others. It also points to something more subtle: an obsession with showing off and the loss of a sense of reality. Such people think that, because they are more "spiritual" or "wise," they are more important than they really are. Paul uses this verb on other occasions, as when he says that "knowledge puffs up," whereas "love builds up" (1 Cor 8:1). Some think that they are important because they are more knowledgeable than others; they want to lord it over them. Yet what really makes us important is a love that understands, shows concern, and embraces the weak. Elsewhere the word is used to criticize those who are "inflated" with their own importance (cf. 1 Cor 4:18) but in fact are filled more with empty words than the real "power" of the Spirit (cf. 1 Cor 4:19).

It is important for Christians to show their love by the way they treat family members who are less knowledgeable about the faith, weak, or less sure in their convictions. At times, the supposedly mature believers within the family become unbearably arrogant. Love, on the other hand, is marked by humility. If we are to understand, forgive, and serve others from the heart, our pride has to be healed and our humility must increase.

Jesus told his disciples that in a world where power prevails, each tries to dominate the other, but "it shall not be so among you" (Matt 20:26). The inner logic of Christian love is not about importance and power; rather, "whoever would be first among you must be your slave" (Matt 20:27). In family life, the logic of domination and competition about who is the most intelligent or powerful destroys love. Saint Peter's admonition also applies to the family: "Clothe yourselves, all of you, with humility toward one another, for 'God opposes the proud, but gives grace to the humble'" (1 Pet 5:5).

Wisdom of the Heart (20:28)[8]

Wisdom of heart means being with our brothers and sisters. Time spent with the sick is holy time. It is a way of praising God who conforms us to the image of his Son, who "came not to be served but to serve, and to give his life as a ransom for many" (Matt 20:28). Jesus himself said: "I am among you as one who serves" (Luke 22:27).

Let us ask the Holy Spirit to grant us the grace to appreciate the value of our often unspoken willingness to spend time with these sisters and brothers who, thanks to our closeness and affection, feel more loved and comforted. How great a lie, on the other hand, lurks behind certain phrases that so insist on the importance of "quality of life" that they make people think that lives affected by grave illness are not worth living!

21
Jerusalem

Hearts of Darkness (21:23–27)[1]

Jesus takes issue with those who seek to burden people's spontaneous faith with formalism and superfluous norms. Recall that when Jesus entered Jerusalem on Palm Sunday and the children sang: "Hosanna to the Son of David," some of the doctors of the law wanted to silence them. But Jesus said: "They cannot be silenced; if they don't cry out, the very stones will cry out!" The Lord then healed many people. When he was hungry, he went over to a fig tree that had no fruit and he cursed it: "May no one ever eat fruit from you again." Afterward the tree withered away, and when his disciples noted this miracle, Jesus replied: "If you have faith, you will do the same and more!" In essence, Jesus preached about faith.

Then he returned to the temple and again healed many people, many sick, and cast out of the temple those who were doing business there, changing money and selling. And this is when, witnessing these things, the chief priests, the doctors of the law, took courage and approached him, asking: "By what authority are you doing these things? We are here and are the ones who rule in the temple."

Responding with a question

Jesus answered with zeal and with great acuity in order to reach the heart of these people. They were people who had insecure hearts, hearts that adapted somewhat easily to circumstances, hearts that, depending on the situation, would go in one direction or another.

Hearts like these might be considered "diplomatic hearts," but such a definition would be inaccurate, because diplomacy is a noble profession, a profession that brings people together, a profession that makes peace; that's not what these people were doing. Their hearts were instead "hypocritical hearts." For them, the truth didn't matter. They pursued their own interests according to how the wind was blowing. In other words, they were weather vanes, all of them. They had inconsistent hearts and negotiated everything: inner freedom, faith, homeland. To them what mattered in any given situation was a good outcome; they were "situationalists," men who adapted to trends: "The wind is coming from there, let's go there." This was what their hearts were like: they took advantage of situations.

What is described in the gospel scene is one of the situations in which they tried to take advantage. They saw a weakness at that moment, or perhaps they imagined it, and decided "this is the time." Thus came the question: "By what authority are you doing these things?" Evidently they felt fairly strong in asking this question. But, once again, Jesus caught them off guard. He didn't argue with them but reassured them, saying "Yes, yes, I will answer you, but first answer this question," and he asked them about John the Baptist. Thus Jesus answered a question with a question, and this weakened them to the point where his questioners didn't know where to turn.

Overcome rigidity

In the prayer recited at the beginning of Mass, we asked the Lord to cast light on the darkness of our hearts. The people of whom the Gospel spoke had much darkness in their hearts. Of course, they observed the law: on the Sabbath they didn't walk more than a hundred meters; and they never sat down at the table without having washed their hands and performed ablutions; they were very law-abiding, very firm in their ways. However, all this has to do only with appearances. They were strong, but outwardly. They were cast in plaster. Their hearts, however, were flaccid. These people didn't know what they believed in. This is why their lives were, externally, completely regulated; but their hearts were weak, they wavered.

Jesus teaches us that Christians must have strong, steadfast hearts that grow on the rock that is Christ and are wise and prudent. Indeed, you don't negotiate with the heart, and you don't negotiate with the rock. The rock is Christ; you don't carry on a negotiation with Christ! This is the drama of the hypocrisy of these people. Jesus, never negotiated his heart as the heart of the Son of the Father, but he was always open with people, always looking for ways to help. His questioners, on the other hand, said: "You can't do this; our discipline, our doctrine say that you can't do this." And they asked him: "Why are your disciples eating grain in the field and walking on the Sabbath? You can't do this." In other words, they were rigid in their discipline and upheld it as something that was not to be touched; for them it was sacred.

A personal fact

When I was a child, Pope Pius XII freed us from the very heavy cross of the eucharistic fast. You couldn't swallow even a drop of water—not even while brushing your teeth. As a child, I myself went to confession and confessed having received communion even though I believed I had swallowed a drop of water before Mass. When the pope changed the discipline—"Ah, heresy! He changed the discipline of the church!"—many Pharisees were scandalized. But Pius XII did what Jesus had done: he saw the needs of the people: "These poor people, with such devotion!" These priests who were saying three Masses a day, the last one at one o'clock in the afternoon, fasting. And the Pharisees—concerned about "our discipline"—rigid in the flesh, but as Jesus says, "decayed in the heart," weak until decayed, with darkness in the heart.

And here lies the tragedy of the people whom Jesus denounced: "Hypocrites, you go where the wind blows, to take advantage!" In fact, they were always trying to benefit from something.

Sometimes when I've seen a Christian man or woman like this, with a weak heart, not firm, not steadfast on the rock, and outwardly so rigid, I have said to the Lord: "Throw a banana peel on the ground in front of him, so that he slips and falls, is ashamed of being a sinner, and thus encounters You, who are the Savior." After all, so many times a sin can shame us and allow us to encounter the Lord, who forgives us.

The Bible says: "The heart of man is a thing of mystery, who can understand it?" And this is why we have asked today, "Lord, cast light on the darkness of our hearts, that our hearts may be steadfast in faith.

Freedom and Rigidity (21:23–27)[2]

In this passage from the Gospel of Matthew, we see instead men who do not have freedom, who have no horizons, men who are closed in their calculations. The chief priests and elders of the people ask the Lord, "By what authority are you doing these things?" When Jesus poses his next question, they start calculating: "If I say this I have this danger, and if I say that..." Then they answer, "We do not know." However, human calculations close the heart and block freedom. It is hope that lightens our load. It is this hypocrisy of the doctors of the law that we see in the Gospel, a hypocrisy that closes the heart: it enslaves. These men were slaves...

How beautiful is the freedom, magnanimity, and hope of a man and a woman of the church. And how awful, and how much harm is done by the rigidity of a man of the church: clerical rigidity, which has no hope.

In this Year of Mercy there are these two paths. On one hand are those who have hope in the mercy of God, who know that God is Father, that God always forgives, and that he forgives everything, that beyond the desert there is the embrace of the Father, forgiveness. On the other path are those who take refuge in slavery, in its rigidity; and they know nothing of God's mercy. The doctors mentioned in the Gospel of Matthew "had studied, but their knowledge did not save them."

Entering the Kingdom of Heaven (21:28–32)[3]

Who does the will of the Father?

Jesus proposes "to the chief priests, to the elders of the people," to the entire "network" of people who were opposed to him, a judgment to reflect upon. He presented the case of the two sons whom the father asks to go and work in the vineyard. One answers: "I won't go to the field. I don't want to." But then he goes. Meanwhile, the other agrees to go but then thinks: "The old man has no strength. I'll do what I want. He can't punish me." And therefore, he doesn't go. He doesn't obey.

Jesus asks his interlocutors: "Which of the two did his father's will? Was it the first, the one who said 'No,' the rebellious one who later thought of his father and decided to obey, or was it the second?"

A severe judgment

At this point Jesus offers his judgment: "Amen, I say to you, tax collectors and prostitutes are entering the kingdom of God before you." They "will be the first." And he explains why:

"When John came to you in the way of righteousness, you did not believe him. You didn't listen to John: the baptism of penitence...The tax collectors and prostitutes believed. You, however, saw these things but then you didn't repent, nor did you believe."

What did these people do to deserve this judgment? They didn't listen to the Lord's voice, they didn't accept correction, they didn't trust in the Lord. One could ask: "But Father, what a scandal that Jesus said this. The tax collectors, the ones who betrayed the homeland by collecting taxes for the Romans, would they really go first to the kingdom of heaven? And the same for the prostitutes, who are sinners?" And finally, "Lord, have you gone mad? And what about us? We are pure, we are Catholics, we partake of communion every day, we go to Mass." Jesus responds: "The tax collectors and prostitutes will go first if your heart is not a contrite heart. And if you have not listened to the Lord, haven't accepted correction, haven't trusted in him, then yours is not a contrite heart."

The Lord doesn't want these hypocrites who were scandalized by what Jesus said about the tax collectors and about the prostitutes but who secretly went to them, whether to do business or to unleash their passions. They considered themselves pure, but in reality, the Lord doesn't want them.

This judgment makes us think. It is a judgment that gives us hope when we look at our sins. Indeed, all of us are sinners. Every one of us is well aware of our list of sins. We know, though, that each one of us can say: "Lord, I offer you my sins, the only thing that we can offer you."

A lesson

We recall the life of a saint who was very generous and offered everything to the Lord: The Lord asked him for something and he did it. The saint always listened and always followed the Lord's will. Yet the Lord once said to him: "You still haven't given me one thing." And he, who was so good, answered:

"But, Lord, what haven't I given You? I've given you my life, I work for the poor, I catechize, I work here, I work there..." The Lord pressed on: "You haven't given me one thing." And the saint repeated, "What Lord?" And the Lord answered, "Your sins."

When we are able to say: "Lord, these are my sins, they aren't this man's or that woman's... They're mine. You take them. This way I'll be saved." When we are able to do this, then we will be that beautiful people—the humble and poor people—who trust in the name of the Lord.

THE PUBLICAN AND THE PROSTITUTE (21:28–32)[4]

Jesus says to the chief priests and elders: "Truly, I say to you, the tax collectors and the harlots will enter the kingdom of God before you." He vehemently reproaches those who were considered masters of "how to think, judge, and live." The prophet Zephaniah, too, takes on the voice of God, and says: "Woe to her that is rebellious and defiled, the oppressing city! She listens to no voice, she accepts no correction, she does not trust in the Lord, she does not draw near to her God" (3:1–2, 9–13). It is basically the same reprimand aimed at the chosen people, at the clerics of those times. Moreover, to say to a priest, to a chief priest, that a harlot is holier than he in the kingdom of heaven is a very strong charge.

What should the church be like?

Jesus had the courage to speak the truth. However, when we think about certain reprimands, we have to wonder: "What should the church be like?" The people we read about in the Bible were indeed "men of the church." They were "heads of the church." Jesus came, John the Baptist came, but those men didn't listen. The prophet recalls that although God chose his people, "this people became a rebellious city, an impure city.

They did not accept how the church should be, how the People of God should be."

The promise of the Lord

Nevertheless, the prophet Zephaniah communicates God's promise to the people: "I will forgive you." That is, in order for the People of God, the church, all of us to be faithful, the first step is to feel we are forgiven. After the promise of forgiveness, there is a description of how the church is supposed to be: "For I will leave in your midst a people humble and lowly. They shall seek refuge in the name of the Lord." Thus, the faithful People of God must have these three traits: humility, lowliness, and trust in the Lord.

Three traits

First, the Church has to be *humble*. In other words, the church should not show off her powers, her grandeur. Humility doesn't mean being a lethargic, weary person with a demure expression, because this is not humility. This is theatrics! This is feigned humility. True humility instead begins with the first step: "I am a sinner." If you are not able to recognize that you are a sinner and that others are better than you, you are not humble. Thus, the first step for a humble church is to acknowledge that she is a sinner; the same is true for all of us. Furthermore, if any of us has the habit of looking at others' defects and gossiping, this is not humility. Instead, it is thinking that we can judge others. The prophet says: "I will leave in the midst of you a humble people." This is a grace, and we must ask for this grace, that the church may be humble, that I may be humble, that each one of us may be humble.

The People of God is *poor*. Poverty is the first of the beatitudes, but what does it mean to be "poor in spirit"? It means being attached only to God's treasures. It definitely does not mean a church that is attached to money, that frets about money, that broods over getting money...For example, there was someone who "innocently" said to the people that in order to pass through the Holy Door you have to make an offering. This is not the church of Jesus, this is the church of the chief priests, attached to money.

Deacon Lawrence—the "treasurer" of the diocese—was once asked by the emperor to bring in the riches of the diocese and hand them over in order to avoid being killed. Saint Lawrence returned with the poor. The poor are in fact the treasure of the church. You can even be the head of a bank as long as your heart is poor, you are not attached to money, and you place yourself at the service of others. Poverty is characterized by the kind of detachment that leads us to serve the needy. We need to ask ourselves: "Am I or am I not poor?"

Finally, the third trait: the People of God *shall seek refuge in the name of the Lord*. This too brings up a very direct question: "Where do I place my trust? In power, in friends, in money? In the Lord!" This is the legacy that the Lord promises us: "I will leave in the midst of you a people humble and lowly. They shall seek refuge in the name of the Lord." They are humble because they know they are sinners; poor because their heart is attached to God's treasures, and if they have them it is only to administer them; seeking refuge in the Lord because they know that the Lord alone can secure what is good for them. This is why Jesus had to tell the chief priests, who did not understand these things, that a prostitute would enter the kingdom of God before they would. As we await the Lord this Christmas, let us ask that he give us a humble heart, a heart that is poor and that above all seeks refuge in the Lord, because the Lord never disappoints.

A Proposal of Love (21:33–43)[5]

The Gospel offers us the parable of tenants to whom a landowner, before leaving, lends a vineyard that he has planted. This is how the loyalty of the tenants is tested: the vineyard is entrusted to them; they are to tend it, make it bear fruit, and deliver its harvest to the owner. When the time comes to harvest the grapes, the landlord sends his servants to pick the fruit. However, the tenants have a possessive attitude. They do not consider themselves to be simple supervisors but rather landowners, and they refuse to hand over the harvest. They mistreat the servants, to the point of killing them. The landowner is patient with the tenants. He sends more servants, a larger number than the previous time, but the result is the same. In the end, still patient, he decides to send his own son. But those tenants, prisoners of their own possessiveness, kill the son, reasoning that, in this way, they will have the inheritance.

This narrative allegorically illustrates the reproaches of the prophets in the story of Israel. It is a story that belongs to us, a story about the covenant that God wished to establish with humanity and in which he has called us to participate. Like any other love story, this story of the covenant has its positive moments but is also marked by betrayal and rejection. In order to make us understand how God the Father responds to the rejection of his love and his proposal of an alliance, the gospel passage puts a question on the lips of the owner of the vineyard: "When therefore the owner of the vineyard comes, what will he do to those tenants?" (Matt 21:40). This question highlights God's disappointment at the wicked behavior of mankind but it is not the last word! Here is the uniqueness of Christianity: a God who, even though disappointed by our mistakes and our sins, does not fail to keep his Word, does not give up and, most of all, does not seek vengeance!

My brothers and sisters, God does not avenge himself. God loves; he does not avenge himself. He waits for us, always ready to forgive us, to embrace us. Through the "rejected stones"—and Christ is the first stone rejected by the builders—through situations of weakness and sin, God continues to circulate "the new wine" of his vineyard, namely mercy. This is the new wine of the Lord's vineyard: mercy. There is only one obstacle to the tenacious and tender will of God: our arrogance and our conceit, which at times turn into violence! Faced with these attitudes that produce no fruit, the Word of God retains all its power to reprimand and reproach: "Therefore I tell you, the kingdom of God will be taken away from you and given to a people who will produce its fruits" (Matt 21:43).

In considering the importance of responding with good fruits to the call of the Lord, who asks us to become his vineyard, we come to understand what is new and original about the Christian faith. It is not so much a matter of precepts and moral norms; rather, it is first and foremost a proposal of love that God makes through Jesus and continues to make with humanity. It is an invitation to enter into this love story by becoming a vibrant vineyard, open to producing rich fruits and hope for everyone. A closed vineyard can grow wild and produce wild grapes. We are called to go out, to put ourselves at the service of our brothers and sisters who are not with us, in order to rouse each other and encourage each other, to remind ourselves that we must be the Lord's vineyard in every environment, even the more distant and challenging ones.

Dear brothers and sisters, let us invoke the intercession of the Most Holy Mary, so that she may help us to be everywhere, in particular at the peripheries of society, the vineyard that the Lord planted for the good of all, to bring to all the new wine of the Lord's mercy.

Those Rejected Become Cornerstones (21:42)[6]

Changes in society begin with the poor and the elderly. As Jesus said: "The very stone which the builders rejected has become the cornerstone" (Matt 41:42). The poor are in some ways this "cornerstone" for building a community. Today, unfortunately, a speculative economy has made the poor even poorer, depriving them of essentials, such as housing and employment. This is unacceptable! Those who live in solidarity don't accept this situation, and they take action. The word "solidarity" is one that many people would like to eliminate from the dictionary, because in some cultures it is seen as a bad word. No! Solidarity is a Christian word! And this is why you [in the Sant'Egidio Community] are the family of the homeless, friends of disabled persons... I also see here many "new Europeans," immigrants who arrived after agonizing and dangerous journeys. The Community welcomes them attentively and demonstrates that a foreigner is one of our brothers or sisters, whom we must recognize and to help. And this rejuvenates us.

22

The Greatest Commandment

The Invitation (22:1–14)[1]

The invitation refused

Jesus speaks to us about the response given to the invitation from God—who is represented by a king—to participate in a wedding banquet. The invitation has three characteristics: it is *freely* offered, it has *breadth,* and it is *universal.* Many people were invited, but something surprising happened. None of the intended guests came to take part in the feast, saying they had other things to do. Indeed, some people were indifferent, impertinent, even annoyed. God is good to us. He freely offers us his friendship. He freely offers us his joy, his salvation, but so often we do not accept his gifts. Instead, we place our practical concerns, our interests first. And when the Lord is calling us, it so often seems to annoy us. Some of the intended guests went so far as to abuse and kill the servants who delivered the invitation.

The invitation welcomed

Despite the lack of response from those called, God's plan is never interrupted. In facing the rejection of the first invitees, he is not discouraged. He does not cancel the feast, but extends another invitation, expanding it beyond all reasonable limits, and sends his servants into the town squares and the byways to gather anyone they find. These people, however, are ordinary, poor, neglected, and marginalized, good and bad alike (even bad people are invited!) without distinction. And the hall is filled with "the excluded." The Gospel, rejected by some, is unexpectedly welcomed in many other hearts.

A universal invitation

The goodness of God has no bounds and does not discriminate against anyone. For this reason, the banquet of the Lord's gifts is universal, for everyone. Everyone is given the opportunity to respond to the invitation, to the call; no one is entitled to feel privileged or to claim an exclusive right. Our awareness of this induces us to break the habit of conveniently placing ourselves at the center, as did the high priests and the Pharisees... We must open ourselves to the peripheries, acknowledging that, at the margins too, even one who has been cast aside and scorned by society is the object of God's generosity. We are all called not to reduce the kingdom of God to the confines of the "little church"—our "tiny little church"—but to enlarge the church to the dimensions of the kingdom of God. There is, however, one condition: wedding attire must be worn; that is, charity toward God and neighbor must be shown.

God and Caesar (22:15–22)[2]

Today's Gospel presents to us with a face-to-face encounter between Jesus and his adversaries. The subject addressed is that of tribute to Caesar: a "thorny" issue about whether or not it was lawful to pay taxes to the Roman emperor, to whom Palestine was subject in Jesus's time. There were various positions. Thus, the question that the Pharisees posed to him—"Is it lawful to pay taxes to Caesar, or not?" (Matt 22:17)—was meant to ensnare the Teacher. In fact, depending on how he responded, he could have been accused of being either for or against Rome.

Here too, however, Jesus responds calmly and takes advantage of the malicious question in order to teach an important lesson. Rising above the polemics and the alliance of his adversaries, he says to the Pharisees: "Show me the coin used for the tax." They present him the coin, and, observing it, Jesus asks: "Whose image is this, and whose title?" The Pharisees can answer only: "Caesar's." Then Jesus concludes: "Render therefore to Caesar the things that are Caesar's, and to God the things that are God's" (cf. Matt 22:19–21). On the one hand, by suggesting that they return to the emperor what belongs to him, Jesus is declaring that paying tax is not an act of idolatry but a legal obligation to an earthly authority. On the other hand—and it is here that Jesus presents the "thrust" of his response, recalling the primacy of God—he asks them to render to God that which is his due as the Lord of life and of history.

The reference to Caesar's image engraved on the coin affirms that Jesus's questioners are correct in seeing themselves as citizens of the state, with all the rights and duties that go along with this. But symbolically, it also makes them think about another image, one that is imprinted on every man and woman: the image of God. He is the Lord of all, and we, who were created "in his image," belong to him first and foremost. From the question posed to him by the Pharisees, Jesus draws out a more radical and vital question for each of us, a question we need to ask ourselves: To whom do I belong? To family, to the city, to friends, to work, to politics, to the state? Yes, of course. But, Jesus reminds us, first and foremost we belong to God. This is the fundamental belonging. It is he who has given us all that you are and have. And therefore, day by day, we can and must live our lives in recognition of this fundamental belonging and in heartfelt gratitude toward our Father, who creates each one of us individually, uniquely, but always to the image of his beloved Son, Jesus. It is a wondrous mystery.

Christians are called to commit themselves concretely in the human and social spheres without comparing "God" and "Caesar." Comparing God and Caesar would be to adopt a fundamentalist approach. Christians are called to commit themselves concretely in earthly realities, but illuminating them with the light that comes from God. Trust in God and hope in him do not imply an escape from reality but rather the diligent rendering to God of that which belongs to him. This is why the believer looks to the future reality, that of God, so as to live earthly life to the full, and to meet its challenges with courage.

The Journey through Life (22:30)[3]

The teaching of the Master (cf. Matt 22:30) and Saint Paul (cf. 1 Cor 7:29–31) on marriage is set—and not by chance—in the context of the ultimate and definitive dimension of our human existence. We urgently need to rediscover the richness of this teaching. By heeding it, married couples will come to see the deeper meaning of their journey through life. In fact, ... no family drops down from heaven perfectly formed; families need constantly to grow and mature in the ability to love. This is a never-ending vocation born of the full communion of the Trinity, the profound unity between Christ and his church, the loving community that is the Holy Family of Nazareth, and the pure fraternity existing among the saints of heaven.

Our contemplation of the fulfillment that we have yet to attain also allows us to see in proper perspective the historical journey that we make as families, and in this way to stop demanding of our interpersonal relationships a perfection, a purity of intention, and a consistency that we will encounter only in the kingdom to come. It also keeps us from judging harshly those who live in situations of frailty. All of us are called to continue striving toward something greater than ourselves and our families, and every family must feel this constant impetus. Let us make this journey as families, let us keep walking together. What we have been promised is greater than we can imagine. May we never lose heart because of our limitations, or ever stop seeking that fullness of love and communion that God holds out before us.

The Greatest Commandment (22:34–40)[4]

The whole of Divine Law can be summed up in our love for God and neighbor. Matthew the evangelist recounts that several Pharisees colluded to put Jesus to the test (cf. Matt 22:34–35). One of them, a doctor of the law, asked him this question: "Teacher, which is the greatest commandment in the law?" (Matt 22:36). Jesus, quoting the book of Deuteronomy, answered: "You shall love the Lord your God with all your heart, and with all your soul, and with all your mind. This is the greatest and first commandment" (Matt 22:37–38). And he could have stopped there. Yet, Jesus adds something that was not asked by the doctor of the law. He says, "And a second is like it: Love your neighbor as yourself" (Matt 22:39). And in this case too, Jesus does not invent the second commandment, but takes it from the book of Leviticus. The novelty is in his placing these two commandments together—love for God and love for neighbor—revealing that they are in fact inseparable and complementary, two sides of the same coin. You cannot love God without loving your neighbor, and you cannot love your neighbor without loving God.

Love of the neighbor reveals the love of God

In effect, the visible sign a Christian can show in order to witness to his love for God to the world and to others, to his family, is the love he bears for his brothers. The commandment to love

God and neighbor is the first, not because it is at the top of the list of commandments. Jesus does not place it at the pinnacle but at the center, because it is from the heart that everything must go out and to which everything must return and refer.

In the Old Testament, the requirement to be holy, in the image of God who is holy, included the duty to care for the most vulnerable people, such as the stranger, the orphan, and the widow (cf. Exod 22:20–26). Jesus brings this covenant law to fulfillment; he unites in himself, in his flesh, divinity and humanity, a single mystery of love.

Now, in light of this Word of Jesus, love is the measure of faith, and faith is the soul of love. We can no longer separate a religious life, a pious life, from service to brothers and sisters, to the real brothers and sisters whom we encounter. We can no longer divide prayer, the encounter with God in the sacraments, from listening to others, closeness to their lives, especially to their wounds. Remember this: love is the measure of faith. How much do you love? Each one must ask ourselves: What is my faith? My faith is as I love. And faith is the soul of love.

In the middle of the dense forest of rules and regulations—the legalisms of past and present—Jesus makes an opening through which one can catch a glimpse of two faces: the face of the Father and the face of the brother or sister. He does not give us two formulas or two precepts: there are no precepts nor formulas. He gives us two faces, actually only one real face, that of God reflected in many faces, because in the face of each brother, each sister, especially of those who are the smallest, the most fragile, the defenseless and needy, there is God's own image. And we must ask ourselves: when we meet one of these brothers or sisters, are we able to recognize the face of God in them? Are we able to do this?

The gift of the Spirit

Jesus offers to all the fundamental criteria on which to base our lives. But, above all, he gives us the Holy Spirit, who allows us to love God and neighbor as he does, with a free and generous heart. With the intercession of Mary, our Mother, let us open ourselves to welcome this gift of love, to walk forever with this twofold law, which really has only one facet: the law of love.

WHO IS A TEACHER'S NEIGHBOR? (22:34–40)[5]

As Jesus taught us, the law and the prophets are summed up in two commandments: love the Lord your God and love your neighbor. We can ask ourselves: Who is a teacher's neighbor? *Your students are your neighbor!* It is with them that you spend your days. It is they who await guidance, direction, a response—and, even before that, good questions!

School certainly involves valid and qualified instruction, but it also involves human relations, which for us are welcoming and benevolent relations, to be offered indiscriminately to all. Indeed, the duty of a good teacher—all the more for a Christian teacher—is to love his or her more difficult, weaker, more disadvantaged students, and those who might make us lose our patience, even more. Jesus would say: If you love only those who study, who are well educated, what merit do you have? Any teacher can do well with such students. I ask you *to love the "difficult" students more*... those who do not want to study, those who find themselves in difficult situations, the disabled and foreigners, who today pose a great challenge for schools.

If a professional association of Christian teachers wants to bear witness to its inspiration today, then it is called to persevere in the peripheries of schools, which cannot be abandoned to marginalization, exclusion, ignorance, crime...

The Christian community has had many examples of great educators who are dedicated to addressing the shortcomings of the educational system or to establishing their own schools. Consider, among others, Saint John Bosco, the bicentenary of whose birth is this year. He advised his priests: teach with love. The first attitude of an educator is love.

The Tender Embrace (22:39)[6]

Christ proposed as the distinctive sign of his disciples the law of love and the gift of self for others (cf. Matt 22:39; John 13:34). He did so in stating a principle that fathers and mothers tend to embody in their own lives: "No one has greater love than this, to lay down one's life for one's friends" (John 15:13). Love also bears fruit in mercy and forgiveness. We see this in a particular way in the scene of the woman caught in adultery; in front of the temple, the woman is surrounded by her accusers, but later, alone with Jesus, she meets not condemnation but the admonition to lead a more worthy life (cf. John 8:1–11).

Against this backdrop of love, so central to the Christian experience of marriage and the family, another virtue stands out, one often overlooked in our world of frenetic and superficial relationships. It is tenderness. Let us consider the moving words of Psalm 131. As in other biblical texts (e.g., Exod 4:22; Isa 49:15; Ps 27:10), the union between the Lord and his faithful ones is expressed in terms of parental love. Here we see a delicate and tender intimacy between mother and child: the image is that of a baby sleeping in his mother's arms after being nursed. As the Hebrew word *gamûl* suggests, the infant is now fed and clings to his mother, who takes him to her bosom. There is a closeness that is conscious and not simply biological. Drawing on this image, the Psalmist sings: "I have calmed and quieted my soul, like a child quieted at its mother's breast" (Ps 131:2). We can also think of the touching words that the prophet Hosea puts on God's lips: "When Israel was a child, I loved him . . . I took them up in my arms . . . I led them with cords of compassion, with bands of love, and I became to them as those who lift infants to their cheeks, and I bent down to them and fed them" (Hos 11:1, 3–4).

23

The Scribes and the Pharisees

Remove the Masks (23:1–12)[1]

Lent invites us to amend our lives, to put them in order. This is precisely what allows us to draw near to the Lord, who is always ready to forgive.

The Lord says to us: "I will change your soul." What does he ask of us? To draw near. To draw near to him. He is a Father; he awaits us in order to forgive us. The Lord also gives us this counsel: "Do not be like the hypocrites." As we read in the Gospel, the Lord does not want this [hypocritical] type of drawing near. He wants us to draw near in sincerity and truth. What do hypocrites do? They mask themselves. They mask themselves as good. They mask their faces so that they look like a holy picture. They pray looking up to heaven to make themselves seen. They feel that they are more righteous than others. They look down on others. And they boast of being good Catholics because they have acquaintances among benefactors, bishops, and cardinals.

This is hypocrisy. And the Lord says no to it. No one should feel self-righteous. We all need to be justified, and the only one who justifies us is Jesus Christ. That is why we need to draw near: to avoid being masked Christians. When appearances vanish, reality comes to light and we see that they are not Christians.

Christians without masks

What is the sign that we are on the right path? Scripture tells us: defend the oppressed; take care of your neighbor, the sick, the poor, the needy, the ignorant. This is the touchstone. Hypocrites are so full of themselves that they are blind to seeing others. But when one journeys a little and draws near to the Lord, the light of the Father enables one to see these things and to go out to help one's brothers and sisters. And this is the sign of conversion.

Certainly this is not the whole of conversion, because conversion is an encounter with Jesus Christ. But this is the sign that we are with Jesus: taking care of our brothers and sisters, the poorest and the sick, as the Lord teaches us in the Gospel.

Lent, therefore, helps us to change our lives, to amend our lives, to draw near to the Lord. Hypocrisy, by contrast, is the sign that we are far from the Lord. The hypocrite saves himself on his own, or at least this is what he thinks, whereas the sign that we have drawn near to the Lord in a spirit of repentance and forgiveness is that we take care of our needy brothers and sisters. May the Lord give us all light and courage: light to be aware of what is happening within us, and courage to be converted, to draw near to the Lord. It is beautiful to be close to the Lord.

Three Words (23:1–12)[2]

The message of the church today can be summarized in *three words*: the invitation, the gift, and the pretense.

In the book of the prophet Isaiah (1:10, 16–20), the invitation is to conversion: "Give ear to the teaching of our God... Wash yourselves; make yourselves clean!" In other words, "Whatever you have inside that isn't good, that which is evil, that which is unclean, must be purified."

... Uncleanliness of heart is not removed like one removes a stain, by going to the dry cleaner's and having it come out clean. It is removed by *doing*. Conversion means taking a different path, a path other than that of evil.

Another question: "How do I do good?" The response again comes from the prophet Isaiah: "Seek justice, correct oppression, defend the fatherless, plead for the widow." These instructions were easily understood in Israel, where the poorest and the neediest were orphans and widows. For each of us this means going to where the wounds of humanity are, where there is so much pain. By doing good you will cleanse your heart, you will be purified! This is the invitation of the Lord...

If we do this, what will the *Lord's gift* be? "Even though your sins are like scarlet, they shall be as white as snow; though they are red like crimson, they shall become like wool."

Even in the face of our fear or hesitation—"But Father, I have so many sins! I have committed so very, very many!"—the Lord insists: "If you take this path, the one to which I invite you, even if your sins are like scarlet, they will become as white as snow."

The third word is *pretense*. In the Gospel according to Matthew (23:1–12) Jesus speaks about the scribes and the Pharisees. As sinners we are all clever, and we always find a path that isn't the right one, in order to seem more just than we are: it's the path of hypocrisy.

Jesus speaks of those who like to boast about being right: the Pharisees, the doctors of the law, who say the right things, but who do the opposite. These "clever ones" find vanity, pride, power, and money pleasing. They are hypocrites because they pretend to convert, but their heart is false; they are liars. Indeed, their heart does not belong to the Lord; it belongs to the father of all lies, Satan. And this is the *pretense* of holiness.

Jesus always spoke very clearly against this attitude. In fact, Jesus preferred sinners a thousand times more than he did hypocrites. This was because at least sinners told the truth about themselves: "Depart from me, for I am a sinful man, O Lord" (Luke 5:8), as Peter once said. A similar phrase would never fall from the lips of a hypocrite, who would instead say: "I thank you Lord, that I am not a sinner, that I am just" (cf. Luke 18:11).

Here, then, are three phrases to meditate on: the invitation to conversion; the gift that the Lord will give us, which is that of great forgiveness; and the trap of making a pretense of converting and taking the path of hypocrisy. With these three words at heart we can take part in the Eucharist, our action of grace, in which we hear the invitation of the Lord: "Come to me, eat of me. I will change your life. Do justice, do good, but please, look away from the leaven of the Pharisees, from hypocrisy."

A Living and Active Word (23:4)[3]

Jesus was angered by those supposed teachers who demanded much of others, teaching God's word but without being enlightened by it: "They bind heavy burdens, hard to bear, and lay them on the shoulders of others; but they themselves will not lift a finger to move them" (Matt 23:4). The apostle James exhorted: "Not many of you should become teachers, my brethren, for you know that we who teach shall be judged with greater strictness" (Jas 3:1). Whoever wants to preach must be the first to let the word of God move him deeply and become incarnate in his daily life. In this way preaching will consist in that activity, so intense and fruitful, which is "communicating to others what one has contemplated."[4] For all these reasons, before preparing what we will actually say when preaching, we need to let ourselves be penetrated by that word which will also penetrate others, for it is a living and active word, like a sword "which pierces to the division of soul and spirit, of joints and marrow, and discerns the thoughts and intentions of the heart" (Heb 4:12). This has great pastoral importance. Today too, people prefer to listen to witnesses: they "thirst for authenticity" and "call for evangelizers to speak of a God whom they themselves know and are familiar with, as if they were seeing him."[5]

Jesus's Emotions (23:13–37)[6]

As true man, Jesus showed his emotions. He was hurt by the rejection of Jerusalem (cf. Matt 23:27) and this moved him to tears (cf. Luke 19:41). He was also deeply moved by the sufferings of others (cf. Mark 6:34). He felt deeply their grief (cf. John 11:33), and he wept at the death of a friend (cf. John 11:35). These examples of his sensitivity showed how much his human heart was open to others.

24
Persecution

The False Prophets (24:1–12)[1]

"Dear children, this is the last hour; and as you have heard that the antichrist is coming, even now many antichrists have come. This is how we know it is the last hour... But you have an anointing from the Holy One, and all of you know the truth... As for you, the anointing you received from him remains in you, and you do not need anyone to teach you. But as his anointing teaches you about all things and as that anointing is real, not counterfeit—just as it has taught you, remain in him"(1 John 2:18, 20, 27).

Every age has its difficulties, as does the life of the believer. The resource for facing them is the one the Lord has shown us: "Remember to not prepare your defense first. I will give you language and wisdom that none of your adversaries will be able to withstand or contradict" (Luke 21:14–15). Saint John reminds us "the last hour" is an eschatological moment, the hour of the antichrist, of the false prophets (Matt 24:11). The last hour is the coming of Christ... and, therefore, it is every coming of Christ in our lives and the reactions that it arouses. To be faithful to this eschatological moment we are asked not to forget the anointing we received.

The false prophets are those who are tired of a humble Christ...
The antichrists are among us: they are the ones who are tired of the humble Christ. Belonging to Christ is not judged solely by being physically in a community. It goes further: it is belonging to the Spirit, letting oneself be anointed by the same Spirit that anointed Jesus. The one who judges our anointing is the same Lord "who knows what is in everyone" (cf. John 2:24–25). To the extent that Christ is accepted by the heart, those who accept him will become a source of division (cf. Matt 10:21). It is the sign of the last times (cf. Luke 21:28). The believer participates in the same Christ who "is destined to cause the falling and the rising of many in Israel, and to be a sign that will be opposed" (Luke 2:34). Whoever does not have the anointing, who does not accept it, can deny this vocation to the cross.

...to reach perfection
The Lord teaches us that those who are perfected and healed are anointed: the dead are anointed (cf. Mark 16:1); the sick man is anointed (cf. Mark 6:13; Jas 5:14); wounds are anointed (cf. Luke 10:34); the penitent is anointed (cf. Matt 6:17). Anointing has a sense of reparation (Luke 7:38, 46; 10:34; John 11:2; 12:3). All this applies to us: we are resurrected, healed, reformed, and renewed by the anointing of the Holy Spirit. Every yoke of slavery is destroyed because of the anointing (cf. Isa 10:27).

The first anointed is the Lord (Luke 2:26; Acts 4:26; Luke 4:18; Acts 10:38). He was anointed with the oil of exultation (cf. Heb 1:3). Rejoicing reminds us of glory. To be anointed means to participate in the glory of Christ, which is his cross. "Father, glorify your Son... Father, glorify your name" (cf. John 12:23, 28). Those who seek peace outside the anointing do not seek the glory of God in the cross of Christ: "How can you believe, since you accept glory from one another but do not seek the glory that comes from the only God?" (John 5:44).

How to Recognize False Prophets (24:4–5, 11, 24)[2]

Jesus warned us: "Beware of false prophets" (Matt 7:15); "Many false prophets will arise" (Matt 24:11); "False Messiahs and false prophets" (Matt 24:24). In fact, this is ancient history: there have been and there will be false prophets (cf. 2 Pet 2:1). And they will usurp the name of the Lord and try to deceive many (cf. Matt 24:4–5). They "will appear and perform great signs and wonders to deceive, if possible, even the elect" (Matt 24:24). The word of God describes in detail these false prophets: "With beautiful words and fascinating discourses, they deceive the hearts of the simple" (Rom 16:18) and "they will exploit you with false words" (2 Pet 2:3). "These are false apostles, fraudulent workers" (2 Cor 11:13). They are called apostles without being so, and they are found to be liars (cf. Rev 2:2). They are "talkers and deceivers" (Titus 1:10) who deceive "men with that cunning that leads to error" (Eph 4:14); they "lure unstable people" (2 Pet 2:14), using every type of "unbridled carnal passions" (2 Pet 2:18).

Waiting for the Coming of the Lord (24:42–51)[3]

The Lord is "the one who comes," and this is the reason why we must watch and watch. We must wait for his revelation. He will manifest himself. To reveal oneself means to reveal something unknown; it is the opposite of hiding oneself. Manifesting implies a transfiguration: it is an epiphany. We can begin this meditation taking inspiration from chapter 60 of the book of Isaiah.

Be vigilant

The Lord announced that he would come as a thief. Watch, therefore; behave righteously (cf. Matt 24:42 and Matt 25:1ff).

The virgins could sleep, but they had to be ready for the slightest sign. Mark (13:33–37) warns us to pay attention, to stay alert. It is an "active vigilance." We are asked to do certain things and not others. From this active vigilance comes fidelity.

Vigilance and infidelity

Lack of vigilance and infidelity go hand in hand. They draw nourishment from one another, mutually. We are not able to accept the Lord's invitation when our heart is dominated by its own judgment, its own inner space, its own interests. Wedding guests refuse to attend so they can take care of business. There is also the unfaithful person who behaves ambiguously: he goes to the party but does not wear the suitable garment, or he proves to be unworthy to take part in the banquet (cf. Matt 22:1–4).

Waiting attentively

There is a vigilance that goes beyond mere attention: it is the "vigilance on hold." We need to re-read the scriptures to see the just men, the pious women, and the faithful people of God who live this hope in expectation: John the Baptist, who sends to ask Jesus if he is "the one who is to come" (Matt 11:3); or Joseph of Arimathea, who "waited" (Mark 15:43); or Simeon (Luke 2:25); or the faithful people to whom Anna spoke (Luke 2:38) and who "had been waiting" (Luke 3:15). We must ask ourselves if our vigilance includes expectant hope, the hope that in nothing will [we] be disappointed" (Phil 1:20), or if "the ardent expectation of creation . . . is extended toward the revelation of the sons of God" (Rom 8:19), and if "awaiting adoption as sons, the redemption of our body" (Rom 8:23) "we wait with perseverance" (Rom 8:25). Such expectation has the virtue of accelerating the coming of the kingdom of God . . . Saint Peter advises us: "While waiting for these events, do your utmost to make God find you in peace, without guilt and without blemish" (2 Pet 3:12–14).

The joy of waiting

The scriptures present us with God himself looking forward to our redemption (2 Peter 3:8–9). To yearn for the manifestation of God is a way of responding to his paternal desire. It requires a vigilant, patient, attentive, and faithful capacity for vigilance, which finds its expression in prayer and daily examination of conscience. It is a waiting for his manifestation (Jas 5:7–9). It is a longing for his coming (2 Tm 4:8), the expectation of the great God and savior Jesus Christ (Titus 2:13). It is expecting Christ, the manifestation of Christ, and nothing else.

Therefore the community prays to God, so that he may be revealed (cf. Num 6:25; 1 Cor 16:22; Rev 22:20). Let us pray so that the One who manifested himself once and for all in glory may bring us hope.

Get Ready . . . to Serve (24:45)[4]

John tells us that, as soon as they reached the shore, the disciples saw a fire of burning coals there with fish on it, and some bread (cf. John 21:9). This is the true image of who Jesus is for us: he who each day prepares the Eucharist for us. And to this we are all invited to participate with our good works. The parables of the Lord . . . push us to "be ready" for his coming. Prepare yourself as "the faithful and wise servant, whom the master has put in charge of the servants in his household to give them their food at the proper time" (Matt 24:45).

25

The Fullness of Life

THE TEN VIRGINS (25:1–13)[1]

There is this "immediate time" between the first and the final coming of Christ, and that is the very time in which we are living. The parable of the ten virgins fits into this context of "immediate" time. There are ten maidens who are awaiting the arrival of the Bridegroom, but he is late and they fall asleep. At the sudden announcement that the Bridegroom is arriving they prepare to welcome him, but while five of them, who are wise, have oil to burn in their lamps, the others, who are foolish, are left with lamps that have gone out because they have no oil for them. While they go to get some oil, the Bridegroom arrives. [When they return], the foolish virgins find that the door to the hall of the marriage feast has been shut. They knock on it again and again, but it is now too late. The Bridegroom answers: I do not know you.

The Bridegroom is the Lord, and the time of waiting for his arrival is the time he gives to us, to all of us, with mercy and patience before his final coming. It is a time of watchfulness; a time in which we must keep alight the lamps of faith, hope, and charity; a time in which we must keep our hearts open to goodness, beauty, and truth. It is a time to live in conformity with God, because we do not know either the day or the hour of Christ's return. What he asks of us is to be ready for the encounter—ready for a beautiful encounter, the encounter with Jesus, which means being able to see the signs of his presence, keeping our faith alive with prayer and the sacraments, and taking care not to fall asleep so as to not forget about God. The life of slumbering Christians is a sad life; it is not a happy life. Christians must be happy, with the joy of Jesus. Let us not fall asleep!

The Use of Our Gifts (25:14–30)[2]

The parable of the talents makes us think about the relationship between how we use the gifts we have received from God and his return, when he will ask us what use we made of them. We are well acquainted with the parable: before his departure, the master gives a few talents to each of his servants to ensure that the talents will be put to good use during his absence. He gives five to the first servant, two to the second, and one to the third. In the period of their master's absence, the first two servants increase their talents—these are ancient coins—whereas the third servant prefers to bury his and to return it to his master as it was.

On his return, the master judges what the servants have done: he praises the first two while he throws the third one out into the outer darkness because, through fear, he hid his talent, withdrawing into himself. A Christian who withdraws into himself, who hides everything that the Lord has given him, is a Christian who...is not a Christian! He is a Christian who does not thank God for everything God has given him!

This tells us that the expectation of the Lord's return is the time of action—we are in the time of action—the time in which we should bring God's gifts to fruition, not for ourselves but for him, for the church, for others. The time to seek to increase goodness in the world is always. In particular, in this period of crisis, today, it is important not to turn in on ourselves, burying our own talent, our spiritual, intellectual, and material riches, everything that the Lord has given us, but, rather to open ourselves, to be supportive, to be attentive to others.

...I ask you who are just setting out on your journey through life: Have you thought about the talents that God has given you? Have you thought of how you can put them at the service of others? Do not bury your talents! Set your sights on great ideals, the ideals that enlarge the heart, the ideals of service that make your talents fruitful. Life is not given to us to be jealously guarded for ourselves, but that we may give it in turn. Dear young people, have a deep spirit! Do not be afraid to dream of great things!

The Meaning of the Parable (25:14–30)[3]

The man in the parable [of the talents] represents Jesus; we are the servants, and the talents are the inheritance that the Lord entrusts to us. What is the inheritance? His Word, the Eucharist, faith in the heavenly Father, his forgiveness..., in other words, so many things, his most precious treasures. This is the inheritance that he entrusts to us, not only to safeguard, but to make fruitful! While in common usage the term "talent" indicates a pronounced individual quality, such as talent in music, in sport, and so on, in the parable talents represent the riches of the Lord, which he entrusts to us so that we make them bear fruit. The hole dug into the soil by the "wicked and slothful servant" (Matt 25:26) points to the fear of risk, a fear that blocks creativity and the fruitfulness of love, because fear of the risks of love stops us. Jesus does not ask us to store his grace in a safe! Jesus does not ask us for this; he wants us to use it to benefit others. All the goods that we have received are to be given to others, and so increase. It is as if he were to tell us: "Here your have my mercy, my tenderness, my forgiveness: take them and make ample use of them." And what have we done with them? Whom have we "infected" with our faith? How many people have we encouraged with our hope? How much love have we shared with our neighbor? These are questions that will do us good to ask ourselves. Any environment, even the most distant and most impractical, can become a place where our talents can bear fruit. There are no situations or places precluded from Christian presence and witness. The witness that Jesus asks of us is not closed, but open. It is in our hands.

Don't hide your faith

This parable urges us not to conceal our faith and our belonging to Christ, not to bury the Word of the Gospel, but to let it circulate in our life, in our relationships, in concrete situations, as a strength that galvanizes, that purifies, that renews. This is also the case with the forgiveness that the Lord grants us, particularly in the sacrament of reconciliation: let us not keep it closed within ourselves, but allow it to emit its power, which brings down the walls that our egoism has raised, enabling us to take the first step in strained relationships, to resume the dialogue where there is no longer communication... And so forth. Allow these talents, these gifts, these presents that the Lord has given us, to be, to grow, to bear fruit for others as a reult of our witness.

It would be a fine gesture for each of you to pick up the Gospel at home today, (Matthew 25:14–30), and read this, and ask yourself: "The talents, the treasures, all that God has given me, all things spiritual, all goodness, the Word of God, how do I make this grow in others? Or do I merely store it in a safe?"

God trusts us

The Lord does not give the same things to everyone in the same way: he knows us personally and entrusts us with what is right for us. But in everyone, in all, there is something equal:

the same immense trust. God trusts us. God has hope in us! And this is the same for everyone. Let us not disappoint him! Let us not be misled by fear, but let us reciprocate trust with trust! The Virgin Mary embodied this attitude in the fullest and most beautiful way. She received and welcomed the most sublime gift, Jesus himself, and in turn she offered him to mankind with a generous heart. Let us ask her to help us to be "good and faithful servants" in order to participate "in the joy of our Lord."

The Last Judgment (25:31–46)[4]

The image used by the evangelist is that of the shepherd who separates the sheep from the goats. On his right he places those who acted in accordance with God's will, who went to the aid of their hungry, thirsty, foreign, naked, sick, or imprisoned neighbor. I said "foreign": I am thinking of the multitude of foreigners who are here in the diocese of Rome. What do we do for them? On the shepherd's left are those who did not help their neighbor. This tells us that God will judge us on our love, on how we have loved our brethren, especially the weakest and the neediest. Of course, we must always have clearly in mind that we are justified. We are saved through grace, through an act of freely given love by God who always goes before us; on our own we can do nothing. Faith is first of all a gift we have received. But in order to bear fruit, God's grace always demands our openness to him, our free and tangible response. Christ comes to bring us the mercy of a God who saves. We are asked to trust in him, to respond to the gift of his love with a good life made up of actions motivated by faith and love.

Dear brothers and sisters, may looking at the Last Judgment never frighten us: rather, may it impel us to live better in the present. With mercy and patience God offers us this time so that we may learn every day to recognize him in the poor and in the lowly. Let us strive for goodness and be watchful in prayer and in love. May the Lord, at the end of our life and at the end of history, be able to recognize us as good and faithful servants.

The Gospel Is for Everyone (25:31–46)[5]

The proclamation of the Gospel is destined for the poor first of all, for all those who so often lack what they need in order to live a life of dignity. To them first are proclaimed the glad tidings that God loves them with a preferential love and comes to visit them through the charitable works that disciples of Christ do in his name. Go to the poor first of all: this is the priority. At the moment of the Last Judgment, as we can read in Matthew 25, we shall all be judged on this. Some, however, may think that Jesus's message is for those who are uneducated. No! No! The apostle affirms forcefully that the Gospel is for everyone, even the learned. The wisdom that comes from the resurrection is not in opposition to human wisdom but, on the contrary, purifies and uplifts it. The church has always been present in places where cultural development occurs. But the first step is always the priority for the poor. Nevertheless, we must also reach the frontiers of the intellect, of culture, of dialogue—the dialogue that makes peace, the intellectual dialogue, the reasonable dialogue.

The Gospel is for everyone! This reaching out to the poor does not mean we must become champions of poverty or, as it were, "spiritual tramps"! No, no, this is not what it means! It means we must reach out to the flesh of Jesus that is suffering. But the flesh of Jesus suffers also in those who, with their study, with their intelligence, with their culture, do not know him. We must go there! I therefore like using the expression "to go toward the outskirts," the outskirts of existence. From the outskirts of physical poverty to those of intellectual poverty, which is also real. All the peripheries, all the crossroads on the way: go there. And sow there the seed of the Gospel with your words and your witness.

Contemplate Jesus (25:31, 34–36, 41–43)[6]

Let us turn to Jesus who is portrayed here as the universal judge. What will happen "when the Son of man comes in his glory, and all the angels with him, then he will sit on his glorious throne"? (Matt 25:31). What does Jesus tell us?

We can imagine this Jesus standing over us, saying a few words to each of us and to the church of Italy. He might say: "Come, O blessed of my Father, inherit the kingdom prepared for you from the foundation of the world; for I was hungry and you gave me food, I was thirsty and you gave me drink, I was a stranger and you welcomed me, I was naked and you clothed me, I was sick and you visited me, I was in prison and you came to me" (Matt 34–36). I am reminded of the priest who welcomed this very young priest who gave testimony.

But he could also say: "Depart from me, you cursed, into the eternal fire prepared for the devil and his angels; for I was hungry and you gave me no food, I was thirsty and you gave me no drink, I was a stranger and you did not welcome me, naked and you did not clothe me, sick and in prison and you did not visit me" (Matt 25:41–43).

. . . and in his gestures

The beatitudes and the words that we have just read on the universal judgment help us to live the Christian life in holiness. The words are few and simple but practical. We have two pillars: the beatitudes and the words of the Last Judgment. May the Lord give us the grace to understand his message! And let us look once again to the features of Jesus's face and to his gestures. We see Jesus who eats and drinks with sinners (Matt 2:16; Matt 11:19); we contemplate him as he converses with the Samaritan woman (John 4:7–26); we perceive him as he meets Nicodemus at night (John 3:1–21); we savor the scene where he allows a prostitute to anoint his feet (cf. Luke 7:36–50); we feel his touch on the tip of our tongue, which is then released (Mark 7:33). We admire the connection shared by all the people who surround his disciples—us, that is—and we experience their "glad and generous hearts" (Acts 2:46–47).

An Open Heart (25:34–37)[7]

The church is a mother with an open heart. She knows how to welcome and accept, especially those in need of greater care, those in greater difficulty. As was Jesus's wish, the church is the home of hospitality. And how much good we can do if only we try to speak this language of hospitality, this language of receiving and welcoming. How much pain can be soothed, how much despair can be allayed in a place where we feel at home! This requires open doors, especially the doors of our heart. Welcoming the hungry, the thirsty, the stranger, the naked, the sick, the prisoner (cf. Matt 25:34–37), the leper, and the paralytic. Welcoming those who do not think as we do, who do not have faith or who have lost it—sometimes, because of us. Welcoming the persecuted, the unemployed. Welcoming those of different cultures, with which our earth is so richly blessed. Welcoming sinners, because each one of us is also a sinner.

So often we forget that there is an evil underlying our sins, an evil that precedes our sins. There is a bitter root that causes damage, great damage, and silently destroys so many lives. There is an evil that, bit by bit, finds a place in our hearts and eats away at our life: it is isolation, an isolation that can have many roots, many causes. It can destroy our life and do much harm to us. It can make us turn our back on others, on God, on the community. It can make us closed in on ourselves. From here we see that the real work of the church, our mother, should not be mainly about managing works and projects, but rather about learning to live in fraternity with others. A welcome-filled fraternity is the best witness that God is our Father, for "by this all will know that you are my disciples, if you have love for one another" (John 13:35).

In this way, Jesus teaches us a new way of thinking. He opens before us a horizon brimming with life, beauty, truth and fulfillment.

Accompanying Migrants (25:35)[8]

"Maintaining and expanding witness to the Gospel is urgently needed today more than ever... Human mobility, which corresponds to the natural historical movement of peoples, can prove to be a genuine enrichment for both families that migrate and countries that welcome them. Furthermore, forced migration of families, resulting from situations of war, persecution, poverty, and injustice, and marked by the vicissitudes of a journey that often puts lives at risk, traumatizes people and destabilizes families.

In accompanying migrants, the church needs a specific pastoral program addressed not only to families that migrate but also to those family members who remain behind. This pastoral activity must be implemented with due respect for [people's] cultures, for the human and religious formation from which they come, and for the spiritual richness of their rites and traditions, even by means of a specific pastoral care...

"Migration is particularly dramatic and devastating to families and individuals when it takes place illegally and is supported by international networks of human trafficking.

This is equally true when it involves women or unaccompanied children who are forced to endure long periods of time in temporary facilities and refugee camps, where it is impossible to start a process of integration. Extreme poverty and other situations of family breakdown sometimes even lead families to sell their children for prostitution or for organ trafficking."[9]

"The persecution of Christians and ethnic and religious minorities in many parts of the world, especially in the Middle East, are a great trial not only for the church but also the entire international community. Every effort should be encouraged, even in a practical way, to assist families and Christian communities to remain in their native lands."[10]

Concern for the Vulnerable (25:40)[11]

Jesus, the evangelizer par excellence and the Gospel in person, identifies especially with the little ones. This reminds us Christians that we are called to care for the vulnerable of the earth. But the current model, with its emphasis on success and self-reliance, does not appear to favor an investment in efforts to help the slow, the weak, or the less talented to find opportunities in life.

It is essential to draw near to new forms of poverty and vulnerability, in which we are called to recognize the suffering Christ, even if this appears to bring us no tangible and immediate benefits. I think of the homeless, the addicted, refugees, indigenous peoples, the elderly who are increasingly isolated and abandoned, and many others. Migrants present a particular challenge for me, since I am the pastor of a church without frontiers, a church that considers itself mother to all. For this reason, I exhort all countries to a generous openness which, rather than fearing the loss of local identity, will prove capable of creating new forms of cultural synthesis. How beautiful are those cities which overcome paralyzing mistrust, integrate those who are different, and make that very integration a new factor of development! How attractive are those cities which, even in their architectural design, are full of spaces that connect, relate, and favor the recognition of others!

I have always been distressed at the lot of those who are victims of various kinds of human trafficking. How I wish that all of us would hear God's cry: "Where is your brother?" (Gen 4:9). Where is your brother or sister who is enslaved? Where is the brother and sister whom you are killing each day in clandestine warehouses, in rings of prostitution, in children used for begging, in exploiting undocumented labor? Let us not look the other way. There is greater complicity than we think. The issue involves everyone! This infamous network of crime is now well established in our cities, and many people have blood on their hands as a result of their comfortable and silent complicity.

26

The Passion—Part 1

The Poor (26:11)[1]

The salvific work of Christ is not exhausted with his person and in the span of his earthly life; it continues through the church, the sacrament of God's love and tenderness for humanity. In sending his disciples on mission, Jesus confers a double mandate on them: to proclaim the Gospel of salvation and to heal the sick (cf. Matt 10:7–8). Faithful to this teaching, the church has always considered caring for the sick an integral part of her mission.

"The poor and the suffering you will always have with you," Jesus admonishes (cf. Matt 26:11). The church continually finds them along her path and sees in those who are sick a privileged way to encounter Christ, to welcome and serve him. To treat the sick, to welcome them, to serve them, is to serve Christ: the sick are the flesh of Christ.

This happens in our own time, when, notwithstanding many scientific breakthroughs, the interior and physical suffering of people raises serious questions about the meaning of illness and pain and about the meaning of death. These are existential questions, to which the pastoral action of the church must respond with the light of faith, having before her eyes the crucifixion, in which appears the whole of the salvific mystery of God the Father, who out of love for human beings did not spare his own Son (cf. Rom 8:32). Therefore, each one of us is called to bear the light of the Word of God and the power of grace to those who suffer, and to those who assist them—family, doctors, nurses—so that service to the sick might always be better accomplished with empathy, with generous dedication, with evangelical love, with tenderness. Mother Church, through our hands, caresses suffering and treats wounds, and does so with the tenderness of a mother.

Let us pray to Mary, Health of the Sick, that every person who is sick might experience, thanks to the care of those who are close to them, the power of God's love and the comfort of her maternal tenderness.

Service, Sacrifice, Friendship, Promise, Betrayal (26:26–35)[2]

The Upper Room speaks to us of *service*, of Jesus giving the disciples an example by washing their feet. Washing one another's feet signifies welcoming, accepting, loving, and serving one another. It means serving the poor, the sick, and the outcast, those whom I find difficult, those who annoy me.

The Upper Room reminds us, through the Eucharist, of *sacrifice*. In every eucharistic celebration Jesus offers himself for us to the Father, so that we too can be united with him, offering to God our lives, our work, our joys and our sorrows . . . offering everything as a spiritual sacrifice.

The Upper Room also reminds us of *friendship*. "No longer do I call you servants," Jesus said to the Twelve, "but I have called you friends" (John 15:15). The Lord makes us his friends. He reveals God's will to us, and he gives us his very self. This is the most beautiful part of being a Christian and, especially, of being a priest: becoming a friend of the Lord Jesus and discovering in our hearts that he is our friend.

The Upper Room reminds us of the Teacher's *farewell* and his *promise* to return to his friends: "When I go . . . I will come again and will take you to myself, that where I am you may be also" (John 14:3). Jesus does not leave us, nor does he ever abandon us; he precedes us to the house of the Father, where he desires to bring us as well.

The Upper Room, however, also reminds us of *pettiness*, of curiosity—"Who is the traitor?"—and of *betrayal*. We ourselves, and not just others, can manifest those attitudes whenever we look at our brother or sister with contempt, whenever we judge them, whenever by our sins we betray Jesus.

When Our Vigilance Diminishes (26:43)[3]

When the servant lets go of his *vigilance*, his loyalty is asleep; and he, who at first dozed off due to laziness and neglect, ends up pretending not to be asleep so as not to lose his pay. It is no longer possible to distinguish restful sleep after the fatigue of honest work from comfortable, false, and complicit drowsiness . . . Whenever we find social sins, we will discover pastors who have fallen asleep, have sold their consciences, or have simply lost the ability to contemplate their Lord, "for their eyes were heavy" (Matt 26:43) and their hearts were "sleeping because of grief" (Luke 22:45) and there was also fear of the cross. Woe to the shepherds who avoid the cross! In one way or another, their own conscience reflects the bravado of Peter: "Lord, I am ready to go with you to prison and to death!" (Luke 22:33), or worse: "Even though all become deserters, I will not" (Mark 14:29).

With Tenderness, Not Violence (26:52–53)[4]

Life must be approached gently, with meekness. Let us recall the episode from the Gospel of Luke, in which Jesus and his apostles were not welcomed in a village of Samaria and James and John proposed to Jesus: "Lord, do you want us to command fire to come down from heaven and consume them?" (Luke 9:54). In response to the bellicose words of his disciples, Jesus "turned and rebuked them" (Matt 26:55). In short, he scolded them; today he would point out to them that it is not a reaction worthy of a good Christian. We also think back to the night when they arrested Jesus and Peter drew his sword, standing as defender of the nascent church (an inappropriate defender, moreover, since a few hours later he would deny him), and Jesus said to him: "Put your sword back into its place... Do you think that I cannot appeal to my Father, and he will at once send me more than twelve legions of angels?" (Matt 26:52–53). With these words, Jesus wanted to make Peter understand that the right attitude is not violence but tenderness, which must be preserved even in the most difficult moments: if someone slaps you, turn the other cheek.

Jesus Was Silent (26:63)[5]

Silence is the highest and most ordinary expression of dignity—all the more so in times of trial and crucifixion, when the flesh would like to justify itself and escape the cross. In the supreme moment of injustice, "Jesus was silent" (Matt 26:63; cf. also Isa 53:7; Acts 8:32). It would not have been right for Jesus to respond to those who told him to come down from the cross. All of God's patience, the patience of centuries, and even his affection emerge here, in this silence of the humiliated Christ. From the silence of the centuries in the history of humanity, the eternal silence of the Word burst forth, the loving "contemplation" of the Father and of the Son and of the Holy Spirit, all the Trinitarian communion. It is Word, but Word that—in the hour of annihilation caused by injustice—becomes silent. *Iesus autem tacebat* ("Jesus remains silent"). We contemplate the whole "journey" of the Word of God (cf. John 1:1; 14:2–3, 10:28), how tenderness is made in the bosom of a Mother. This Mother "kept all these things, pondering them in her heart" (Luke 2:19). The memory of the church is situated in the silent heart of Mary. The "incarnate" silence of the Word is expressed in that moment of injustice, of humiliation, of annihilation, in the hour of the power of darkness. That is the dignity of Jesus, and it is also ours.

27
The Passion—Part 2

Enemies of Jesus (27:18)[1]

There is a primordial cruelty, inherent deep within us, which rebels against God, and which is triggered when a weakness appears in someone who threatens us. Jeremiah makes it clear: "But I was like a gentle lamb led to the slaughter. And I did not know it was against me that they devised schemes, saying, 'Let us destroy the tree with its fruit, let us cut him off from the land of the living, so that his name will no longer be remembered'" (Jer 11:19). The "songs of the suffering servant" (Isa 53:1f.) describe this cruelty in a prophecy that will be fulfilled in the passion of Christ.

I want to make a couple of comments regarding this. First, people rage against those they consider weaker; against Jesus they did not dare to do anything for fear of the people (Matt 26:5): they saw him as strong because everyone followed him and many believed in him (John 7:40–52; 8:30; 10:42). Only when he was "weakened" by the betrayal of one of his own (Matt 26:14–16) could they come forward.

Second, at the root of all cruelty there is a need to downplay one's own faults and limitations. Jesus was a living reproach. Like the goat in Leviticus (16:20–22), Jesus becomes the one on whom all their iniquities are placed. There are also those who are aware of this, but let it go. Pontius Pilate realized that "they had handed him over to him out of envy" (Matt 27:18) and, despite this, the ranks of silent witnesses expand.

Jesus's response

In moments of darkness and great tribulation, when the "snags" and the "knots" cannot be untangled, when things cannot be clarified, then we must be silent. The meekness of silence will make us look even weaker, and then it will be the Demon himself who, emboldened, will fully manifest himself and, no longer camouflaged as an angel of light, will reveal his real intentions. We must resist him in silence, "remain steadfast" (Eph 6:13), but with the same attitude as Jesus.

The Experience of Exile (27:39–46)[2]

The servant of God feels deep loneliness: it is the profound experience of exile. Reality itself seems to be making fun of the man of faith. Where is the Word of God? What has finally been accomplished? (Jer 17:15).

It seems that God did not keep his promise when he chose Jeremiah: "I am with you to deliver you" (Jer 1:8). Jeremiah feels mocked for having placed his trust in God, and the same situation is played out again at the height of Jesus's drama on Mount Calvary: "You who would destroy the temple and build it in three days, save yourself! If you are the Son of God, come down from the cross . . . He saved others; he cannot save himself. He is the King of Israel. Let him come down from the cross now, and we will believe in him. He trusts in God; let God deliver him now, if he wants to" (Matt 27:39–44).

In the silence of God we discover that the relationship of obedience to him in prayer is not an exchange, that the promise and fidelity of his word is a very different thing from what we imagine... [And], on this journey our heart is changed.

The silence

The experience of the silence of God and the silence of men coincides with the experience of exile itself. We are stripped of what we have. We too find ourselves "along the rivers of Babylon." With our lyres hanging, we sit and weep remembering Zion (Ps 137:1). Exile occurs at the height of its drama of the passion of the Lord, especially in the prayer in Gethsemane, which is one of the most human and dramatic supplications of Jesus (Mark 14:32–34; Matt 26:36–46; Luke 22:40–46).

The plea of an exile, feeling far from the Lord, is filled with sadness and anguish. It reaches its climax in the sadness of Jonah, who does not understand God's plans (Job 4:9). "My God, my God, why have you forsaken me?" (Matt 27:46). One who prays in the moment of exile enters the path of a particular purification. The heart is not at peace, but strives for understanding. Attitudes, words, and thoughts alternate in a contradictory way. The person passes from tiredness to resignation (Job 29:4), or slips into bitter irony (Job 7:20), or seeks logical explanations (Job 10:8), or assumes attitudes of distrust (Job 10:2). But beyond all this, one who knows he is in exile remembers his country, lets the heart sigh, does not bargain, does not turn back, but takes a step forward and looks for God beyond the conventional shelters. He starts from his loneliness, from his exile, from that silence which he does not understand, from his world wounded by pain.

The Temptations of Jesus on the Cross (27:39–40, 63–66)[3]

[In the desert], Jesus resisted the temptation that presented him with the possibility of "doing his work" in his own way, as he preferred, disconnecting himself from obedience to the Father. And the proposal was subtly presented: "If you are the Son of God" (Matt 4:3 6), show me . . . The same temptation will appear later in the life of Jesus and from time to time he will be asked for a sign (Luke 11:29). Now, toward the end, he will be challenged to come down from the cross (Matt 27:39–40) or to break the seals of the tomb (Matt 27:63–66). Jesus's response to this temptation is illuminating. He does not enter into theological dialogue with the tempter. In the desert he responded with fidelity to memory rooted in the history of his people (Matt 4:4–10); at other times he called "wicked and adulterous" the generation that demands a sign (Matt 12:39), or spoke in a mysterious way of the "sign of Jonah" (Luke 11:29–30). In the end, on the cross he is silent (Matt 27:14).

Then, when the time comes, "the hour" will blow open the seals of all human control with the power of the resurrection. Jesus responds with faith and obedience. [He asks the same of us], "and to each one in particular he addresses the words: 'whoever wishes to join me in this enterprise must be willing to labor with me, that by following me in suffering, he may follow me in glory.'"[4] Furthermore, "Those who wish to give greater proof of their love . . . will not only offer themselves entirely for the work, but will act against their sensuality and carnal and worldly love, and make offerings of greater value and of more importance."[5]

Mysteriously suggestive is the apparently anachronistic rereading of Moses's choice by the author of the letter to the Hebrews: "Choosing rather to share ill-treatment with the people of God than to enjoy the fleeting pleasures of sin, he considered abuse suffered for Christ to be of greater value than the treasures of Egypt, for he was looking ahead to his reward" (Heb 11:25–26). Moses's obedient disposition [enables him to] set aside his personal project and [dedicate himself to] that of God.

Hope Is Measured on the Cross (27:42–46)[6]

Two types of people, two attitudes toward life. Some, even in the midst of misfortunes and contradictions, are able to maintain hope—and even cheerfulness—willing to greet the promises even from afar (cf. Heb 11:13). Others, disillusioned by God because things go wrong, attribute to him the guilt: "This trouble is from the Lord! Why should I hope in the Lord any longer?" (2 Kings 6:33). The former consider the delay in the fulfillment of the promise a push to move forward, because they choose not to question the Word of the Lord; the latter—in the face of failure—become defensive, using self-justification to deal with their disappointment.

Both behaviors converge . . . in the cross: one, [the taunt of] "let him come down from the cross now, and we will believe in him" (Matt 27:42), the other, the cry of (trusting) abandonment of Jesus: "My God, why have you forsaken me?" (Matt 27:46) and the dignified silence of Our Lady. This is hope, and its value is always measured on the cross. It is unlikely that those who have not suffered the disappointment of losing what they wanted could know the experience of true hope.

God's Silence (27:46)[7]

[Jesus] abandons himself, [places himself in] the hands of God without trying to control the results of the crisis, of the storm. [This kind of] abandonment, however, is not naïve. It is the abandonment that the Lord himself recommended before his death: "When they hand you over, do not worry about how you are to speak or what you are to say; for what you are to say will be given to you at that time; for it is not you who speak, but the Spirit of your Father speaking through you" (Matt 10:19–20). Such abandonment implies trust in God, but it does not exempt one from agonizing suffering, because this abandonment does not receive an immediate answer. Indeed, it is even put to the test by the silence of God that can lead to the temptation of distrust, the shocking cry at the culmination of the test: "My God, my God, why have you forsaken me?" (Matt 27:46).

28
The Resurrection

BEFORE THE TOMB (28:5–7, 10)[1]

Everyone here is spiritually resurrected...

It is an extraordinary grace to be gathered here in prayer. The empty tomb, that new garden grave where Joseph of Arimathea reverently placed Jesus's body, is the place from which the proclamation of the resurrection begins: "Do not be afraid; I know that you are looking for Jesus who was crucified. He is not here, for he has been raised, as he said. Come, see the place where he lay. Then go quickly and tell his disciples, 'He has been raised from the dead'" (Matt 28:5–7). This proclamation, confirmed by the testimony of those to whom the risen Lord appeared, is the heart of the Christian message, faithfully passed down from generation to generation, as the apostle Paul, from the very beginning, bears witness: "I handed on to you as of first importance what I in turn received: that Christ died for our sins in accordance with the scriptures, that he was buried, and that he was raised on the third day in accordance with the scriptures" (1 Cor 15:3–4). This is the basis of the faith that unites us, whereby together we profess that Jesus Christ, the only-begotten Son of the Father and our sole Lord, "suffered under Pontius Pilate, was crucified, died and was buried;

he descended into hell; on the third day he rose again from the dead" (Apostles' Creed). Each of us, everyone baptized in Christ, has spiritually risen from this tomb, for in baptism all of us truly became members of the body of the One who is the firstborn of all creation; we were buried together with him, so as to be raised up with him and to walk in newness of life (cf. Rom 6:4).

...to be men and women of resurrection

Let us receive the special grace of this moment. We pause in reverent silence before this empty tomb in order to rediscover the grandeur of our Christian vocation: we are men and women of resurrection, not of death. From this place we learn how to live our lives, the trials of our churches and of the whole world, in the light of Easter morning. Every injury, every one of our pains and sorrows, has been borne on the shoulders of the Good Shepherd who offered himself in sacrifice and thereby opened the way to eternal life. His open wounds are like the cleft through which the torrent of his mercy is poured out upon the world. Let us not allow ourselves to be robbed of the basis of our hope, which is this: *Christos anesti!* Let us not deprive the world of the joyful message of the resurrection! And let us not be deaf to the powerful summons to unity that rings out from this very place, in the words of the One who, risen from the dead, calls all of us "my brothers" (cf. Matt 28:10; John 20:17).

The Announcement of the Resurrection (28:8–15)[2]

On this Easter Monday the Gospel presents to us the narrative of the women who, on arriving at Jesus's tomb, find it empty and see an angel who announces to them that he is risen. And as they run to tell this news to the disciples, they encounter Jesus himself, who says to them: "Go and tell my brethren to go to Galilee, and there they will see me" (Matt 28:10). Galilee is the "periphery" where Jesus began his preaching; it is from there that he will share the Gospel of the Resurrection, for it to be proclaimed to all so that everyone might encounter him, the Risen One, present and working in history. Today too he is with us, here in Saint Peter's Square.

This, therefore, is the proclamation that the church repeats from the first day: "Christ is risen!" And, in him, through baptism, we too are risen. We have passed from death to life, from the slavery of sin to the freedom of love. Behold the Good News that we are called to take to others and to every place, inspired by the Holy Spirit. Faith in the resurrection of Jesus and the hope that he brought us is the most beautiful gift that Christians can and must give to their brothers and sisters. To all and to each, therefore, let us not tire of saying: Christ is risen! Let us repeat it all together, today here in this Square: Christ is risen! Let us repeat it with words, but above all with the witness of our lives. The happy news of the resurrection should shine on our faces, in our feelings and attitudes, in the way we treat others.

We announce the resurrection when…

We proclaim the resurrection of Christ when his light illuminates the dark moments of our life and we can share that with others; when we know how to smile with those who smile and weep with those who weep; when we walk beside those who are sad and in danger of losing hope; when we recount our experience of faith with those who are searching for meaning and for happiness. With our attitude, with our witness, with our life, we say: Jesus is risen! Let us say it with all our soul.

Radical news

We are in the days of the Easter Octave, during which the joyful atmosphere of the resurrection accompanies us. It's curious how the liturgy considers the entire octave as one single day, in order to help us enter into the mystery, so that his grace may impress itself on our hearts and our lives. Easter is the event that brought radical news for every human being, for history, and for the world: the triumph of life over death. It is the feast of reawakening and of rebirth. Let us allow our lives to be conquered and transformed by the resurrection!

To Go Out (28:16–20)[3]

The Gospel of Matthew reports Jesus's mandate to his disciples: the invitation to go out, to set out in order to proclaim to all nations his message of salvation. "To go" or, better, "depart" becomes the key word of today's feast: Jesus departs to the Father and commands his disciples to depart for the world.

Jesus departs…

Jesus *departs,* he ascends to heaven, that is, he returns to the Father from whom he was sent into the world. He has finished his work, and thus he returns to the Father. But this does not mean a separation, for he remains forever with us, in a new way. By his ascension, the Risen Lord draws the gaze of the apostles—and our gaze—to the heights of heaven to show us that the end of our journey is the Father. He himself said that he would go to prepare a place for us in heaven.

Yet, Jesus remains present and active in the affairs of human history through the power and the gifts of his Spirit. He is beside each one of us, even if we do not see him with our eyes, He is there! He accompanies us, he guides us, he takes us by the hand and he lifts us up when we fall down. The risen Jesus is close to persecuted and discriminated Christians; he is close to every man and woman who suffers. He is close to us all. He is here, too, here in Saint Peter's Square. The Lord is with us! Do you believe this? Then let's say it together: the Lord is with us!

... and brings his gift to the Father

When Jesus returns to heaven, he brings the Father a gift. What is the gift? His wounds. His body is very beautiful: no bruises, no cuts from the scourging—but he retains his wounds. When he returns to the Father he shows him the wounds and says: "behold Father, this is the price of the pardon you have granted." When the Father beholds the wounds of Jesus he forgives us forever, not because we are good, but because Jesus paid for us. Beholding the wounds of Jesus, the Father becomes most merciful. This is the great work of Jesus today in heaven: showing the Father the price of forgiveness, his wounds. This is the beauty that urges us not to be afraid to ask forgiveness. The Father always pardons, because he sees the wounds of Jesus; he sees our sin and he forgives it.

A clear mandate

Jesus is present also through the church, which he sends to extend his mission. Jesus's last message to his disciples is the mandate to depart: "Go therefore and make disciples of all nations" (Matt 28:19). It is a clear mandate, not just an option! The Christian community is a community "going forth," "in departure." Moreover, the church was born "going forth." And you will say to me: What about cloistered communities? Yes, [this is true for them] also, for they are always "going forth" through prayer, with a heart open to the world, to the horizons of God. And the elderly, the sick? [It is true for them] too, through prayer and union with the wounds of Jesus.

To his missionary disciples Jesus says: "I am with you always, to the end of the age" (Matt 28:20). Alone, without Jesus, we can do nothing! In apostolic work our own strengths, our resources, our structures do not suffice, even if they are necessary. Without the presence of the Lord and the power of his Spirit, our work, though it may be well organized, winds up being ineffective. And thus, we go to tell the nations who Jesus is.

Disciples – Missionaries (28:19)[4]

In virtue of their baptism, all the members of the People of God have become missionary disciples (cf. Matt 28:19). All the baptized, whatever their position in the church or their level of instruction in the faith, are agents of evangelization, and it would be insufficient to envisage a plan of evangelization to be carried out by professionals while the rest of the faithful would simply be passive recipients. The new evangelization calls for personal involvement on the part of each of the baptized. Every Christian is challenged, here and now, to be actively engaged in evangelization; indeed, anyone who has truly experienced God's saving love does not need much time or lengthy training to go out and proclaim that love. Every Christian is a missionary to the extent that he or she has encountered the love of God in Christ Jesus: we no longer say that we are "disciples" and "missionaries," but rather that we are always "missionary disciples." If we are not convinced, let us look at those first disciples, who, immediately after encountering the gaze of Jesus, went forth to proclaim him joyfully: "We have found the Messiah!" (John 1:41). The Samaritan woman became a missionary immediately after speaking with Jesus, and many Samaritans came to believe in him "because of the woman's testimony" (John 4:39). So too, Saint Paul, after his encounter with Jesus Christ, "immediately proclaimed Jesus" (Acts 9:20; cf. 22:6–21). So what are we waiting for?

Bibliography

Vatican Documents

The texts (homilies, meditations, speeches, Angelus, etc.) after the beginning of the pontificate are adapted from: http://w2.vatican.va/content/vatican/en.html.

Francis. *Evangelii Gaudium,* Apostolic Exhortation on the Proclamation of the Gospel in Today's World (November 24, 2013).

Francis. *Lumen Fidei,* Encyclical Letter on the Faith (June 29, 2013).

Francis. *Laudato Si',* Encyclical Letter on Care for Our Common Home (May 24, 2015).

Francis. *Amoris Laetitia,* Post-Synodal Apostolic Exhortation on Love in the Family (March 19, 2016).

Italian Sources

Pope Francis. *Non fatevi rubare la speranza. La preghiera, il peccato, la filosofia e la politica pensati alla luce della speranza.* Milan: Oscar Mondadori–Vatican City: LEV, 2014.

Jorge Mario Bergoglio–Pope Francis. *Aprite la mente al vostro cuore.* Milan: BUR–Rizzoli, 2014.

Jorge Mario Bergoglio–Pope Francis. *Il desiderio allarga il cuore. Esercizi spirituali con il Papa.* Bologna: EMI, 2014.

Jorge Mario Bergoglio–Pope Francis. *In lui solo la speranza. Esercizispirituali ai vescovi spagnoli* (January 15–22, 2006). Milan: Jaca Book; Vatican City: LEV, 2013.

Jorge Mario Bergoglio–Pope Francis. *La misericordia è una carezza. Vivere il giubileo nella realtà di ogni giorno*. Edited by Antonio Spadaro. Milan: Rizzoli, 2015.

Jorge Mario Bergoglio, *Le parole di Papa Francesco,* vols. 1–20. Milan: Corriere della Sera, 2014–2015.

Jorge Mari Bergoglio–Pope Francis. *Nel cuore di ogni Padre. Alle radici della mia spiritualità.* Introduction by Antonio Spadaro. Milan: Rizzoli, 2014.

Notes

Introduction

1. Pope Francis, *Misericordiae Vultus,* Bull of Indiction of the Extraordinary Jubilee of Mercy, no. 8.

2. Pope Francis's 2016 Message for Lent: "I desire mercy, and not sacrifice" (Matt 9:13).

1. Origins of Jesus

1. Pope Francis, Morning Meditation, "We Are History," Chapel of *Domus Sanctae Marthae,* December 18, 2014.

2. Pope Francis, Morning Meditation, "In the Little Things," Chapel of *Domus Sanctae Marthae,* September 8, 2015.

3. Pope Francis, Morning Meditation, "Small and Holy," Chapel of *Domus Sanctae Marthae,* September 8, 2014.

4. Pope Francis, Homily for Opening of the "Holy Door of Charity" and Celebration of Holy Mass, Rome, December 18, 2015.

5. Pope Francis, Angelus, Fourth Sunday of Advent, December 22, 2013.

2. The Magi

1. Pope Francis, Encyclical, *Lumen Fidei,* no. 35.
2. Pope Francis, Angelus, January 6, 2016.
3. Pope Francis, Angelus, January 6, 2015.
4. Pope Francis, Homily, January 6, 2016.
5. Pope Francis, Homily, January 6, 2016.
6. Pope Francis, Homily, Arena Sports Camp, Salina Quarter, Lampedusa, July 8, 2013.

7. Pope Francis, Homily, Ciudad Juárez Fair Grounds, Mexico, February 17, 2016.

8. Pope Francis, Address at the Meeting with Families, Mall of Asia Arena, Manila, January 16, 2015.

3. John the Baptist

1. Pope Francis, Angelus, December 6, 2015.

2. Pope Francis, Morning Meditation, Chapel of *Domus Sanctae Marthae*, "Christians Who Can Humble Themselves," June 24, 2014.

3. Pope Francis, Angelus, Feast of the Baptism of the Lord, January 12, 2014.

4. Pope Francis, Speech at the Meeting with Refugees and Disabled Young People, Latin Church, Bethany beyond the Jordan, May 24, 2014.

5. Pope Francis, General Audience, Saint Peter's Square, April 6, 2016.

4. Jesus's Public Life Begins

1. J. M. Bergoglio – Pope Francis, "*La manifestazione del peccato*," in *Aprite la mente al vostro cuore* (Milan: BUR / Rizzoli, 2014), 101–3; Pope Francis, *Non fatevi rubare la speranza: La preghiera, il peccato, la filosofia e la politica alla luce della speranza* (Milan: Oscar Mondadori / Vatican City: LEV, 2014), 60–63.

2. Pope Francis, Angelus, January 26, 2014.

3. Pope Francis, Apostolic Exhortation, *Evangelii Gaudium*, no. 20.

4. J. M. Bergoglio – Pope Francis, "*Misericordia*," in *La misericordia è una carezza. Vivere il giubileo nella realtà di ogni giorno*, ed. Antonio Spadaro (Milan: Rizzoli, 2015), 47–75.

5. Pope Francis, Angelus, January 26, 2014.

6. Pope Francis, Apostolic Exhortation, *Evangelii Gaudium*, no. 288.

7. Pope Francis, Homily, Barthélémy Boganda Stadium, Bangui, Central African Republic, November 30, 2015.

5. The Sermon on the Mount

1. Pope Francis, Homily, Solemnity of All Saints, November 1, 2015.

2. Pope Francis, Message for the Twenty-Ninth World Youth Day, 2014.

3. Pope Francis, Angelus, November 1, 2013.

4. Pope Francis, Morning Meditation, Chapel of *Domus Sanctae Marthae*, "The Christian Identity Card," June 9, 2014.

5. Pope Francis, Morning Meditation, Chapel of *Domus Sanctae Marthae*, "The Navigator and the Four Woes," June 6, 2016.

6. Pope Francis, Message for the Twenty-Ninth World Youth Day, 2014.

7. Pope Francis, Apostolic Exhortation, *Evangelii Gaudium*, no. 227.

8. Second Vatican Council, Decree on Ecumenism, *Unitatis Redintegratio*, no. 4.

9. Pope Francis, Morning Meditation, Chapel of *Domus Sanctae Marthae*, "The Last Word," June 9, 2015.

10. Pope Francis, Angelus, February 16, 2014.

11. Pope Francis, Morning Meditation, Chapel of *Domus Sanctae Marthae*, "How to Safeguard the Heart," June 15, 2015.

12. Pope Francis, *Il nome di Dio è misericordia. Una conversazione con Andrea Tornielli* (Milan / Vatican City / LEV, 2016), 102–3.

6. Prayer

1. Pope Francis, Morning Meditation, Chapel of *Domus Sanctae Marthae*, "Appearance and Truth," October 14, 2014.

2. Pope Francis, Morning Meditation, Chapel of *Domus Sanctae Marthae*, "The Strength in Our Weakness," June 18, 2015.

3. Pope Francis, Morning Meditation, Chapel of *Domus Sanctae Marthae*, "Space and Atmosphere," June 16, 2016.

4. Pope Francis, Morning Meditation, Chapel of *Domus Sanctae Marthae*, "In Heaven's Stock Exchange," June 19, 2015.

5. Pope Francis, Encyclical, *Laudato Si*, no. 226.

6. Pope Francis, Angelus, March 2, 2014.

7. A True Christian

1. Pope Francis, Morning Meditation, Chapel of *Domus Sanctae Marthae*, "No One Can Judge," June 23, 2014.

2. Pope Francis, Apostolic Exhortation, *Evangelii Gaudium*, no. 172.

3. Pope Francis, Apostolic Exhortation, *Evangelii Gaudium*, no. 179.

4. Pope Francis, Morning Meditation, Chapel of *Domus Sanctae Marthae*, "Listen First," June 25, 2015.

5. Pope Francis, Morning Meditation, Chapel of *Domus Sanctae Marthae*, "Founded on Rock," December 4, 2014.

6. Pope Francis, Apostolic Exhortation, *Amoris Laetitia*, 8.

7. Pope Francis, Homily, Nairobi University Campus (Kenya), November 26, 2015.

8. Pope Francis, Morning Meditation, Chapel of *Domus Sanctae Marthae*, "Speakers without Authority," June 26, 2014.

8. The Miracles of Jesus

1. Pope Francis, Morning Meditation, Chapel of *Domus Sanctae Marthae*, "Let Us Close the Distance," June 26, 2015.

2. Pope Francis, Apostolic Exhortation, *Amoris Laetitia*, no. 64.

3. *Relatio Finalis*, Final Report of the Synod of Bishops to the Holy Father, Pope Francis, 2015, 41.

4. Pope Francis, Morning Meditation, Chapel of *Domus Sanctae Marthae*, "Martyred with White Gloves," June 30, 2014.

5. Pope Francis, Encyclical, *Laudato Si'*, no. 98.

6. Pope John Paul II, Encyclical, *Laborem Exercens*, no. 27.

9. Compassion

1. Pope Francis, Morning Meditation, Chapel of *Domus Sanctae Marthae*, "Let Us Close the Distance," June 26, 2015.

2. Pope Francis, Homily, Plaza de la Revolución, Holguín, Cuba, September 21, 2015.

3. Pope Francis, Morning Meditation, Chapel of *Domus Sanctae Marthae*, "Mercy, Celebration and Remembrance," July 5, 2013.

4. Pope Francis, Morning Meditation, Chapel of *Domus Sanctae Marthae*, "The True Fast," March 3, 2017.

5. Pope Francis, Address to the Parish Priests of the Diocese of Rome, March 6, 2014.

6. Pope Francis, Address to Participants in Rome's Diocesan Conference: "A People That Leads Its Children, Communities, and Families in through the Great Stages of Christian Initiation," June 16, 2014.

7. Pope Francis, Address at the Celebration of Vespers with Priests, Men and Women Religious, Seminarians and Various Lay Movements, September 21, 2014.

10. The Mission of the Disciples

1. Pope Francis, Morning Meditation, Chapel of *Domus Sanctae Marthae*, "Key Words," June 11, 2015.

2. Pope Francis, Apostolic Exhortation, *Evangelii Gaudium,* no. 180.

3. Pope Francis, Address to Participants in the General Assembly of the Focolare Movement, September 26, 2014.

4. Pope Francis, Apostolic Exhortation, *Evangelii Gaudium,* no. 21.

5. Pope Francis, Apostolic Exhortation, *Amoris Laetitia,* nos. 101–2.

6. Thomas Aquinas, *Summa Theologiae,* II-II, q. 27, art. 1, ad 2.

7. Thomas Aquinas, *Summa Theologiae,* II-II, q. 27, art. 1.

8. Pope Francis, Address at the Meeting with Young People, Estadio "José María Morelos y Pavón." Morelia, February 16, 2016.

9. Pope Francis, Angelus, December 26, 2014.

10. Pope Francis, Apostolic Exhortation, *Amoris Laetitia,* no. 18.

11. Jesus's Way

1. Pope Francis – J.M. Bergoglio, "*Consolazione,*" in *La misericordia è una carezza. Vivere il giubileo nella realtà di ogni giorno,* ed. Antonio Spadaro (Milan: Rizzoli, 2015), 247–79.

2. Pope Francis, Homily at the Mass for Italian Parliamentarians, March 27, 2014.

3. Pope Francis, Morning Meditation, Chapel of *Domus Sanctae Marthae,* "Christians? Yes, but…" March 24, 2015.

4. Pope Francis, Apostolic Exhortation, *Evangelii Gaudium,* no. 269.

5. Pope Francis, Encyclical, *Laudato Si',* no. 96.

6. Pope Francis, Address to the Participants in the Pilgrimage of Families during the Year of Faith, October 26, 2013.

7. Pope Francis, Angelus, June 9, 2013.

8. Pope Francis, Homily at Mass in Saint Francis Square, Assisi, October 4, 2013.

12. Jesus and the Pharisees

1. J. M. Bergoglio, "*Introduzione,*" in *Cambiamento* (*Le parole di Papa Francesco,* 19) (Milan: Corriere della Sera, 2014), 5–13.

2. Pope Francis, Apostolic Exhortation, *Evangelii Gaudium,* no. 149.

3. John Paul II, Post-Synodal Apostolic Exhortation, *Pastores Dabo Vobis* (March 25, 1992), 26. *AAS* 84 (1992), 698.

4. John Paul II, Post-Synodal Apostolic Exhortation, *Pastores Dabo Vobis* (March 25, 1992), 26. *AAS* 84 (1992), 696.

5. Pope Francis, Address to the Camaldolese Benedictine Nuns, November 21, 2013.

13. The Parables

1. Pope Francis, Address to Participants in the Meeting Sponsored by the Pontifical Council for Promoting New Evangelization, September 19, 2014.

2. Pope Francis, Apostolic Exhortation, *Evangelii Gaudium*, no. 225.

3. Pope Francis, Apostolic Exhortation, *Evangelii Gaudium*, no. 24.

4. Pope Francis, Apostolic Exhortation, *Evangelii Gaudium*, nos. 278–79.

5. Pope Francis, Angelus, July 20, 2014.

6. Pope Francis, Apostolic Exhortation, *Amoris Laetitia*, no. 287.

7. Cf. *Relatio Finalis*, Final Report of the Synod of Bishops to the Holy Father, Pope Francis, 2015, 13–14.

8. Augustine, *De sancta virginitate* 7,7: PL 40, 400.

9. Catechesis (August 26, 2015): *L'Osservatore Romano*, August 27, 2015, p. 8.

10. *Relatio Finalis*, Final Report of the Synod of Bishops to the Holy Father, Pope Francis, 2015, 89.

11. Pope Francis, Address to the Plenary of the Congregation for the Clergy, October 3, 2014.

12. Pope Francis, Angelus, July 27, 2014.

13. Pope Francis, Apostolic Exhortation, *Amoris Laetitia*, no. 182.

14. Faith

1. Pope Francis, Morning Meditation, Chapel of *Domus Sanctae Marthae*, "The Great One's Darkest Hour," February 6, 2015.

2. Pope Francis, Angelus, August 3, 2014.

3. Pope Francis, Address to Participants in the Meeting Sponsored by the Fondazione Banco Alimentare (Food Bank Foundation), October 3, 2015.

4. Pope Francis, Angelus, August 10, 2014.

5. Pope Francis, Angelus, June 28, 2015.

15. Encountering Jesus

1. Pope Francis, Angelus, August 20, 2017.

2. J. M. Bergoglio – Papa Francesco, *"L'incontro con Gesù,"* in *Aprite la mente al vostro cuore* (Milan: BUR–Rizzoli, 2014), 18–20.

3. Pope Francis, Jubilee Audience, May 14, 2016.

4. Pope Francis, Address to the Participants in the Fifth Convention of the Italian Church, November 10, 2015.

16. Who Is Jesus?

1. Pope Francis, Angelus, June 29, 2018.
2. Pope Francis, Homily at Artemio Franchi Municipal Stadium, Florence, November 10, 2015.
3. Pope Francis, Homily, Vatican Basilica, June 29, 2016.
4. Pope Francis, Angelus, August 24, 2014.

17. The Transfiguration

1. Pope Francis, Address of Pope Francis to the Bishops Appointed over the Past Year, September 10, 2015.
2. Pope Francis, Angelus, Second Sunday of Lent, March 12, 2017.
3. Pope Francis, Angelus, Second Sunday of Lent, March 16, 2014.

18. Who Is the Greatest?

1. Pope Francis, Morning Meditation, Chapel of *Domus Sanctae Marthae,* "The Angel and the Child," October 2, 2015.
2. Pope Francis, Apostolic Exhortation, *Evangelii Gaudium,* no. 3.
3. Paul VI, Apostolic Exhortation, *Gaudete in Domino,* May 9, 1975, 22. *AAS* 67 (1975), 297.
4. Pope Francis, Morning Meditation, Chapel of *Domus Sanctae Marthae,* "Going Out to Give Life," December 9, 2014.
5. Pope Francis, Apostolic Exhortation, *Amoris Laetitia,* no. 297.
6. *Relatio Synodi,* Report of the III Extraordinary General Assembly of the Synod of Bishops, 2014, 25.
7. Pope Francis, Morning Meditation, Chapel of *Domus Sanctae Marthae,* "A God Who Reconciles," January 23, 2015.
8. Pope Francis, Morning Meditation, Chapel of *Domus Sanctae Marthae,* "An Open Door," March 10, 2015.

19. From Galilee to Judea

1. Pope Francis, Apostolic Exhortation, *Amoris Laetitia,* no. 71.
2. *Relatio Finalis,* Final Report of the Synod of Bishops to the Holy Father, Pope Francis, 2015, 38.
3. Pope Francis, Apostolic Exhortation, *Amoris Laetitia,* nos. 61–66.

4. *Relatio Synodi*, Report of the III Extraordinary General Assembly of the Synod of Bishops, 2014, 14.

5. *Relatio Synodi*, Report of the III Extraordinary General Assembly of the Synod of Bishops, 2014, 16.

6. *Relatio Synodi*, Report of the III Extraordinary General Assembly of the Synod of Bishops, 2014, 2014, 16.

7. *Relatio Finalis*, Final Report of the Synod of Bishops to the Holy Father, Pope Francis, 2015, 41.

8. Pope Francis, Apostolic Exhortation, *Amoris Laetitia*, no. 19.

9. Pope Francis, Morning Meditation, Chapel of *Domus Sanctae Marthae*, "The Food of Jesus," January 27, 2015.

20. The Margins

1. Pope Francis, Address to Participants in the Meeting Sponsored by the Pontifical Council for Promoting New Evangelization, September 19, 2014.

2. Pope Francis, Message for the Celebration of the Forty-ninth World Day of Peace, "Overcome Indifference and Win Peace," January 1, 2016.

3. Pope Francis, Address to the Bishops of the Episcopal Conference of Portugal on the "*Ad limina*" Visit, September 7, 2015.

4. Pope Francis, Apostolic Exhortation, *Amoris Laetitia*, no. 25.

5. Pope Francis, Address in the Meeting with the Bishops of Mexico, February 13, 2016.

6. Pope Francis, Encyclical, *Laudato Si'*, no. 82.

7. Pope Francis, Apostolic Exhortation, *Amoris Laetitia*, nos. 97–98.

8. Pope Francis, Message for the Twenty-third World Day of the Sick, February 11, 2015.

21. Jerusalem

1. Pope Francis, Morning Meditation, Chapel of *Domus Sanctae Marthae*, "Darkness of the Heart," December 15, 2014.

2. Pope Francis, Morning Meditation, Chapel of *Domus Sanctae Marthae*, "A Grandmother's Lesson," December 14, 2015.

3. Pope Francis, Morning Meditation, Chapel of *Domus Sanctae Marthae*, "They Shall Be First," December 16, 2014.

4. Pope Francis, Morning Meditation, Chapel of *Domus Sanctae Marthae*, "Three Traits," December 15, 2015.

5. Pope Francis, Angelus, October 8, 2017.

6. Pope Francis, Address to the Sant'Egidio Community, June 15, 2014.

22. *The Greatest Commandment*

1. Pope Francis, Angelus, October 12, 2014.
2. Pope Francis, Angelus, October 22, 2017.
3. Pope Francis, Apostolic Exhortation, *Amoris Laetitia*, no. 325.
4. Pope Francis, Angelus, October 26, 2014.
5. Pope Francis, Address to Members of the Italian Union of Catholic School Teachers, Managers, Educators and Trainers [UCIIM], March 14, 2015.
6. Pope Francis, Apostolic Exhortation, *Amoris Laetitia*, nos. 27–28.

23. *The Scribes and Pharisees*

1. Pope Francis, Morning Meditation, Chapel of Domus Sanctae Marthae, "Christians without Makeup," March 18, 2014.
2. Pope Francis, Morning Meditation, Chapel of Domus *Sanctae Marthae*, "When the Lord Exaggerates," March 3, 2015.
3. Pope Francis, Apostolic Exhortation, *Evangelii Gaudium*, no. 150.
4. Thomas Aquinas, *Summa Theologiae*, II-II, q. 188, art. 6.
5. Pope Paul VI, Apostolic Exortation, *Evangelii Nuntiandi*, December 8, 1975, 76. *AAS* 68 (1976), 68.
6. Pope Francis, Apostolic Exhortation, *Amoris Laetitia*, no. 144.

24. *Persecution*

1. Pope Francis–J. M. Bergoglio, "*Il Signore ci unge*," in *In lui solo la speranza. Esercizispirituali ai vescovi spagnoli* (January 15–22, 2006) (Milan: Jaca Book; Vatican City: LEV, 2013), 85–90.
2. Pope Francis–J. M. Bergoglio, "*Veracità e conversione*," in *Il desiderio allarga il cuore. Esercizi spirituali con il Papa* (Bologna: EMI, 2014), 57–63.
3. Pope Francis–J. M. Bergoglio, "*Aspettando l'Epifania*," in *Aprite la mente al vostro cuore* (Milan: BUR-Rizzoli 2014), 104–7; Pope Francis, *Non fatevi rubare la speranza. La preghiera, il peccato, la filosofia e la politica alla luce della speranza* (Milan: Oscar Mondadori; Vatican City: LEV, 2014), 54–57.
4. J. M. Bergoglio, "*Gesù, pane di vita*," in *Vita* (*Le parole di Papa Francesco*, 13) (Milan: Corriere della sera, 2015), 78–88.

25. The Fullness of Life

1. Pope Francis, General Audience, April 24, 2013.
2. Pope Francis, General Audience, April 24, 2013.
3. Pope Francis, Angelus, November 16, 2014.
4. Pope Francis, General Audience, April 24, 2013.
5. Pope Francis, Address to Participants in the Ecclesial Convention of the Diocese of Rome, June 17, 2013.
6. Pope Francis, Address at the Meeting with the Participants in the Fifth Convention of the Italian Church, November 10, 2015.
7. Pope Francis, Homily at Campo Grande de Ñu Guazú, Asunción, July 12, 2015.
8. Pope Francis, Apostolic Exhortation, *Amoris Laetitia*, no. 46.
9. *Relatio Finalis*, Final Report of the Synod of Bishops to the Holy Father, Pope Francis, 2015, 23; cf. Message for the World Day of Migrants and Refugees on January 17, 2016 (September 12, 2015), *L'Osservatore Romano*, October 2, 2015, p. 8.
10. *Relatio Finalis*, Final Report of the Synod of Bishops to the Holy Father, Pope Francis, 2015, 24.
11. Pope Francis, Apostolic Exhortation, *Evangelii Gaudium*, nos. 209–10.

26. The Passion—Part 1

1. Pope Francis, Angelus, February 8, 2015.
2. Pope Francis, Homily for Mass with the Ordinaries of the Holy Land and the Papal Entourage, May 26, 2014.
3. J. M. Bergoglio–Pope Francis, "*Le due bandiere*," in *Nel cuore di ogni Padre. Alle radici della mia spiritualità, Introduzione di Antonio Spadaro* (Milan: Rizzoli, 2014), 162–69.
4. J. M. Bergoglio–Pope Francis, "*Consolazione*," in *La misericordia è una carezza. Vivere il giubileo nella realtà di ogni giorno*, ed. Antonio Spadaro (Milan: Rizzoli, 2015), 247–79.
5. J. M. Bergoglio, "*Il silenzio*," in *Natale* (*Le parole di Papa Francesco*, 1) (Milan: Corriere della Sera, 2014), 67–83.

27. The Passion—Part 2

1. Pope Frances, "*L'accanimento*," in *Non fatevi rubare la speranza. La preghiera, il peccato, la filosofia e la politica pensati alla luce della speranza* (Milan: Oscar Mondadori; Vatican City: LEV, 2014), 103–5.
2. J. M. Bergoglio–Pope Francis, "*L'esilio della carne: la preghiera della carne in esilio*," in *Aprite la mente al vostro cuore* (Milan: BUR-Rizzoli, 2014), 199–203.

3. Pope Frances, "*Ambizione*," in *Non fatevi rubare la speranza*, 90–92.

4. Saint Ignatius of Loyola, *The Spiritual Exercises*, no. 95–97, trans. Louis J. Puhl, SJ, 1951; http://spex.ignatianspirituality.com/SpiritualExercises/Puhl.

5. Saint Ignatius of Loyola, *The Spiritual Exercises*, no. 97.

6. Pope Francis, "*In lui solo riporre la speranza*," in *Non fatevi rubare la speranza*, 161–72.

7. J. M. Bergoglio, "*Croce e senso bellico della vita*," in *Pace* (*Le parole di Papa Francesco*, 5) (Milan: Corriere della Sera, 2014), 31–46.

28. The Resurrection

1. Pope Frances, Address at the Ecumenical Celebration on the Occasion of the 50th Anniversary of the Meeting between Pope Paul VI and Patriarch Athenagoras in Jerusalem, May 25, 2014.

2. Pope Francis, Angelus/Regina Caeli, April 6, 2015.

3. Pope Francis, Angelus/Regina Caeli, June 1, 2014.

4. Pope Francis, Apostolic Exhortation, *Evangelii Gaudium*, no. 120.